UNEARTHING the CHURCH

IN SCRIPTURE AND IN

Turkey

David Winwood

McKnight & Bishop Ltd

About the Publisher

McKnight & Bishop are always on the look-out for new authors and ideas for new books. If you write or if you have an idea for a book, please e-mail us at: **info@mcknightbishop.com**

Some things we love are undiscovered authors, open-source software, Creative Commons, crowd-funding, Amazon/Kindle, social networking, faith, laughter and new ideas.

Visit us at **www.mcknightbishop.com**

More copies of this book are available through bookstores, online retailers (like Amazon), libraries, and academic institutions.

ISBN 978-1-905691-54-8

A CIP catalogue record for this book is available from the British Library

First published in 2018 by McKnight & Bishop Inspire, an imprint of:

McKnight & Bishop Ltd. | 26 Walworth Crescent, Darlington, DL3 0TX
http://www.mcknightbishop.com | info@mcknightbishop.com

This book has been typeset in Arial Narrow, Comic Sans MS, Euphorigenic, Monotype Corsiva, Panettone and Walkway Semibold

Printed and bound in Great Britain by United Print Ltd.

This book is dedicated to my dear Wilma,
in deep gratitude for fifty years
of love and loyal support.

Image Rights

The line drawings and coloured photographs are, unless otherwise indicated, by the author.

Text Dividers Created by Freepik.com

With thanks to Steven Braman for his kind permission to use his images of the Aqueduct in Antioch in Pisidia p231 and Lystra and Derbe mounds and excavations p232. You can visit Steven's blog about his trip to Turkey at www.bramanswanderings.com/turkey

We also acknowledge, with gratitude, permission to use the following images, adapted a little for the purposes of this publication -

- Asclepion Tunnels, Bergama : Adam Jones (ⓒⓘⓞ 2.0) p90
- Ruins of Alexandria Troas : Elelicht (ⓒⓘⓞ 3.0) p169
- Second image of Troas : Austrian National Library (ⓒ Bild ID 15547039) p169
- Coin, image of Apollo: © Marie-Lan Nguyen / Wikimedia Commons p 169
- Antioch in Pisidia p231 -
  - Across Archaeological site : Maderibeyza (ⓒⓘⓞ 3.0)
  - Roman Theatre : Klaus-Peter Simon (ⓒⓘⓞ 3.0)
  - Exhibits : Maderibeyza (ⓒⓘⓞ 3.0)
  - Horse Stone Carving : Basak (ⓒⓘⓞ 4.0)
- Lystra Ruin of Arch : Dursunbal (ⓒⓘⓞ 4.0) p232

Acknowledgements

I am indebted to Bill Davies, who has led groups to some of the New Testament sites in Turkey, and to Philip Beuzeval, who was my tutor in New Testament Greek many years ago. They were both willing to read through my first rough draft of this manuscript and make perceptive and constructive suggestions.

Thankfully, my wife, Wilma, who taught secondary English for twenty years before switching career to psychotherapy, kindly checked through all my punctuation and syntax.

I am more grateful than words can express to friends, companions and colleagues who have encourage me through the years, to a number of preachers, writers and theologians, whose inspiration has sustained me, and to Christian communities in the UK, and in several parts of the world, whose witness has illuminated the authentic New Testament message for me. I cherish memories of those who have accompanied me on some trips to Turkey and, above all, I'm earnestly aware of the enduring grace of God that keeps me going.

I would also like to express my gratitude to Mark McKnight of McKnight & Bishop Ltd., for his care and expertise, advice, guidance and keen interest in publishing this book. I am thankful for his kindness in responding to my many suggestions and enquiries.

Nevertheless, no one but me can be blamed for my views or mistakes.

Contents

Why Turkey?   13
Personal experience | Inspiration from land & people | New Testament lives

Chapter 1: The Island of Patmos   27
The Island | St. John's Cavern | The Book of Revelation

Chapter 2: Ephesus   51
In the 1st century | St. Paul | Mary's House | Hagios Theologos | Love

Chapter 3: Smyrna   75
The city | St. Polycarp | Suffering and witness

Chapter 4: Pergamum   91
The Acropolis | The Theatre | Asclepion | Red Basilica | Truth

Chapter 5: Thyatira   107
Excavations and remains | The Church | Godliness

Chapter 6: Sardis   123
The city | Gymnasium | Temple | Synagogue | Church | Kosher living

Chapter 7: Philadelphia   137
Small archaeological site | Open doors | More contemporary witness

Chapter 8: Laodicea   151
In New Testament times | The Church | Hierapolis | Pamukkale | Colossae

Chapter 9: The Aegean Coast   175
Troy | Alexandria Troas | Priene | Miletus and the Epehsians | Didyma

Chapter 10: The Aegean meets the Mediterranean   197
Dalyan | Patara | Xanthus | Myra | St. Nicholas | Attalia | Perge | Aspendos

Chapter 11: Tarsus and Antioch   223
History | Man of Tarsus | Antioch | Poverty

Chapter 12: Pisidian Antioch to Iconium –   255
Antioch | Iconium | The Dervishes | Lystra | Derbe

Chapter 13: Cappadocia and Nemrut Dagi   277
The land | Goreme | Churches | Kaymakli | Pentecost |
Caravanserai | Mt. Nemrut

Chapter 14: Constantinople   307
Brief history | Christian city | St. Irene | Hagia Sophia | St.
Saviour in Chora

Chapter 15: Nicaea   323
The town | First Ecumenical Council | Nicene Creed | The Seven
Councils

Congratulations!   339
New Testament Turkey   346
Bibliography   348

Why Turkey?

Why Turkey?

I was spellbound on my first visit to Turkey, in the late nineties, by the beauty, history and mixture of ancient cultures, and by discovering the context in which the Christian church first took root. I was bowled over by the abundance of ancient ruins of towns and cities, which were virtually undisturbed since earthquakes or conquests brought their better days to an end. I returned time and time again, exploring sites, searching out some of the lesser known places, researching their background, making sketches for illustrations, taking hundreds of photographs of archaeological remains and restorations, learning from local people and studying the appropriate New Testament texts more thoroughly than before.

Ignorance wasn't Bliss!

Prior to that first visit, I had no real interest in Turkey! Holiday makers were obviously having a wonderful time with the bargain package–deals, fun loving night life and hours of sun-tanning on wonderful, sandy beaches but I wasn't persuaded that it would be an ideal holiday destination for me. In my ignorance, I had no idea of the wealth of history and culture or of the beauty and variety of the fascinating landscapes in that vast country.

I was aware that modern Turkey had been ancient Anatolia, or Asia Minor, where St. Peter, St. Paul and many others gave all their energy in Christian mission but I had no knowledge of the hundreds of ruins of ancient temples and cities, in almost every part of the land. I had no concept of the way in which the excavations and reconstruction work of archaeologists had made it possible to walk the streets of Ephesus, paddle in the pools of Pamukkale or go into the underground cities and rock - hewn churches of Cappadocia. Equally I didn't realise that to visit the home town of St. Paul at Tarsus, or the cavern of St. John on Patmos

Island could so vividly bring the New Testament Church and New Testament experience to life.

Some of the sites are truly stunning, although others are not so impressive. Nevertheless, with a little creative imagination and a bit of background knowledge, what may seem like just a pile of old stones can be rebuilt, in the mind, into a magnificent first century city – like virtual reality, in the head!

Cradle of Faiths

I have come to realise that Anatolia, the central region of Turkey, has cradled great civilizations. Throughout its long history, it has been a meeting point of languages, arts, cultures, philosophies, political ambitions, trade, military exploits and religious convictions coming from Europe, Asia and Africa. It has been appropriately described as the 'Cradle of Faiths'. The city of Ur, home of Abraham, towards the east of Turkey and the area of the nearby rivers Tigris and Euphrates were background to early Hebrew faith. Abraham is considered to be the 'grandfather' of Judaism. Mohammed is thought of as a descendent of Ishmael (son of Abraham) and Abraham, the great patriarch, was 'Father' to the race and faith into which Jesus was born. Quite apart from temples and monasteries, in which the worship of a vast variety of ancient gods flourished for centuries, Turkey was the 'cradle' of the three great world faiths – Judaism, Christianity and Islam.

What Changed?

If you are wondering what changed my mind about Turkey, I should say that it was as much a change of heart as it was a change of mind. I read John Stott's writing on the letters to the seven churches of Asia Minor (Anatolia), from the first three chapters of the Book of Revelation. That's what grabbed me! The photographs of archaeological sites, the information about those places, studies of the letters, and inspiration as early Christian mission, planted among those people in those places, came to life. That's what took me on my first visit to Turkey. Just one visit and I was hooked! It was the beginning of about twenty years of research. I made many visits, when I could fit them in, often travelling alone so that I could move quickly from one place to another, exploring areas I didn't know. I usually hired a car to enable me to get around swiftly to locations mentioned in the New Testament, like Patara, Myra, Attalia, Perga, Tarsus or Antioch and others far from the tourist's trail.

The quality of the roads has improved enormously over the years but not the quality of all the drivers or of some of the near-vintage cars. There were times when driving in Turkey was rather a nightmare. Thinking back to my earliest jaunts, it seemed that the Aegean coastal road attracted some crazy, 'hell for leather' drivers but now there are generally good, safe roads, modern cars and professional driving instruction. Throughout Turkey, widespread development of all kinds is quite astounding: in housing, business, the economy, investment in poorer areas, education, the infrastructure serving archaeological sites, tourism and probably in other ways.

What a joy it was driving through beautiful scenery, along the Aegean coast, by the blue lagoons, through the snow-capped Taurus mountains or into the geological vista of Cappadocia. I felt a sense of adventure, searching out places I'd hardly ever heard of like Xanthus, Letoon, Termessos and Aspendos…. sometimes scrambling up rocks to ruins of high level cities or clearing away undergrowth to reach what remains of unexcavated archaeological sites, overgrown with weeds.

One time, I hired a car and was trying to find my way out of Ankara. It was during a period of massive road improvement. At last, I saw a direction sign pointing left for Cappadocia, where I was heading. I took the turning onto a really good, new road out of the town. After about half a mile, the road was rising to a fly-over, I thought, but suddenly - there was no road! It was the end (almost for me) and a long drop beyond. To be fair there was a rope across the road but not quite enough to bring a car to a halt, if not spotted in time.

John Stott did not, of course, include directions or road warnings but I am grateful to him for all that he did include and I am thankful for many other valued sources, from which I've learned about background, history and archaeological detail, even though the experts have contradicted each other here and there! I would like to acknowledge my gratitude to the authors of, and contributors to, the books mentioned in the bibliography. I have picked up so much from a wide variety of sources that I can't identify the origin of most things I now understand about Turkey and the biblical sites. The same applies to my understandings of the New Testament text. I have been gaining some knowledge and insight regarding the Scriptures for most of my life and, of course, much of that has found its way into these chapters. I'm sure that I'll be entirely to blame for some thoughts in what lies ahead, which probably arise from my own peculiar interpretations. Nevertheless, I cannot express my appreciation enough, for the way in which learning from others has enriched my life and knowledge.

My main source has been the experience of being on the spot, 'walking in the footsteps' (as the Church travel industry now says) of St. Paul, St. John, St. Peter, St. Luke, Mark, Barnabas, Silas and so very many others, whose names we do not know. On the spot, I have been seeing for myself, learning from local people, listening to archaeologists, consulting professional guides, doing my best to make sense of the New Testament and reflecting on its message for us today.

Local People

Learning from local people has been an enriching part of the total experience. I have found the Turkish people to be courteous, friendly, generous and hospitable, although frequently too anxious to sell me a carpet! Turkish carpets are beautiful and I did buy one. However, one time in Kusadasi my wife and I had to avoid passing one carpet shop because the invitation to buy became far too militant, even though it was accompanied by the usual offer of Turkish apple tea. In Konya, I gave in and agreed to share apple tea with an enthusiastic salesman, although I made it clear that I wasn't buying. We must have been chatting enjoyably for at least half an hour and I picked up a lot about local life, but no carpet. As I left he said to me, "You have broken my record. I never fail to sell to a man of your age when they join me for apple tea!"

I have been impressed by the way in which total strangers have been willing to offer help. For example – in the confusion of a rush hour traffic jam in central Adiyaman, I lowered the car window to ask a man, hurrying by, if he could direct me to a hotel. He started to give directions but, realising that it could be a bit complicated, he said, "If I may come into the car, I will take you there." Readily, he interrupted his own timetable to help me out. In Tarsus, Mustafa approached, offering to take me to see places relating to St. Paul but would not accept any reward. I met Tezer on a flight to Istanbul. He, and his work colleagues who were sitting behind, had been at the Birmingham Exhibition Centre on business. He asked about my destination and then immediately leapt up to reach for his lap top, from the overhead locker. He and his young wife had been there for their honeymoon, just a few weeks before, and he was eager to show me photographs of all the sites I was aiming to see. A young waiter, working part time in a hotel in Nevsehir, to provide income while at university, told me about the expanding opportunities for university education throughout Turkey. I'm sure there had been no university in that town on my previous visits and the last had been only two or three years before.

I think people are more likely to talk to you when you are on your own – Taxi drivers and people on market stalls, even though they have limited English and I have no Turkish. I gained from talking with Whirling Dervishes in Konya and from the Imam at Esrefoglu Mosque at Beysehir. (I must tell you that it was built in 1297 and famed for its wooden interior and flat wooden roof, with an opening in the middle for snow to fall into the mosque and land in a well just below floor level). I valued time with evangelical Christians at Alasehir (Philadelphia), as well as with Eastern Orthodox Christians in Istanbul. I must not forget groups of children who were always curious about visitors. They approached asking, "What is your name?" They'd want to sing to you and, if they spotted a camera, they'd love to pose for a photograph.

I would always remind visitors to be careful about their security in strange places but generally local people are a delight and they often have local knowledge, even about the ancient sites. That prompts me to mention the Turkish Tour Guides from whom I learned so much. I think particularly of AJ, with whom it was a pleasure to work on the last occasion a group accompanied me to the biblical sites. She was knowledgeable, sensitive, professional, friendly and caring towards members of the group. She was keen for us to work well together, which we did, so that the prayer times and scriptural insights blended with the archaeological and historical information. I remember, perhaps above all, that AJ, as she had suggested we call her, had a great sense of humour and there were times when we couldn't stop laughing.

People and Places

P laces contribute to the shape of people's lives: and people contribute to the shape of life in those places. Perhaps I am stating the obvious but I have discovered that to understand the communities in which people live is essential, if we want to understand the people. Awareness of this is vital in pastoral sensitivity and for communication. It is therefore, vital in Christian mission. The apostles and saints of the New Testament were mindful of this but they were not the only New Testament people. The letters, sermons, and gospels were addressed to particular groups of people from different places and with different backgrounds. They were also New Testament people. The message was designed to speak God's word to them, within their own context, using images, language and ideas that were part of their culture and way of life. The more we are able to understand life in those various places the more likely we are to understand the message and, hopefully, to be able to interpret it for our own life and society.

It is clear that the ministry of Jesus was primarily among the Jews. He quoted the Old Testament frequently; in his parables he used images from the everyday life of the people; he took account of the Roman occupation and of the religious authority overshadowing the community. His message went beyond these things but clearly he knew and understood the life, culture and beliefs of the people and he spoke to them within their context. The apostle Paul did the same in preaching his first sermon to the Jewish community at Antioch of Pisidia. However, his approach in Athens was completely different, as he quoted Greek poets and philosophers.

The letters to the seven churches, in the Book of Revelation, were addressed to people in different towns of Anatolia. They took account of the population, Jewish, Greek or mixed, of the influence of religious life in the temples, the social morality of the community, the wealth or poverty of the people, the types of business that flourished in the towns and even the water supply. These things may not be referred to directly but were used as images and illustrations to communicate, indicating that the writer knew and understood those places and the local way of life. He was seeking to bring God's truth right into those situations.

Being in the New Testament places, on the spot, learning about the first century communities and their lives, soaking up the atmosphere, listening to the stories and reading the scripture can help to bring the mission and the message of the early church to life. It can speak to you, heart, mind and spirit. When I've been able to introduce groups to some of those New Testament places, I have been thrilled to see and hear a number of them saying how it strengthened their faith to be there, rooted their Christian experience or made the scripture real. To know that is inspiring for me.

Using the Book

Perhaps there is no need to say that I would encourage you to visit some of the places described in the pages ahead. You can't beat seeing for yourself and reading the scripture on the spot. But if you go, may I suggest that you travel with an organised pilgrimage: check that there will be good pastoral and spiritual leadership; ensure that the tour company is working with Turkish partners who will be informed about the current situation in the areas you'll be visiting; make sure that there will be a professional Tour Guide, as required by Turkish regulations. The hotels are very good (although I do recall a few frozen nights in a rock hewn hotel bedroom in Cappadocia!), the sun shines most of the time, the scenery is outstanding and I'm sure you'll have a great time. I hope that you'll read the relevant chapters of this book before you go and during the visit, and that the content will enrich your trip.

For some years, the archaeological sites in Turkey had been attracting increasing numbers of visitors, including many tours to sites of Christian significance but the outbreaks of violence, political and religious conflict, hostile internal division together with migration tensions reduced the popularity of Turkish tourism for a while. I am, therefore, well aware that, understandably, you may not feel that this is a good time to visit. Nevertheless, now that things have settled a little the places of interest are busy again. Whether you manage such a trip, or not, I hope that this publication could take you there in imagination and give you a feel of the places and communities into which the infant church was born. Let the stories get under your skin. Think and feel your way into first century life. Allow your imagination to take you for a stroll in some of the impressive Roman cities with their fabulous architecture and among the people who were changed by the flame of faith burning in the mission of the apostles - and so open up the meaning, significance and challenges of the Gospel message, through which God may speak anew.

I have used much of this material for Bible study groups and I hope that you may be able to do the same. It encourages a different way into the study, not starting with the text but with the people and their communities who were first addressed by the letters and gospels. If you can think and feel your way into their lives and circumstances, you may get a bit nearer to reading the message almost as one of them, feeling some of its force for them and then discussing the implications for us. I've been told that some groups found it was a powerful way into a better understanding of the scripture. That doesn't necessarily require a group, of course, you can do the same in private study.

Many people today regard scripture as discredited by science, psychology, assumptions about historical and factual unreliability and by contemporary morality. Alongside that, the Church and its theology has lost a great deal of authority, influence, relevance, credibility and respect in the minds of everyday people. Christians are also likely to share many of these thoughts and face some difficulty in holding and defending their own faith. Archaeological explorations, in places where the Christian faith first grasped hearts and minds, is enabling us to know more of the human experience of New Testament people and of their profound sense of the reality and presence of God, despite life's doubts and troubles. With these things in mind, careful study of the New Testament may enrich our understanding of the early church's witness and of those for whom the scriptures were originally written. In so doing, renewed authenticity, inspiration and confidence in the Bible's deeper truth can emerge for us.

You'll find that questions arise along the way from the circumstances of the people or from the scriptural text. I have tried to identify some of those questions but I expect that others will also arise for you. I have highlighted a number of the issues for 'Reflection', to encourage space for thinking and to stimulate discussion. In some places, the message of the scripture or the circumstances of the people have brought to mind bits of my own life-experience which were unrelated to Turkey. Why not allow your reading to do the same for you, so that, in your exploration, God's Spirit may search your mind and heart ... and your whole experience. I hope you'll enjoy the book.

Turkey Transformed

History has changed Turkey time and again, inevitably for good and for bad. Many of the places of interest to Christians had been Greek/Roman towns and temples where Christian churches were built alongside them or within them. Christianity spread across the nation and tumbled out into the world. By the 4th Century, Constantinople (Istanbul) was the head of the 'civilised' world and of the western church. Then, about a thousand years later, in 1453, Sultan Mehmet, after conquering Constantinople, imposed Islam on Turkey and ordered that Christian Churches be turned into mosques. It follows, therefore, that many of the sites which interest us, also have significance for Muslims. In 1934, Mustafa Kemal Ataturk ordered that the historical, religious sites become museums under the care of the secular, liberal state. Now worship is allowed in a few of those buildings but only on specified occasions. The majority remain museums.

Many Turkish Muslims are orthodox but others are liberal in their theology and politics. Large numbers regard themselves as practically secular Muslims, although they may observe the festivals. They are open minded and welcome an exchange of ideas. Conversations with Turkish people have made it plain to me that our concerns about human rights and terrorism are widely shared in Turkey, though certainly not by all. It seems vital that we should understand as much as we can about the life and faith of Muslim people, especially as we are now in a world confronted by a clash between Islamist politics and western democracy. In many places, violent destruction, with an Islamist label attached, is being inflicted upon innocent people. Greater understanding on our part will enable us to be much clearer about what is truly Islamic and what bears an Islamic label for political reasons but has no place in the faith of Muslim people.

Vision

If you are able to visit these New Testament sites in reality or in imagination, through creative bible study, you may be able to visualise the mob in the Roman theatre in Ephesus, where St. Paul caused a riot, or think yourself into being among the crowds in Smyrna , listening to the resolute witness of St. Polycarp, before the Emperor ordered the guards to burn him alive. You may be bewitched, as I am, by the domes and minarets which dominate the Istanbul skyline, stunned by the bizarre and dream-like landscape of Cappadocia, intrigued by the underground cities and impressed by the frescos in the rock-hewn churches.

I confess, I am now completely hooked! One good reason is the photogenic beauty of the strange and wonderful scenery. Another is a sense of trying to get to the roots of our faith, when exploring the ancient cities and early churches, where the foundations of Christian community were being laid. A further reason for me is that, as it leads to a deeper understanding of New Testament faith, it therefore stimulates my own. There are also the challenges of ancient civilizations, of contemporary cultures and religious convictions in modern Turkey. I have to add that another good reason for me is because I enjoy being there. I love the place and I'm grateful that it has given me so much.

A final thought along these lines is that it offers me perspective. When I see the evidence and hear of the testimony of Christian communities which, from the time of the apostles, have persisted through the struggles of history, poverty and suffering, and have survived the affluence and power of dominant empires, it brings the problems of life and the troubles of the church today into perspective.

If the eternal God is working His purpose out as century succeeds to century, then the fuss and worries of the Church in this century pale into insignificance, as I think I can see signs of the fingerprints of God on the landscape of history.

It reminds me to trust Him a little more and, like Peter, Paul, John and the others, it stirs up Christians today to offer all we can in God's mission … and then to leave the eternal bits to Him.

The Island of Patmos

Monastery of the Apocalypse

Mosaic – Prochorus, St John's scribe, recording the Apostles words.

Pilgrim's stone road to the Cavern

11th/12th century icon of St John

The Sacred Cavern

The Monastery of St John the Divine

Mosaic – St John entrusts the monastery to Christodoulos

The Monastery is in the village of Chora

The courtyard and narthex of the Monastery Church

Chapter 1

The Island of Patmos

"I was put on the Island of Patmos because I proclaimed God's word and the truth that Jesus revealed."

Revelation 1 v. 9

St. John was there, on Patmos, when he addressed seven letters to churches in Anatolia. He had been exiled by the fanatical Emperor Domitian (AD 51 – 96) for preaching and teaching God's word, for acknowledging the Lordship of Jesus Christ and for refusing to regard Caesar as supreme lord. I am tempted to take our trip into Turkey straight away but Patmos is a Greek island, even though it's only sixty kilometres from the coast of Turkey. I hope you won't mind a detour, while we look around this island, where John had been banished when he first put his pen to parchment. Tertullian, second century lawyer and Christian historian, tells us that John was among the victims of bitter persecution, having been dropped into boiling oil before being exiled to the rocky and windswept island of Patmos. Tertullian also states that (somehow) John survived without major injury.

Reading even John's first letter to the Church in Ephesus is enough to convince anyone of his understanding and profound concern, expressed in each of the letters, for that Christian community and for the other churches. It therefore seems right for us to set out from Patmos, as John was there when his heart went out to the people he cared about in seven towns of Anatolia.

On our approach to the island, as we drifted towards the harbour, the engines were switched off. The sun was glistening on the water lapping against the side of the boat. Seagulls were gliding overhead, shining white against the deep blue sky and chanting like a tuneless choir. My first impression was of an inviting, homely looking little island. Spending time there confirmed that view, although I also discovered that, for a very little island, it had quite a chequered history.

The Pedigree of Patmos

According to ancient mythology, the 'sacred' powers of Apollo and Zeus brought this island out of the depths of the sea to please the goddess Artemis who, on seeing it bathed in moonlight, fell in love with the island. Archaeologist's, however, speak of pottery and other objects which testify to the presence of human inhabitants from the middle bronze-age, rather than of indulgent pleasures of the gods.

The Dorians and then the Ionians had settled on Patmos by the fourth century BC and built a flourishing civilization. A town developed around the port (now Skala) and a track was trodden from there to the acropolis at the top of Kasteli hill (Acropolis means 'higher city'). There, a temple was built to the glory of Artemis, where the Monastery of St. John is today. From the first century AD, the Romans occupied the island and used it as a place of exile. In 95 AD, St. John was among the exiles, although his ministry continued to bring Christian faith to the island. The population was then around ten thousand people, whereas today it is about three thousand. Following the early Christian era, until the eleventh century, the island's history seems to have been lost, except for the knowledge that Patmos was plagued by pirate raids and thousands of people drifted away.

Hosios Christodoulos came to Patmos and founded the Monastery of St. John in 1088. Spasmodic pirate raids and Arab attacks continued and the Turks infiltrated the island, even though the Venetians and the Knights of St. John were supposed to be keeping the island safe.

The Turks established power in 1523 but, apart from demanding taxes, they were quite easy going. The sixteenth to seventeenth century brought a period of trade and prosperity and the Turks remained in power until 1912. 1713 saw the famous Patmian School founded and many Greek scholars came to the island to study. Patmos gained reputation as a significant intellectual centre and the school continues today as an important seminary. One political power after another dominated life on Patmos including the Venetians, Turks, Greeks, Italians, the Nazis and the British until March 1948, when the Greek flag was officially raised. The economy of Patmos is now almost entirely dependent on tourism and, although it is an inviting holiday island with its own quiet appeal, St John is the best tourist attraction.

The Sacred Cavern

Near to Grikos, in the south of the island, there's a small cave with a little church built over the entrance to protect it. This is where, it is believed, St. John first settled on Patmos. Higher, on the other side of the hill, about half way between Skala and Chora, is the cavern most likely to have been St John's mission base. Supported by later research and scholarship, it is regarded as the place where St. John received a revelation from God. Here he wrote the book of the Revelation, with assistance from his scribe Prochorus, who was one of the seven deacons ordained by the apostles (Acts 6 v.3 – 6). Later, Prochorus became Bishop of Nicomedia. The cavern is now enclosed in the Monastery of the Apocalypse and forty steps down will take you to the open courtyard of the most sacred place on the island.

There are various mosaics and icons of St. John. In one, above the entrance to the cavern, we see him dictating to his disciple Prochorus. Other icons of him could easily make me feel that I'd rather not bump into him on a dark night. Reading his words, however, makes it clear that the severe representations in some of the icons may be rather misleading. In the seven letters, we discover that he must have been close to the people, understanding their life and experience, encouraging, commending and warning them. Beauty and poetry are found in later chapters of Revelation (4, 7v.9f, and chpts.19 – 22) which convey his sensitivity and his compassion for those who were suffering. He may have been a solemn saint, but not severe.

The inscription above the entrance to the cavern reads -

> "How dreadful is this place!
> It is none other than the house of God
> And this is the gate of heaven."

The Church of St. Anna was built on the open side of the cavern, to enlarge and protect a worship area. It was here that St. John gathered Christians to worship and grow in discipleship and where he received the Revelation. On my first visit, I was thrilled to stumble into the excitement of crowded worship, including a service of Christian Baptism for a little child. It was a superb reminder that 'this *is* the house of God' and not simply an archaeological site or tourist attraction. Later, I was glad to be there again for some quiet moments, seeking to be conscious of the presence of God, as John was when he spoke of hearing God's word -

> "I am Alpha and Omega, the beginning and the ending …
> which is, which was, and which is to come."

In the cavern, official guides usually draw attention to a niche where they suggest 'St. John laid his head to rest'; and to a small protruding rock to the right above it, which 'St. John gripped to pull himself up from prayer', as well as a flatter rock surface 'used by John's scribe to record his dictation' … and an ancient cross in the rock face which was 'carved by St. John'. The fissures in the roof of the cavern which divide the rock face into three are regarded as a reminder of the Holy Trinity. Visitors may be told that, 'St. John heard God's voice through the clefts in the rock'.

After listening to a guide, we followed the group of visitors leaving the church. An elderly lady, who was among them, quietly stood aside. Her scarf-covered head was bowed a little and I thought that perhaps she had stopped for a moment to reflect or pray but as we passed, having heard our English accent, she lifted her head and said, with feeling, "What a lot of bloody nonsense!"

Fact or Fiction?

Extravagant and unnecessary claims about unimportant details seem somewhat 'over the top' and could easily undermine confidence in the validity of this historic site. Who knows where John laid his head and what does that matter? I have even heard a guide telling his group that 'Christ was physically present in the cave at the time of the Revelation, as John heard His voice and saw Him in a vision'. If it was all at this level, I would soon be a signed up sceptic. Thankfully, guides at all of the ancient sites in Turkey are required to be archaeologically qualified. The nation prides itself on their high level of training and ability. Some of the guides on Patmos do not inspire me with quite the same trust in the accuracy of their scholarship.

Perhaps, to be kinder, I should keep in mind the fact that icons and religious symbols play a very important part in Orthodox devotion. For many it is, therefore, less likely that a clear distinction would be drawn between devotional tradition and archaeological fact. The focus would be upon spiritual meaning and experience, rather than precise historical detail. For centuries, the very presence of this cavern and its careful preservation has helped pilgrims to breathe a little of the spirit of Revelation and the experience of St. John and there's no need for exaggeration.

We are surrounded by icons every day, although we may not immediately be aware of them. Images and symbols quietly communicate their meaning. A heart shape is an icon for love or romance. The cowboy with a white hat is recognised as the 'good guy'. A red poppy prompts us to remember those who died in war. Little icons are used in computers nowadays but traditionally icons represent significant meaning or deep belief. For a Christian, a cross points to the heart of the Christian faith. Ancient artistic images speak of the character of Christian saints and are of great importance in Eastern Orthodox faith. The icon helps worshippers to focus on the spiritual beyond the image. It is also true that places where, for centuries, Christians have gathered to pray evoke devotion and bring blessing to many. Holy Island (Lindisfarne) on the Northumberland coast or each of the three possible sites of Emmaus in Israel/Palestine, even though only one can be the historic Emmaus: they are all good examples. A devout response is then not wholly dependent on archaeological evidence but on spiritual meaning.

Nevertheless we must not allow hyped imagination to bring serious professional, historic discovery into disrepute. There is a consistent thread of tradition from the time of St. John that authenticates the considerable probability that this cavern was the place.

The cavern became a place of Christian worship when St. John was there. When he returned to Ephesus, the cavern not only continued to be a gathering place for Christians but also a place of pilgrimage, soon after the end of the first century. Excavations indicate that the original Church of St. Anna, extending the cavern, was from the fourth century.

The ancient stone road from Skala to Chora ran from the harbour, with its Temple of Apollo, to the acropolis and the Temple of Artemis at the top of the hill, where the Monastery of St. John the Divine now stands. On the way, a branch from the road was created by pilgrims coming to worship at the Holy Cavern of the Apocalypse, probably trodden by their feet in the earliest years. The present cobbled surface was laid quite recently ... in 1794.

Sacred Music

Within the campus of the Holy Cavern of the Apocalypse, cut into the rock around St. John's cavern, there is an open-air amphitheatre frequently presenting some awesome programmes of music. My wife and I happened to catch a Mozart evening, celebrating the 250th anniversary of his birth. It was part of the Sixth Festival of Sacred Music and an unforgettable experience – a high standard of music and excellent technical presentation. The setting was inspirational - surrounded by rock and a variety of trees, through which we could look down to the sea or up into the warm crimson sky, whilst being cooled by the breeze and soothed by the music. If you should ever be there don't miss out. You may even be touched by the Spirit.

The Monastery of St John the Divine

Approaching the island from the sea, the towering stone walls of the Monastery of St. John the Divine stand out from quite a distance. Being at the highest point of the island, it looks rather like a medieval castle. This majestic monastery, founded by Hosios Christodolos in 1088, dominates the skyline.

St Christodoulos

'Doulos' is the Greek word for 'servant', which is a most appropriate name by which the monk was known. This great saint was a dedicated 'servant of Christ'. When he arrived on the island, he said that there was not a single house standing, only 'a humble chapel built in the name of the Evangelist'. The monk fell in love with the island and sensed God's call to stay and establish a monastery. He sought support from the Emperor Alexius Comnenus, in Constantinople, and received more than he could have expected - the island and the right to a private ship, free of tax. A mosaic of Christodoulos in the courtyard sees him holding a scroll from the emperor in one hand and the monastery in the other. The actual scroll is mounted flat in a tall picture frame in the monastery museum

A hundred and fifty monks, as well as experienced builders and other workers, were brought to the island by Christodoulos. First, they replaced the 4th century church at the cavern by building the Church of St. Anna.

The monastery church high on the mountain was completed about 1090. It replaced the ruins of an early Christian basilica, which had been built on the site of the temple dedicated to Artemis (Diana). Marble slabs and pillars from the temple were used in the construction of the exonarthex (the covered forecourt to the church) and in the church itself. It took five years to complete the monastery buildings. Christodolous died on March 16th 1093 in Euboea: a date which is honoured each year on Patmos.

The monk left behind his testimony, including some personal words of witness expressing the convictions that bound him to the island.

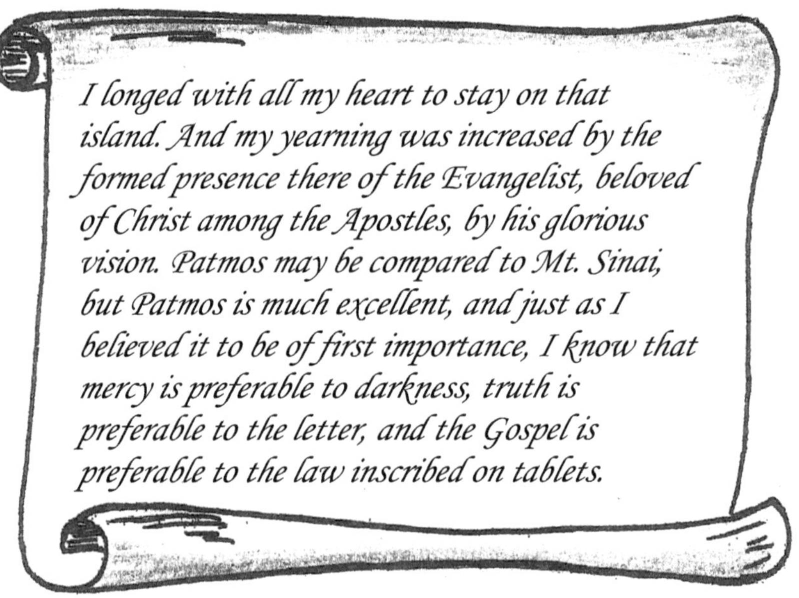

The Convent of Evangelismos

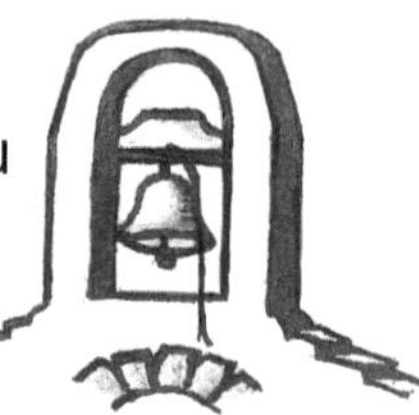

The Convent of Evangelismos Mitros Egapimenou (The Annunciation to the Mother of the Beloved One) overlooks a magnificent bay just south west of Chora. It was built in 1613 by Nikiphorus Kretas, a monk from the Monastery of St. John the Divine. As he had struggled to recover from the plague, he dedicated the first church of the Convent to St. Luke the Physician. In the chapel, an El Greco icon of Christ broke the 'rules' of iconography by showing emotion in the face of Jesus. You can see His sorrow. Later, Sister Olympiada, one of the nuns, encouraged by this approach, went on to portray more humanity and sensitivity in her work. Her splendid talent can be seen in the Chapels of the Convent, in her icon of St. John and others.

I wondered how the nuns fill their days in modern times. One described the work. It included running an orphanage and a primary school on the island of Rhodes. Others look after the vineyard, flower garden, vegetable plot and bees and honey at the Convent.

A Holy Island

There's no difficulty in understanding why Patmos is regarded as a holy island. It's a place of inspiration and beauty that helps you to listen inwardly for the voice of God. Wherever you are on this island, you are not far from the sea. Everything is bathed in sunshine. The light breeze is refreshing and the crystal clear waters of the Mediterranean, inevitably brilliant. The island is a spiritual oasis.

I sat on a rock by the sea, soaking up the scenery. I was below the cavern of St. John and not far from Agios Theologos beach, where John baptised islanders. Some ruins of a later Baptismal font remain. I was wondering if it really was the blast of a trumpet that broke into the mind of St. John, as his writing says. For the moment, it seemed incongruous that God would break this sacred silence with a blast! Could it have been the clarity, purity or glory in the strain of a trumpet that brought the Word of God to St. John? As I sat in the silence, that seemed more appropriate to me … but they were simply the wanderings of my imagination.

Chapels and Churches

They say that there is a church for every day of the year, on this island, but that claim has been exceeded. The total number is now over four hundred! Bishop Georgarinis visited Patmos early in the eighteenth century and observed that there were eight hundred houses in Chora and two hundred and fifty churches. Islanders raise funds to build the chapels. Many are family memorial chapels, dedicated to saints. They are mainly small, whitewashed buildings, many with red-tiled domes and often with a bell tower. The chapels are all over the island, each one representing devoted family life and each an expression of local art and a witness to faith.

Skala

Skala is a lively small town, with a picturesque island atmosphere. It was little more than a port for many years. From AD1600, increasing trade and, therefore, increased shipping, made it a busy working town. From the early 20th century, Skala, being a desirable place, became the most populated town on the island. Later in the century, it developed modest accommodation and facilities to welcome an increasing number of tourists and pilgrims.

Chora

Chora is the highest town on the island, to where most islanders moved for safety in the long period of pirate raids. At first, the houses were built at a distance from the monastery to observe the requirement for monks to be apart from the community. After 1132, however, the people were invited to build around the monastery walls, to increase protection for the monastery and to enable the people to shelter inside its massive walls, at times of danger. Many small houses were built close together on the slopes, linked by steps and narrow streets which, together with its churches, bright bougainvillea and friendly cats characterise this attractive town.

Barren or Beautiful

Biblical text books had given me the idea that Patmos was an inhospitable, barren, rocky island and so I was surprised by its charm and tranquillity. It's not a green island, as the trees were rapidly reduced to build ships when the port flourished after 1600. In 1935, Amphilochios Makris became Abbot of the Monastery of St. John the Divine and later concentrated on the work of the nuns at the Monastery of the Annunciation. At some time, he introduced a penance requiring islanders to plant a tree. In time, the hills were, to some extent, replenished with healthy trees. We can therefore, with clear conscience, rejoice in the sins of the Patmanians! It's fascinating to find that an ecological element became rooted in the concerns and practice of the church at this comparatively early stage, although we do also know about this monk's specialist skill in wood carving ... perhaps that could have been his motivation!

Reflection

The Cavern of St. John raised questions about the authenticity of some claims that are made about historic sites. We shall return to the discussion about 'truth' at a later stage but, at this point –

- Do you think that the absolute authenticity of historic sites is of any importance to you as far as your faith is concerned?

- These questions are not seeking to undermine the professionalism of archaeologists in any way but what about the dependability of claims that this is the Cavern of St. John or of the 'grotto' where Jesus was born in Bethlehem, the place of crucifixion, the site of a certain miracle, the statue that shed tears, the bones of a saint?

- In your view, do these places help to assure us of the historic roots of our faith or do they build up an arsenal of weapons of mass deception?

- Would you raise the same questions about some theological claims made with certainty by some Christians about – what happens when we die; how sure we can be about salvation; the reality, nature or will of God; the absolute certainty that some aspects of social behaviour, moral conviction or tenets of faith are right and others are wrong?

- Amphilochios brought another matter to our mind by his campaign to plant trees – ecology. Why should this be on the agenda for the church? Isn't it primarily a concern for scientists and politicians? What positive action can Christians take besides protesting?

Who wrote Revelation?

Our aim is to get a bit closer to some of the New Testament people, to understand more of their message and the communities to which they ministered. We'll begin with seven letters in Revelation chapters 1 – 3, which were written from Patmos and addressed to some of the churches taking shape in the Roman province of Asia (in modern

Turkey) from the second half of the first century. Who wrote these letters?

In Revelation 1 v.9, the author speaks of himself as a 'brother and companion in their suffering'. That is, in the suffering of Christians in the seven churches, to whom he is writing. There is long tradition and some archaeological support for the belief that John the Apostle, in his later years, came to Ephesus, one of the seven churches, bringing Mary the mother of Jesus ... following from John 19 v. 26 and 27. It is understood that he led the Church in Ephesus and ministered to other churches in the region, before being exiled to the mines on Patmos. A number of early Christian communities and the early buildings in and around Ephesus were linked to the name of St. Mary or St. John. The cross associated with St. John was scratched into some stone walls and floors or carved into pillars. This can be seen at some of the early church sites today. These things, together with the knowledge and understanding of the seven churches and their communities, shown by the author of the letters, could point to the writer being St.John the Apostle.

Victorinus, an African Theological scholar and teacher in Rome, and Jerome, whose scholarship was probably unsurpassed in the early church, both writing of the apostle in the fourth century, referred to the 'revelation that John received from God on the island of Patmos, to give hope and strength to Christians facing suffering and persecution under the authority of Rome.' Further testimony came from Eusebius. He is looked upon as the first church historian. When referring to the Book of Revelation, in the third century, he wrote -

> "The apostle and evangelist, John, related these things to the
> churches when he returned from exile on the island, after the death
> of Domitian."

About the year 140 AD, Justin Martyr suggested that the author was John the Apostle but Dionysius, principal of the great centre of Christian learning in Alexandria, questioned the authorship as early as 250 AD. He was the first to recognise the considerable differences in grammar, style and theology between Revelation and John's Gospel. In my student days, it was considered unscholarly to link John the Apostle with the Book of Revelation. The author has sometimes been called John the Elder, John the Divine or John the Theologian. He certainly seems to have been a significant leader of the early church who knew about and had shared the life and suffering of the churches in Roman occupied Asia. He understood their social and spiritual condition and was regarded by Christians as someone of authority.

We don't really know which John to thank for these letters so, on this one, I have to sit on the fence!

The Style of Writing

The style of writing in the Book of Revelation is described as 'Apocalyptic'. The Greek word 'apokalupsis' is about 'revealing', 'unveiling', 'disclosing', although, at first, the style seems to obscure, rather than reveal!

It is a strange piece of literature, full of bizarre symbolism that conveys little to people of our generation without explanation, although it spoke powerfully to first century people. We are likely to be baffled by the curious cast of angels and demons, lambs, lions, horses and dragons! If you are a fan of 'Harry Potter' or 'Lord of the Rings' you may be in your element but the broken seals, the sound of trumpets, the seven bowls being emptied on the earth, the thunder and lightning, hail, fire, blood and smoke are all rather weird and mysterious.

It's not difficult to see why this New Testament book has been given some 'crazy' interpretations. No wonder it is not often read throughout by many Christians today and yet it has been of immense value to Christians through the years, particularly at times of crisis and persecution.

Apocalyptic writing starts from the belief that the world is beyond mending: it's too evil and must be replaced or renewed. The author anticipates a 'new heaven and a new earth' (Rev 21 v1– 4) and that God is bringing that transformation through Jesus Christ. It would seem that, by AD 90 – 95, this author believed that life had reached such a level of suffering and destruction that Christ's triumph would bring the current state of affairs to an end.

At the time I am writing, I think it would be true to say that among the Islamic Jihadists there are some who sincerely have a similar understanding as they look upon the western world. They even believe that they have been chosen to be God's instrument in the destruction of evil, through suicide bombing and terrorist activity. The overwhelmingly major difference is that Revelation is bringing the Good News that God has taken suffering upon Himself, in Christ, as His will is to relieve and heal suffering. The purpose of Revelation is to strengthen, purify, challenge, encourage and inspire the churches through times of suffering and persecution ... to find victory in Christ, carrying them beyond their agony and yet also finding Him sharing in the pain and oppression.

God's Revelation

John's Introduction 1 v. 1 – 20

We have mentioned that the Greek word 'apokalupsis' means 'revealing', 'unveiling', 'disclosure'.

v.1–2 affirms that this message has been revealed by God and given to John by Christ. This book is John's testimony. He circulated the message among the new, growing churches in western Asia Minor (Anatolia) because it was speaking to their immediate circumstances and about the years directly ahead. "The things which must happen very soon" (v.1) were calling them to change their lives. It was not like a crystal ball predicting future events but God's message for now.

Blessings

1 v.3 Adopts the style of the beatitudes, assuring God's blessing and joy

- for those who read this record of God's revelation
- for those who listen to its message
- and for those who put its message into action in obedience to God

Six other similar blessings are assured later in the Book of Revelation

- 14 v. 13 – for those who "die in the Lord"
- 16 v. 15 - for those who are "united in the wedding feast of the lamb"
- 20 v. 6 - for those who "share in the Resurrection"
- 22 v. 7 - for those who act upon God's prophetic word in this revelation
- 22 v. 14 - for those who prepare themselves in repentance to eat the fruit from the tree of life, and so enter the new city of God.

It is likely that the author was familiar with the beatitudes in Matthew chpt. 5, as collections of some of the sayings of Jesus had been in circulation for a while. John may therefore be presenting these blessings in the way in which readers could recognise Christ's own words, following the pattern used in the Sermon on the Mount. Perhaps this should stir us to ask which blessings from Christ apply to our contemporary life and why? And to ask what we can hear or discern, from within our life and times, that could be regarded as 'revelation' or 'blessing' from God today.

To the Churches

1v. 4 – 6 John has first addressed the message to seven of the churches in Asia Minor, that is to Christians among whom he had shared in ministry, as a leader of the church.

11 v.4 Blessing comes from one 'Who was and is and is to come' i.e. from the Eternal God. What does the author have in mind when he

speaks of the 'the seven spirits'? It could be a reference to seven messengers who carried the letters to the churches. Our understanding of 'angel' is 'messenger'. Could it be a reference to the sevenfold gifts of the Spirit – wisdom, understanding, counsel, might, knowledge, true piety and reverence for God?

Jesus is Lord

1 v. 5 – 6 In expressing honour and praise to Jesus Christ, the author uses a concept found often in John's Gospel. Jesus is referred to as "the faithful witness". Then follows a summary of the gospel, focused in the love of Christ and His death on the cross, out of which the whole revelation comes.

1 v. 7 This verse declares that the work begun in Christ, through suffering, is for all people. Even those who crucified Christ will see him come in glory.

1 v.8 The completeness found in Christ is of God. He is eternal and whole from beginning to end and He is Lord. The word translated as 'almighty' is the word 'pantocrator'. It was used frequently in the New Testament church to describe the ultimate triumph of Christ. It greatly influenced early Christian art and iconography. In the face of persecution and the power of Rome, 'Pantocrator' had great significance because it acknowledged Christ as the Supreme Lord. The Roman Emperor had authority on earth and the means to inflict torture and death but Christ had ultimate and eternal authority: greater mastery than the might of Rome, in fact mastery over all.

Light of the World

1 v. 9 – 20 The book has opened with a brief statement of faith and theology and now moves towards introducing the more down to earth and practical guidance of God in the letters to the seven churches. The 'vision' is described. The Son of Man, the victorious living Christ, is speaking from among seven lamp stands and in his hands are seven stars. Verse 20 explains that the seven lamps are

the seven churches, each called to shine with the love and truth of Christ. Jesus said –

"You are the light of the world" and "Let your light shine before all people" (Mat.5v14 &16).

Christ is already within the churches. His light is shining through His people. The stars are explained as angels or messengers, bringing God's word to the churches. There is a powerful concept in these images of revelation coming from Christ who is among His people in the churches. It seems to be about recognising the living Christ in the life and experience of Christian people and about receiving and responding to God's message in our midst! Is this image relevant for us in the contemporary church? Then how can we hear what God is saying?

1 v. 16 reminds us that God's message is like a 'two edged sword'. Not simply words of comfort at times of suffering but a message that 'cuts both ways'. The seven letters include commendation and praise but also judgement and exaltation about the living faith and the active role of Christian people.

Reflection

What would you think of someone today who hears voices and sees strange symbols like stars, swords and angels that have brought a message from God?

What are today's beatitudes? What blessings are we receiving from within our own life and times?

If God's message is like a two edged sword of praise and of judgement, what praise and judgement do you think is being spoken by God to your local church?

Christians often hope to hear the voice of God as though from 'on high', spiritually, spoken into our hearts and minds but if Christ is speaking from among the lamps today, that is from within the churches and from among His people, as well as in other ways, how can we recognise and discern the message for us now?

Ephesus

The Celsus Library

The Roman Theatre

The Temple of Hadrian on Curetes Street

Artemis, goddess
of Ephesus Temple

Marble Street directions to the 'Love House'

Nike
goddess
of
victory

Icthus symbol - scratched
into marble pavements to
declare 'Jesus Christ,
Son of God and Saviour'

Hagios Theologos The Cathedral of St John

Ephesus

A capital from a supporting pillar

The Church of St John – his burial place

House of Mother Mary

A statue of Mary welcomes
visitors to this devotional place

It is thought that, possibly, this was the site
of Mary's house, about five miles from Ephesus

The house is regarded as a place of devotion rather than a museum

Ephesus

This place is immensely impressive. I could revisit Ephesus time and again. To walk on Marble Street is enough to enable anyone to see why this city rivalled Rome in its magnificence. Aphrodisias boasts of the finest craftsmanship but if you want to feel that you are in a Roman town, Ephesus is the place to be. Most of the surviving structures are from the Greek and Roman period, although its earliest days were many centuries before the Greeks. There are a variety of views regarding the foundation of Ephesus but tangible evidence, from excavations in 1990, dated some unearthed remains back to 3000 BC. From 189 BC to the first century AD, the city grew in importance under the Romans, becoming the main port of the Aegean and the fourth greatest city in the ancient world. St. Paul and St. John were here in its heyday, at the height of its political importance and religious distinction, when crowds flocked to the great Temple of Artemis (Diana). The Temple ranked among the seven wonders of the ancient world.

Marble Street is about nine hundred yards long and Curetes Street is well over a thousand. They are lined with the remains of columns, statues, shop fronts, temples and fountains, all bearing the stunning decoration of skilled stonemasons and gleaming white in the baking sun. I did once get my feet very wet when the streets were gushing with rain, like overflowing rivers, but generally it's a warm, dry place. The streets would have been swarming with busy traders, pilgrims and grand visitors to this wealthy Roman town when John and Paul mingled with the people. The local population was more than a quarter of a million people.

Ephesus was the principal commercial centre in western Anatolia. Here trade routes from the west linked with routes to the east. Commercial banks grew up handling foreign exchange. Banking, as we know it, could have originated in this town. Looking around today, it's not easy to visualise Ephesus as a busy port, because the Cayster River and the harbour became silted up over the years and the sea has retreated some six miles. In the first century, the Roman historian, Pliny the Elder, made a note of the waters from Ephesus harbour spilling onto the end of the Arcadian Way.

Incredible Discoveries

During the construction of the railway from Izmir to Aydin in the 1860's, an English engineer, John Turtle Wood, became interested in searching for the ruins of the ancient Temple of Artemis. By 1866, with the authorisation of the Turkish Government, the British started excavations but only a few remains from the temple were found. Austrian archaeologists took up the reins in 1894 and were later joined by a team from the British Museum. Step by step, as astounding treasures were unearthed, the elegant Greco-Roman city of Ephesus emerged from the rubble. Excavations and restoration continued to 1970 when work began on the Celsus Library. It was completed in 1978. Nevertheless there was more to unearth and the work has been continued by the Museum of Ephesus.

Daily life in Ephesus

Restoration of the buildings and monuments of the town give us a good idea of the daily life of the people or perhaps of the aristocratic people of the town. Roman baths, where wealthy men would be pampered, were found near the market, by the Celsus Library, and at the harbour. Four gymnasiums provided facilities to keep them fit and their bodies beautiful! The Odeum was like a small theatre, where the Advisory Council would meet to deliberate. You can go into a couple of houses on the slopes of Curetes Street to see the courtyards, fountains, mosaic floors and frescoes. The restored latrines show clearly where the men sat all in a row. On wintry days, some of them even made their servants sit first to warm the marble slabs. It may surprise you to know that this was a place for gossip and even for entertainment, as the small stage area in the middle was for musicians! Whenever I've been there with a group, somebody has usually had the bright idea of entertaining visitors by sitting just where the Romans sat, as demonstrated by the two young 'Romans' in the photograph. They'd come from Australia with their Mum and Dad, good friends I'd arranged to meet in Turkey, as they were keen to see some of its historic wonders.

Fountains were built on the main streets to keep people cool. One of them, dedicated to Trajan, had a large statue of the Emperor in the centre but only his right foot remains today. The Emperor's power is represented by his foot resting on a large ball, believed to represent the globe, which suggests that the Romans thought of the world as spherical, long before this was known for sure.

Photo by Steve Bennett, Brisbane

The ruins of the 'Love House' remain and a story that there was an underground tunnel from the library to the brothel is still going around. On Marble Street, an advertisement for the Love House is cut into the pavement: it depicts a foot indicating the direction, a lady, a heart, some text and a bag of money. Another story suggests that, if your foot was smaller than the one in the sign, you were too young to go there!

A number of monuments and gates have fine statues and reliefs cut into them, mainly of heroes and gods. On Domitian Square, there's a striking relief of a Greek goddess whose name still receives a great deal of attention today ... the goddess Niké! She symbolised victory. Various temples are dedicated to Apollo, Serapis, Domitian, Hadrian, Isis, Dea Roma and Divus Julius, as well as the Temple of Artemis which is just outside the town.

The Temple

Only part of one pillar remains of the great Temple of Artemis (erected out of pieces in 1972 – 73). The earliest period of the temple dates back to the 7th century BC, although it was destroyed and rebuilt seven times according to Strabo (Greek historian 64BC – 24 AD). He also said that people from all over the world came to see it. In 356 BC, it was burned down 'by a lunatic' and then rebuilt in even greater splendour by the Ephesians, at considerable sacrifice. This building was there in New Testament times. It was destroyed for the last time by the Goths in 265 AD. Writing in the first century, Pliny records that there were 127 columns in the temple.

Thirteen steps all round led into the massive building. It was the size of a football pitch. In the centuries ahead, as the town began to decline, the temple eventually fell into disrepair and much of the marble and stone was used in building the Church of St John and even St. Sophia in Constantinople. Two statues of Artemis and other treasures found in the area of the Temple can be seen in the Museum of Ephesus, in the nearby town of Sejuk.

Celsus Library

At the end of Curetes Street, beside the sturdy three-arched gate to the Agora, the shopping centre of Ephesus, you can see the stunning facade of the Celsus Library. It's probably the best known building in Ephesus, built by Gaius Julius Aquila to honour his father Celsus, who had been a Roman Senator and Governor of Asia. He was buried in a vault beneath the west wall. Gaius chose to build a library because Celsus loved books. There were 12,000 of them, papyri scrolls, housed in this library. A statue stood in each of the eight niches on the beautifully sculptured façade. Four of them remain, representing 'wisdom', 'knowledge', 'destiny and 'virtue'. The building was completed in 120 AD. Its collapse was the result of a tenth century earthquake.

The Theatre

The great theatre was the scene of one of the most dramatic incidents in the ministry of St. Paul, to which we will return later. It was built in the Hellenistic period, on the slope of Mount Pion and in a most impressive position for traders and visitors arriving from the port. Harbour Street, or the Arcadiana, runs directly from the harbour to the theatre. The Roman Emperor Claudius (41 – 54 AD) had a building programme underway to enlarge the theatre, around the time that St. Paul came to Ephesus.

Seating about 24,000, this theatre reached the highest capacity of any in Turkey. Together with the Stadium, the theatre provided entertainment, including drama, wild animal fights and gladiatorial contests. The acoustics were brilliant. Some of the wealthy Ephesians set up schools to train gladiators. The orchestra area was probably about six foot below the level of the audience and the stage. There were times when it was flooded and sea battles were played out.The back-stage buildings were three storeys high, elaborate and imposing.

The Church of the Virgin Mary

This is thought to have been the first church to be dedicated to the Virgin Mary. Excavations unearthed a sixth century inscription, indicating that the great Ecumenical Council meeting was held there in 431 AD. Records tell us that the Church was 'made for the Virgin Mary' and the Council recorded that Mother Mary was brought to Ephesus by the Apostle John and lived in a house on this spot for a short while. I know of no other reference to this house.

It strikes me that St. Mary's popularity in Ephesus could have given quite a boost to the church and been helpful in gaining followers. For centuries, Ephesus had been a focus for the worship of female deities. The ancient Anatolian fertility goddess, Cybele, was worshipped on the site of the Great Temple of Artemis of Ephesus, possibly a thousand years before. There was also a Temple to Serapis, the Egytian goddess, in the town. Towards the end of the first century, into the second and beyond, when the Temple was losing its influence, perhaps the 'cloak of Artemis' (Diana) could have fallen upon Mary'.

Was it also significant that this Council, when affirming the divine nature of Christ, that He is God, went beyond that conviction to argue that Mary should not be thought of as only 'Mother of Jesus' but also 'Mother of God' - 'Theotokos'? It was a controversial issue.

The church, constructed in the fourth century, was not as long as the original building but it incorporated three sides of an earlier building. Later, when another church was built alongside, it led to the Church of St. Mary being known also as the 'Double Church'. A festival of worship is held here each year on 15th August, as this is acknowledged as the date of the Assumption of Mary into Heaven

Symbols of Faith

A menorah has been carved roughly into the steps of the Celsus Library - early graffiti, I suppose, but a witness to the faith of the many Hebrew people who lived in Ephesus. The cross had not become the predominant Christian symbol in the early days but the 'Ichthus' fish sign was scratched into the paving on First Street and is still clearly visible. It is a Christian testimony, declaring a very basic creed 'Jesus Christ, Son of God and Saviour'. The circular Icthus sign can be seen in the bath house, on the steps of the library and on the pavement beyond the theatre. The circular icthus sign is less well known to us than the fish symbol but it was widely used in Anatolia and may be seen in many places.

The Circular symbol of Icthus

Graffiti declares Christian faith

ΙΧΘΥΣ (ichthys), or also ΙΧΘΥϹ with a lunate sigma, is an acronym/acrostic for "Ἰησοῦς Χριστός, Θεοῦ Υἱός, Σωτήρ" (Iēsous Christos, Theou Yios, Sōtēr, which translates into English as "Jesus Christ, Son of God, Saviour".

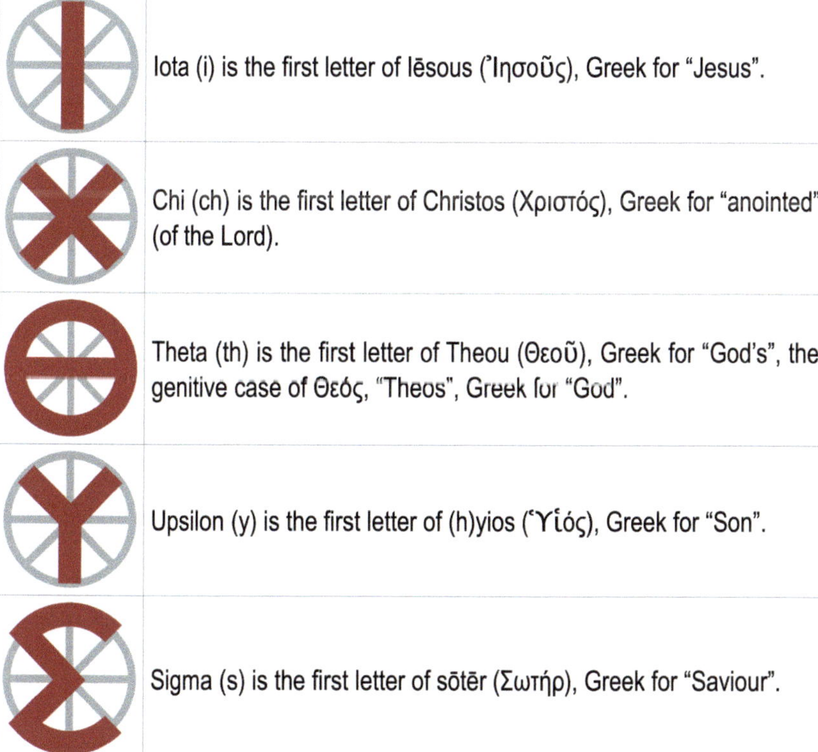

	Iota (i) is the first letter of Iēsous (Ἰησοῦς), Greek for "Jesus".
	Chi (ch) is the first letter of Christos (Χριστός), Greek for "anointed" (of the Lord).
	Theta (th) is the first letter of Theou (Θεοῦ), Greek for "God's", the genitive case of Θεός, "Theos", Greek for "God".
	Upsilon (y) is the first letter of (h)yios (Ὑιός), Greek for "Son".
	Sigma (s) is the first letter of sōtēr (Σωτήρ), Greek for "Saviour".

St. Paul in Ephesus

Luke tells us that St. Paul was prevented from visiting Ephesus on his second missionary trip. Consequently, he called in briefly, on his return journey, promising to come back (Acts 18v.18 – 21). Perhaps he recognised the extensive opportunities for Christian mission in this town, with people coming and going from all over the world. He kept his word and returned on his next venture in mission. He then stayed in Ephesus for two and a half years, AD 54 – 57. At first, Paul was welcomed into the Synagogue where he spoke regularly for three months, discussing the 'Kingdom of God' and the 'Way of the Lord' but, after a while, stubborn opposition emerged from some of the Jews and Paul transferred his ministry to the Hall of Tyrannus. Many of the group went with him and he continued teaching every day (Acts 18 v. 8 -10).

Recently, a cave on the hillside, overlooking the town, came to light. Archaeologists suggest that it may have been St. Paul's headquarters. Inside there are early frescoes and a later 6th century picture of St. Paul. I think that the cave is not open to the public. Paul's mission work in many places was shared by others like Epaphras (Col. 1 v. 7), Aquila and Priscilla, (1 Cor 16 v. 19) plus twenty three other 'fellow workers' referred to by name in Romans 16 v. 3 – 15. From Ephesus, Christian mission spilled over into surrounding towns including Colossae (Col. 1 v.1 – 2), Hierapolis and Laodicea (Col. 4 v. 13) and the other towns referred to in Revelation chapters 1 - 3. In the second century, there was a Bishop Onesimus, who led the church in Ephesus. Could that have been the slave who was adopted by Paul, about whom Paul wrote to Philemon (Philemon v. 10 – 21)? If so, he is bound to have come under Paul's personal influence.

He wrote to Christians in Ephesus

A number of scholars date this letter after Paul's death but there is little doubt that the content came from him, even if compiled later. His prayer in Chpt 3 v. 14 – 19 conveys the passion he brought to his ministry and the affection he felt for his fellow Christians. It is a moving prayer, well worth pondering over. His words can search our own soul to find even a little of the same love, care and earnest, hopeful longing for others to find strength, faith and the inner power of God's love.

In some editions of the New Testament, the translators have missed a bit of the Greek text at the beginning of his prayer. It should begin: "For this reason.... I kneel in prayer...". Paul's specific purpose for prayer is summarised in v17-18: "That you are rooted and grounded in love ... and grasp how wide and long and high and deep is the love of Christ." What a concept! What an aspiration to know that God's love is around us in all directions and we are at the heart of it ... and, at the same time, to have God's love at the heart of ourselves!

No illustration can be adequate for such life changing truth but I recall a children's address from when I was six or seven. A bottle was thrown into the sea. When it was in the water, the waves bounced it around and it began to fill until the bottle was full of sea and floating in the sea. Then the question was asked, "Was the bottle in the water or the water in the bottle?"

I don't remember his punch-line but clearly he was illustrating Paul's message about being filled by God's love and being enveloped in God's love - all at the same time. It was his attempt to find a pictorial image of what can only be known in experience, by faith.

Big Brawl at the Theatre: Acts 19 v 23 - 41

On many occasions, Paul needed some of that assurance himself, perhaps in Ephesus, when a riot threatened his life. He'd been preaching that 'gods made with hands are not gods at all', which provoked the people. They blamed him for decline in the numbers of pilgrims coming to the Temple and for the falling trade of the silversmiths. The Temple's silver souvenirs were not selling well. Their business was threatened. Demetrius, a silversmith himself, stirred up other workers and Paul found himself clashing with a huge crowd of them. At festival times, great crowds usually brought big business to every sales point in the city, in the same way that tourism brings economic growth to places that attract visitors today. Other protesters joined in as their businesses were suffering too. Consequently, huge numbers gathered at the theatre shouting for Paul's blood. Demetrius, who seems to have been president of the Guild of Silversmiths, hyped up the crowd.

The shouting didn't stop for a couple of hours as they kept repeating their 'slogan', "Great is Artemis of Ephesus". Two Macedonians were dragged into the theatre, as the mob rushed in on impulse. They were Gaius and Aristarchus who had arrived with Paul. Anxious to speak to the people, Paul wanted to go into the theatre but fellow Christians held him back, as he would have been lynched. He then received a message from some high ranking officials, who were his friends, begging him not to risk his life. Luke describes the chaos. People were yelling contradictory demands. He says that many had been swept along and didn't even know what it was all about. There are times when that happens today, of course, when some protesters are happy to join any protest they can find.

A respected Jew, Alexander, tried to speak above the bellowing but the mob was still chanting, "Great is Artemis of Ephesus." Eventually, the town clerk's diplomatic speech managed to calm the people. He convinced the rabble that no one could threaten the greatness of Artemis. He reminded them of their belief that Artemis had descended from the sky and could not be thought of as 'made with hands'. He said that if anything illegal had been said or done, it should be  taken to the courts and he warned them that they must be careful to avoid the sanctions of Rome descending upon them for riotous disturbance. It was the speech of a shrewd politician, which brought some order. After a quiet word of encouragement to the Christian leaders, Paul bade farewell and left.

I am smiling as I remember reading aloud Luke's version of that action-packed chapter to a pilgrimage group. They were sitting in rows on the stone seats, quite high in the theatre, away from the many visitors, but as I read others gathered to listen. I became aware of a creeping silence as more people stopped to hear. When I reached the end, they burst into applause! I was a bit embarrassed but also delighted. It is a thrilling chapter and well worth reading.

Unemployment

This may sound like nonsense but it occurs to me that, if it were possible to have been present, with our contemporary insight, we may have been a little more aware, than the apostles, of the likely hardship being faced by the families of the silversmiths, if hundreds of them found themselves out of work. We may have proposed some action in response. You can imagine the power of feeling in the theatre, as the crowd hollered in helplessness, anxiety and anger. It helps me, a little, to get closer to that situation, when I think of the powerful feeling present as a great crowd gathered in Hyde Park for the final rally of The People's March for Jobs in 1983. A few hundred had set out from Glasgow, a couple of months before. Support increased as they were welcomed at churches and community halls whilst walking all the way to London. By the time of this final rally, numbers were estimated at 150,000, but who knows!

The mood was not aggressive but there was a strong atmosphere of intense solidarity, hopelessness and yet expectation. There was a sense of people listening earnestly, as I tried to acknowledge to the crowd that the churches were frequently seen to be identified with the establishment, rather than with the vulnerable as Jesus had been. I recounted how when He carried a cross, the burden that bore Him down was not just the weight of the wood but much more the burden he shared of people's failure and shame, their loss of hope, self-respect and human dignity. That's the kind of pain carried by communities from which many of the crowd had come, especially in the north. People who were plunged into long term unemployment. Remembering the crowd in Hyde Park helps me to better understand Paul's burning desire to speak God's word to distressed people, whose livelihoods were at stake. I was quite moved later when Tony Benn and a couple of leading politicians made their way through the crowd to talk further with me about the teaching of Jesus.

Admiration

Reading Acts 19 fills me with deep regard for St. Paul, not only for his courage and 'foolishness' in wanting to face the roaring crowd in Ephesus but even more for the dynamics of his approach to the tasks of ministry and mission.

Mission Strategy. Paul identified the strategic opportunities for mission based in Ephesus, where people were coming from all over the known world. If he could engage them in the Christian faith and community, it may be likely that many would return to their homes with faith to share. Possibly they would gather new Christians to build up new churches in places far from Ephesus. In the UK, some churches follow the same path today and look for appropriate mission strategy, identifying social phenomena that could provide a helpful framework by which Christian life can spread. In many places, however, it seems there's little strategy.

Focussed Ministry. St. Paul concentrated resources, working consistently. Every day, he was bringing groups together at the hall of Tyrannus. He continued that work for two and a half years, building firm foundations and avoiding the 'hit and run' syndrome. Today our churches, in many situations, have to spread resources more thinly than ever and, therefore, inevitably limit the scope of pastoral care, teaching, preaching, social justice and evangelistic ministries.

Group Work. Within the context of regular group gatherings, St. Paul used a variety of communication skills to strengthen the life and faith of his followers. Long before anyone had heard of group dynamics, they were building each other up through discussion, prayer and sharing in mission work. Since New Testament times, and at every point of renewal in the life of the church, the fellowship group has been as vital in the nurture and development of Christians, as is the gathering for worship. In our present generation, there seem to be fewer such groups in many congregations but where they are in place, it's more likely there will be evidence of growth and of strength in fellowship.

Pastoral Care. Developing personal relationships with other Christians must have been a priority for Paul. His pastoral care and personal links are clearly evident in his letters, as he sent greetings to many by name and enquired about others. His leadership role in the mission of the church was manifest and respected and yet he regarded those who shared God's mission, not as subordinates in any way, but as his fellow-workers. It would seem to be vital today, in our understanding and practice, that God's mission is in ministry shared by all Christians, within which there is close, consistent and supportive pastoral care.

Sustained Encouragement. Paul's letters also tell us that he maintained supportive contact with his fellow workers, when he moved to minister in other places. He sent greetings but he also helped to sustain their faith: he encouraged them, expressed gratitude for their gifts and their commitment, prayed for them and assured them of God's blessing – setting a great example for us. I am thankful and moved by the faith, commitment and sheer hard work of many contemporary church leaders and Christian people and am inspired by the variety and often outstanding gifts that are used in God's service. I am aware, however, that although we live in a vastly different social and cultural context, there's still a great deal for us to learn from the New Testament church.

Depth in Teaching. Most of Paul's letters were probably intended not for the recipient church alone but for circulation to other towns. In this way, he shared his response to pastoral issues arising in the new churches, gave guidance on ethical matters, on social/community problems facing the churches and communicated Christian Theology in some depth. Sadly, today, I hear and read of many Christians in local congregations who are hungry for substantial teaching.

Social Witness. I cannot imagine that Paul would deliberately undermine the income of workers and, consequently, the stability of their family life but it happened when their work was sustaining falsehood, injustice or oppression. When he became aware that his preaching was affecting business life in Ephesus, he was ready to take the risk of facing the mob to explain. What a difficult task! The whole business world in Ephesus was exploiting the ancient spiritual life of the town to make money from the festivals and the pilgrims, rather like the commercialisation of Christmas today. His message of justice, liberation and God's grace would challenge many basic structures, values and the spirituality of Ephesian society and ours today.

Economic Insight and Honesty. When it comes to economic matters and public policy, we tend to compromise our values in the church, nowadays. We are likely to soft peddle on economic matters. We avoid possible accusations of being political. Thankfully, like St. Paul, there are some prophets, nowadays, who stick their heads above the parapet. We are among the wealthy, not the poorest millions of the world. We are part of the global economic system that sustains the disparity between wealth and poverty. Our gospel loses its cutting edge, when we fail to speak and act for radical truth and justice over such matters, as an integral dimension of Christian salvation.

Prayer. Paul prayed for and prayed with his people. I try to pray his prayer for the Ephesians with him so that, "Out of the glorious richness of His resources, God will enable us to know the strength of the Spirit's inner reinforcement, and that Christ may live in our hearts by faith." (Ephesians 3 v. 16 J.B.Phillips). I long for us to keep learning from Paul's mission priorities and strategies, alongside contemporary needs.

Reflection

- What do you admire about St. Paul?

- Read Ephesians 3 v 14-19 and ask who you would pray for, with passion, in this way.

- If your church has lost much of its passion and joy - why? What would rekindle it?

- What mission strategy do you recognise in your denomination or your congregation?

- We mentioned that fellowship groups have a vital role at times of reformation, renewal or revival. Why are there so few groups in many congregations?

- Identify areas of substantial teaching which have been shared with the ordinary folk of your church on Christian Theology, ethics or social/community matters.

- To what extent should unemployment be of concern to the church and, if it is, in what ways should that concern be expressed or acted upon?

- How does the Christian Gospel challenge structures, values, beliefs and spirituality in our society?

- Is it true that we compromise our Christian values in the church? Do we soft peddle on some things to avoid upsetting people, do our best to keep happy those who contribute generously and avoid possible accusations of being political? Does this mean that in so doing, vital truth of the Gospel loses its cutting edge?

Mary's House

There's a small stone house about five miles from Ephesus, in a forest on Mount Bulbul, above the town. Tradition supports the belief that this could have been the home of Mary, the Mother of Jesus, in her final years. There is a conflicting tradition which suggests that Mary died on Mt. Zion in Jerusalem. We therefore approach 'Mary's House' with an element of uncertainty, although the possibility of this having been the site of her home is feasible. The main building is from the sixth century but the foundation walls from the first.

In John 19 v. 27, Jesus entrusted the care of His mother to the disciple John. In 190 AD, Eusebius, Bishop of Caesarea and church historian, refers to John's ministry in Ephesus and to his burial place there. Irenaeus, a disciple of the martyr Polycarp (Bishop of Smyrna), who later became Bishop of Lyon, also wrote about John in Ephesus.

In 1818, an Austrian peasant nun, Katerina Emmerich, who had been paralysed and bedridden for twelve years, gave a detailed description of the house and the surrounding region, even though she had never been near Ephesus. A research team from Izmir College, under the leadership of Priest Fr. Yung, although sceptical about the nun's account, started exploring in 1891. When they reached the area around Mt. Bulbul, local people told them of Christian Turks who came to worship at a small ruin, nearby, on 15th August each year. (The date which many Christians associate with the Assumption of Mary.) When the house was found, the details exactly matched the nun's description.

The ruin was restored, with a small entrance space leading into the main room which now provides a small chapel. The exit is through a smaller side room, which is thought to have been Mother Mary's bedroom. Silence is requested on entry. It is a lovely, simple, devotional place. The surrounding woods are beautiful and the whole setting provides a peaceful place for prayer. The 'House of Mother Mary' is visited by Christians and Muslims. On November 29th 2006, Pope Benedict 16th was the most recent Pope to visit.

Whether or not this is the authentic site of the home of the Mother of Jesus doesn't seem to be a vital matter. It provides a symbolic focus and evokes spiritual reflection. If that's your intention, it's best to visit in the earlier part of the day, before the crowds arrive.

From the early days of the Church, Mary has been a devotional focus for a significant number of Christians but it would be a mistake to think of her as only gentle mother Mary, 'meek and mild'. It is probable that Mary had gentle qualities but it seems that she also had a dynamic radical vision of God's intention for the world, perhaps even thinking of the profound changes that would be fulfilled by the life and ministry of her son. The song of praise, known as the Magnificat (Luke 1 v46 – 56) has been heard from the lips of Mary since this Gospel was put together in about AD 65 – 70. In it, Mary expresses joy - because God gives value and recognition to the lowly and reduces the high profile of the proud and superior. He brings thorough moral change. God sweeps away the powerful and the oppressors to make room for the humble, bringing fundamental social transformation. God provides for the poor and hungry but sends the rich away empty handed, bringing extensive economic re-formation.

This beautiful poem of praise enshrines deep seated hopes that have not yet become reality. Christians in every generation have to learn again the pattern of human life and society which was inspired and modelled in Jesus Christ. The Gospel tells the story in a style which could suggest that Mary originally learned this from Old Testament teaching, on which this hymn of praise seems to have been based and, as an elderly lady, she may have brought her deep convictions to Ephesus and shared them with the growing Christian fellowship there.

Hagios Theologos:
Cathedral of St. John

This magnificent Cathedral Church was built in the 6th century. When I look at church buildings, I'm reminded of my gratitude for the excellent architects who worked with us on two major church development projects in the UK. That quality of ecclesiastical understanding and architectural flare is not easy to find nowadays, nor was it then, but Emperor Justinian (527 – 565 AD) and the Empress Theodora must have known just where to look. Their monograms were carved into the capitals of columns on the first floor of this church. It was built over the site of the tomb of St. John. John's death was probably around the year 100AD. He was buried outside the town on Ayaskuluk Hill. A basilica was built over the tomb in the 4th century.

The Mediterranean doesn't have tides that can clean the coasts and wash away sediments from river mouths, so over centuries the coastline has moved into the sea. Ephesus Harbour and the river were among those that were silted. The low level ground around the Temple of Artemis became a malarial swamp. Consequently, part of the town moved to higher ground around the Cathedral and became known by the name that was given to the burial place of St. John and later adopted by the Cathedral Church – Hagios Theologos. The town was not renamed, 'Seljuk', until 1914. In the 7th - 8th century a protective wall was built around the Cathedral and the nearby 5th century fortress. A large, sturdy, stone, arched gate has been unearthed.

The design of the Cathedral was a masterpiece. In size and beauty, it could have been built to rival the Temple of Artemis. The church was in the form of a cross. The roof, with six domes, was supported by fine, tall, gleaming marble columns and arches, some of which have been reconstructed in their former position. The central dome was over the burial place of St. John. Remaining fragments of mosaics give some idea of the care given to internal decoration. The Cathedral treasury, on the north side, was turned into a chapel in the 10th – 11th century. Its apse bears a fresco of Jesus. St. John is on one side of Jesus and, on the other, is an unrecognised saint. The keyhole shaped Baptistry, with steps descending for emersion, is thought to have been from the 4th century church building. Outside the Cathedral, laid out on the ground, are a large number of capitals from columns, many of which depict the cross of St. John. The remaining stump of one column from the Temple of Artemis, down the hill, is clearly visible from here.

The area over St. John's tomb is marked by a marble platform, with a pillar at each corner. This had been the place of the high altar. Invariably, visitors show extra respect in this part of the ruins. Pilgrim groups have appreciated a few moments to stand quietly around the tomb. It has proved to be a helpful place for brief devotions and for reading the letter, from the book of Revelation, which was addressed by John to the Church at Ephesus (Rev. 2 v.1 – 7.)

The letter to the Church at Ephesus

Love - Revelation 2 v 1 – 7

"You have abandoned the love you had at first."
Revelation 2 v 4

2 v 1 describes Christ walking among the golden lampstands. As the lamps symbolise the churches, so Christ is speaking from within the church at Ephesus. In His hand, He is holding the seven stars which symbolise the angels or messengers who are representatives of the churches. This indicates that He is holding and supporting the seven churches. In fact, the Greek text is stronger. It means He is holding the whole church: not only one congregation or the church in this town; not only one ethnic group or one denomination; not only people of one theological identity but the whole church.

2 v 2 The good deeds and hard work of the Christians in Ephesus are acknowledged and commended. These followers are active in God's work. Christ praises them for their perseverance and endurance, without which their faith would not have survived. This city was famous for its pagan worship and magical arts. It was part of the

culture. Discrimination against Christians in business had become common place, because Christianity was seen to be undermining business. Nevertheless Christians had remained constant and patient through difficult times.

Being a Christian was not a soft option. Like St. John, I am moved by Christian courage during hardship, when I've seen grace and joy among those who suffer. This brings to mind Christians I knew in Zimbabwe, struggling with poverty, who have faced oppression and hunger year after year. Nearer home, the Christian endurance of many who are grieving and lost brings equal challenge to me. Here, in this letter, Christians in Ephesus were being praised for their resilient faith and fortitude.

The Nicolaitans

The Ephesian Church had stood up to 'those who said they were apostles but were not'. By this time, the understanding of 'Apostles' had broadened beyond the twelve. It now referred to those who were the appointed or recognised leaders and who had authority within the church. There was a group, the Nicolaitans, who tried to assume that role but they were misleading the church. They were infiltrating the fellowship, spreading corrupt teaching and immoral behaviour. They believed that 'liberation in Christ' gave the freedom to do anything and that sinning gave God's grace the opportunity to 'abound'. They were causing harm to people but Christians in Ephesus resisted. The true leaders tested those who were leading the church astray and found them false. No one could accuse this church of being naïve or too easy going.

2 v 3 They had endured hardship for the sake of Christ.

2 v 4 But they had lost the zeal of their first love! Active, committed Christians, enduring hard times, persisting in their faith, holding on to the truth even when infiltrators brought false teaching and action into the church – and yet they had lost their passion! The quality of their devotion and their love for God had lost its freshness, its depth

and its joy. They were doing everything right but their hearts were getting cold.

O how easily that can happen at times of pressure. Perhaps we can see it in our own lives. New rules and regulations are introduced in our churches to keep us on the straight and narrow regarding health and safety, charity law, safeguarding discipline and tax regulations, plus a thousand and one directives within each denomination. But what is inspiring, rekindling and nurturing Christian passion and love for God, with heart and soul and mind and strength and for our neighbour, as Jesus said?

Without genuine love, all the hard work of a church would be lifeless. It is the first mark of a true and living church. St. Paul emphasised that it is the highest and best gift of all. (1 Cor. 12 v 31 and 1 Cor. 13). In signing off his letter to the Church in Ephesus, Paul wrote - 'Grace be with all who have undying love for our Lord Jesus Christ.' (Eph. 6 v 24)

2 v 5 So "Repent". That is - be sorry for letting go of God's most precious gift and turn to Him. God's love is always ready and waiting. That's the first step that was required of the Christians in Ephesus. The second step was to "Begin again" – to think, love and act as they did at first. Then they would not simply be going through the motions but living fully, with their being and their doing inspired and motivated by God's grace ... that is, by God's active loving kindness, which we meet most generously and plentifully in Jesus Christ. We must be clear, of course, that John is not pleading for effervescent hype in the church but for deep and genuine love for God and for our neighbours. The message of the letter could not be clearer - without love, the true life and light of the church will fade away. There will be no witness to right-living or loving care for others radiating from the church. The lamp will no longer be there to shine.

2 v 6 The warning about the Nicolaitans is repeated.

2 v 7 God's promise of eternal life will belong to those who overcome the pressures. What is eternal life? John's Gospel gives us a good guide in chapter 17 v 3, in telling us that Eternal Life is to know God and to know Jesus Christ. It is to live in communion with Him - a communion that cannot be limited by life or death. The secret of eternal life is love.

Reflection

- Ask your self - Would it have been appropriate for my church to have received a letter along these lines? And if we did receive such a letter, what would we say in reply?

- The church in Ephesus was praised for holding on to Christian endurance and joy through some very difficult times. Think of Christians in whom you have seen the same courage.

- In Ephesus, some leaders within the church were leading the church astray. Are there any dangers of this happening in the church today?

- As Christians, have we lost our first love?

Smyrna

Modern Izmir from Mount Pagus

The Church of
St Polycarp (1693)
Izmir

Fresco, in the
Church, of the
burning and
death of Polycarp

Fort Velvet on
Pagas Mount

Colonnade in the
main street of
the market

Arches onto
the central
market
street

Storage space
beneath the
shops

Chapter 3

Smyrna

The city of Izmir gave me my first glimpse of Turkey, some years ago. My wife and I arrived late at the airport and, because of delays, we were shuttled to a hotel which had probably seen better days, in a down-market area of Izmir. I should add that the hotel staff were delightful and that the worn out building was not typical of the high quality of hotels throughout Turkey. The first sign or 'sound' of life, rather early the next morning, was the call to prayer from the local mosque. From the hotel window, we watched the sun rise over the town's smoky rooftops, illuminated by the sun's glow, drifting up from industrial areas beyond the shops and houses. Soon, people were scurrying along the streets below, giving us our first fascinating glimpse of 'everyday' in a Turkish town.

Izmir, on the Aegean coast of Turkey, is now the nation's third largest city but there are indications that its earliest settlers, who lived on the northwest side of the bay, probably came before 2000BC. Archaeologists tell us that the ancient town, Smyrna, was built on a small peninsular jutting into the bay and that a seventh century BC Temple of Athena attracted pilgrims. The coming and going of visitors inevitably gave rise to trade, which led to the development of wealth and status for the ancient city. According to tradition, Homer, author of the 'Odyssey' and the 'Illiad', came from this area sometime between the 12th and 8th century BC. Information is rather imprecise and expert sources have widely differing views about his dates. Herodotus, 5th century philosopher, who was born just south of Smyrna, describes a period of decline of over half a century, when the Lydians captured the city in 600BC, before the Persians seized power in 545BC.

Growth of a City

Towards the end of the 4th century, some of the population moved round the bay to the slopes of Mount Pagus. The story goes that, in 334BC, Alexander the Great dreamed that Nemesis, the goddess of that mountain, told him to present Smyrna with a gift. He then consulted the oracle at the Temple of Apollo, who instructed him to build a fort on a hill. Work then began on Fort Velvet, part of which remains today, in its high strategic position on Mt. Pagus. The town grew up around it. Later, after ancient Smyrna spent some years under the rule of the Pergamon Empire, it was passed to the Romans, who constructed a huge water cistern for the city, inside the fortress walls. Its remains are interesting to see. The deep harbour contributed to the successful life of Smyrna, which soon became an important town, competing with the cities of Miletus and Ephesus. The theatre and stadium were built on the high ground, while the monuments and temples were built alongside the agora (market) below. Having seen the brilliant view from Mount Pagus, across the town to the sea, it is obvious why ancient Smyrna was thought to be 'the loveliest in Asia'.

Historic documents report that Mithridates VI of Pontus (120-63BC), who challenged the power of Rome from the Black Sea to Syria and Armenia, slaughtered 80,000 Romans in Smyrna in 88BC. Persians and Greeks acclaimed him a 'Saviour' from Roman oppression but his legacy in Smyrna was of bitter suffering and bereavement.

The modern city is built over Greco-Roman Smyrna so excavation has been very limited. We know that most of its public buildings were faced with gleaming marble which, together with the natural surroundings of sea, mountains and green fields, as well as dazzling sunshine, softened by the cooling onshore breezes, made this a most attractive and comfortable place to live. It was home to a large Jewish community. A Christian community that took root in Smyrna, during the first century, was among those addressed by one of the letters of Revelation. A number of sixth century marble crosses found during excavation in the agora, indicated that a church building had been in the central area.

Thirteen Corinthian columns provide a good land mark for locating the open square of the agora. There had been an altar to Zeus in the centre. Statues of Demeter, goddess of agriculture, harvest and fertility, and of Poseidon, god of the sea, stood side by side. These two deities were especially appropriate for the commercial community. An impressive two storey construction formed part of the agora, providing space for separate shops and storage facilities. The stone vaulting of the lower level can be seen, with a corner of the vault supported by five ribs – built to withstand earthquakes. Remains of a short stretch of road and a Roman aqueduct also survive but, as opportunities come along, further excavation will take place and I think that, in time, more of ancient Smyrna will emerge.

St Polycarp

A man who inspires me was Polycarp. He was the fourth Bishop of Smyrna, who lived between about AD65 and AD155. Tertullian and Irenaeus, two of the Church Fathers from the same period, both record that Polycarp was consecrated as Bishop of Smyrna by St. John. He was almost certainly there, when the letter of Revelation chapter two was addressed to the Church in Smyrna. Around AD110, Polycarp received a letter from Ignatius, Bishop of Antioch. This letter has become one of the main sources of information about organisation in the early church and particularly about the role and responsibilities of a bishop. Polycarp wrote a number of letters but only one survives – to the Christians in Philippi. It refers to letters of St. Paul and of Ignatius and it includes some details of procedures in the early church.

The Anatolian Church, of which Polycarp was part, celebrated Easter on 14th Nisan (April), in line with the date mentioned in St. John's Gospel but this differed by a week from the date observed by Rome. As it had become a matter of contention, Polycarp was appointed to travel to

Rome to seek a way forward. It was resolved, without hindering communion between east and west, as the Pope agreed that the celebrations of Easter Day could continue to be a week apart. It was, then, significant that Polycarp, from the east, was invited to celebrate mass in Rome.

During the reign of Emperor Domitian (AD 81 – 96), Roman rule became increasingly autocratic and its preoccupation with supremacy quite fanatical. The Emperor began to think of himself as a god, demanding supreme allegiance, which created great difficulty for faithful Christians, and many suffered. Pernicious and bloody attitudes filtered down into the culture of Roman authority. After Domitian, even the Emperors were not safe. Three took their own lives, two were lynched by soldiers, one was executed and one was poisoned. No wonder Polycarp wrote, "O God, what an awful age you have caused me to live in." Antoninus Pius, Emperor from AD138 to 161, was considered to be capable and dedicated but his character was not reflected in those who were entrusted with authority at a more local level.

Polycarp was persuaded by his congregation to leave the city and hide, to avoid the increasing danger. However, he was soon tracked down. When soldiers came to arrest him, under the authority of the Roman Governor, he first offered them food and then retired to pray before being taken away. He was subjected to a public trial in the crowded stadium in Smyrna. The same day, Christians from Philadelphia were being slaughtered in the stadium. This stirred up the crowd to point a finger at Polycarp. It's likely that many were silent but thousands jeered and ridiculed him, some, possibly, to ensure that they would not be accused along with him. The Governor tried to persuade him to "swear by the genius of Caesar and revile Christ." Polycarp replied –

> "If you vainly suppose that I will acknowledge Caesar as sovereign,
> and if you pretend that you don't know who I am, listen plainly: I am
> a Christian. For eighty and six years I have served Jesus Christ and
> He has done me no wrong. How can I blaspheme my King who
> saved me?"

This was high treason! The Proconsul threatened to throw him to the beasts but then decided that Polycarp should be burned at the stake. As the fire was lit, Bishop Polycarp prayed –

"O Lord, Almighty God, the Father of your beloved Son Jesus Christ, through whom we have come to know you, I thank you for counting me worthy this day and hour of sharing the cup of Christ, and being among the number of your martyrs."

The wind was blowing the flames about and, although he was terribly burned, the flames did not kill him. His suffering was prolonged until a soldier brought his life to an end with the thrust of a sword. 2nd February AD 155 or 156.

Christian Witness Today

Witness is, of course, an essential element of Christian living but rarely do we have first-hand experience today of the high level of threat and risk that faced Polycarp. The Greek word 'martyr' means 'witness'. When it is used in the New Testament, it does not only refer to those who gave their lives for their faithful convictions and action but to every act of Christian witness. Some Christians I knew in Zimbabwe, who had taken action for justice and peace were beaten up, others were imprisoned, escaped the country, disappeared or were found dead.

You may know of the danger faced by Henry Olonga, as his action attracted international media attention. Thankfully, he managed to escape. Now well settled with his wife and children in Australia, his superb tenor voice and creative media skills are enabling him to develop a ministry in music, art and communication. I first heard him singing in a Gilbert and Sullivan production, when he was a student at Plumtree School, on the western edge of Matabeleland, although I didn't know him then.

In 1995, Henry became the first black and, at only eighteen, the youngest ever international test cricketer to play for Zimbabwe. As he learned of the 'unspeakable atrocities' being carried out in the name of the president, Robert Mugabe, and discovered more of the oppression and suffering of Zimbabwe's people, he became increasingly uncomfortable, not with cricket itself, but in representing his nation. In 2003, together with his team mate, Andy Flower, he decided to wear a black armband during a Cricket World Cup match in Zimbabwe. They issued a statement of protest against the policies of Zimbabwe's Government, mourning the death of democracy. Immediately, a warrant was issued for Henry's arrest on charges of treason, which could incur the death penalty in Zimbabwe. He was forced into hiding. Emails issuing death threats and intimidation by Zimbabwe's Youth Militia increased the pressure. He received an urgent message from a sympathetic supporter in central intelligence warning him to leave the country quickly. It led him to take a trip to South Africa and then to the UK.

Whilst in the UK, Henry performed a number of concerts, during which he thrilled audiences with a variety of impressive songs and told us his story. He explained that making his protest had been the biggest challenge of his life. He had known that he could have been bundled away at any moment but he'd had to take a stand. I asked him "Why?" These were his words –

> "I became a Christian at sixteen and couldn't have made this protest unless I was sure that it was something God wanted me to do. A lot of people blame God for their actions saying, 'God told me to do it', but for me it was a step of faith. I knew there would be consequences. I didn't know what would happen to me. God called me to do what I did. I just knew that I should take action."

> "As I look back I have no doubt that He has always provided for me and I've never been disappointed with Him."

Letter to the Church in Smyrna
Suffering - Revelation 2 v. 8 – 11

> "I know your affliction … do not fear what you are about to suffer."
> Revelation 2 v.9 & 10

There is no mention of the church in Smyrna in the Acts of the Apostles or in the New Testament letters, only here in Revelation. Yet, it seems inevitable that St. Paul visited this church, while he was based in Ephesus and was building up the churches in western Anatolia. Early tradition suggests that he had been there. This letter in Revelation clearly indicates that St. John had been in Smyrna and knew the church and wider community.

Many Christians in Smyrna had faced the experience and challenges of suffering. There was a large Jewish community in the town and, if the account in Acts 5 v 40 – 41 was typical, the Jewish hierarchy could have been responsible for inflicting some of the pain. Some members of the Sanhedrin in Jerusalem wanted the Apostles to be put to death (v 33) but eventually they were whipped and ordered never again to speak in the name of Jesus. The Apostles did not, of course, agree to be silenced about Christ. They were quite willing to be considered as worthy of suffering disgrace for the name of Christ. Bitter opposition from Jews followed Paul throughout his missionary travels, in Antioch, Iconium, Lystra, Thessolonica. It was also ingrained in the Jewish community in Smyrna.

2 v 8 The message in this letter comes from 'the one who is first and last', that is from the eternal one who endured human suffering and death but was victorious.

2 v 9 The persecution of Christians in Smyrna is addressed directly – "I know your troubles and your poverty." The Greeks had two words for poverty. 'Penia' meant 'not wealthy, having no luxury', and 'ptocheia', meaning more extreme, 'absolute poverty and destitution'. That is

the word used here because it describes the Christians in Smyrna. This city was very loyal to Rome. It was the first city in the world to build a temple to the goddess 'Roma'. Then in AD 25, when Asian cities were competing to build a temple to the Emperor Tiberius, Smyrna alone was selected and the temple was the pride of the city. Not surprisingly, Christians became unpopular for not taking part in Emperor worship. This added to the antagonism being stirred up by Jews. (2 v 9)

Society in Smyrna was wealthy and prosperous. Christians were among the poor, lower classes and were probably frozen out of the business community by the powerful and corrupt. At times, they were attacked by the mob. Homes were wrecked, possessions stolen and as much bad gossip as possible was spread.

2 v 9 Refers to the slander of those who claimed to be Jews but who are not. What does it mean? It means false rumours and accusations were being put about by Jews, for example:

- Christians must be cannibals – eating bodies and drinking blood

- organising orgies – agape meals or love feasts

- breaking up families – as devout Jews rejected those who became Christian
- being atheists – no images of their god and no temples for their worship
- being politically disloyal and disruptive – because they would not swear that Caesar is Lord, thus undermining the unity and stability of Rome
- plotting arson – as they spoke of the world ending in flames and disintegration.

The Jews, to whom the letter refers were no longer taking their guidance from God, as true Jews would. Paul made it clear (Rom 2 v28 – 29) that a man is not a Jew if he is only a Jew outwardly (circumcision). Being a true Jew is a matter of the heart. The Jews in

Smyrna were being described as a 'Synagogue of Satan', devoted to evil ways. Synagogue means 'assembly' and Jews loved to call themselves the 'Assembly of the Lord'. So here is a play on their own words – the 'Assembly of Satan'.

2v10 'Do not fear what you are about to suffer'. The letter is based on the experience of many who had suffered persecution, imprisonment and death. Christians in Smyrna were warned that some would be imprisoned and that their troubles would last for ten days. There was no penalty of custody and imprisonment was costly. Prisoners would be kept for ten days and then led out to die. The warning was to strengthen them and encourage them to remain faithful and true. It was to offer them victory over the power of suffering and those who inflicted it. It was to strengthen their hope of life with Christ, here and beyond.

I wonder if this letter was known to young Polycarp and if he remembered it when he most needed to. It could have helped to sustain him throughout his life, as well as when he sought faith and courage to face the final test, in his eighty sixth year.

Costly Faith

> "Suffering is the badge of the true Christian. The disciple is not above His master. Luther reckoned suffering to be among the true marks of the church … discipleship means allegiance to the suffering of Christ, and it is therefore not at all surprising that a Christian should be called upon to suffer."
>
> Dietrich Bonhoeffer. From 'The Cost of Discipleship.'

Bonhoeffer was hanged by order of Himmler in Flossenburg concentration camp on April 9th, 1945.

It seems that God was able to work through life's suffering, since earliest Old Testament times. The suffering of the cross is central to the Christian

Gospel. St Paul and the Apostles faced imprisonment and martyrdom. Suffering was a fact of life for many faithful Christians in the early church.

In the face of that reality, v 10 God offers comfort and grace – "Be faithful until death" and "I will give you the crown of life" (v10). To be faithful is to trust Christ. It is to depend on Him even in danger and death. The reasons given for confidence in Christ right to the end are because:

2 v 8 He is eternal, 'The first and the last.' because Christ is not limited to this mortal life – 'Who was dead and yet He lives.'

2 v 9 He has first-hand experience of human sorrow, suffering and death. Therefore we can confide in Christ who knows and understands the turbulence of our life and death, because Jesus recognised the true value and spiritual worth of every person. God looks on the heart (v9). "I know …. your poverty, even though you are rich".

God's Grace is in Christ. It is not God's will that people should suffer.

2 v 10 God can bring purpose and meaning into suffering. The suffering of the people of Smyrna was being caused by evil intention not by godly action ... and yet at times, 'victory' can be seen in the radiant witness of some Christians, like Stephen or Polycarp, even in their pain. It is not God's will that anyone should suffer but sometimes He will work for good through suffering that comes.

God is generous. God will give "the crown of life"(v 10) and a faithful Christian "will not be harmed by a second death" (v11). Those whose evil actions can destroy physical life have no power over spiritual life and cannot, therefore, bring about spiritual (second) death.

The sustaining, strengthening grace of God does not deliver us from suffering. The Revelation is not suggesting there will be salvation or protection from suffering but rather victory within it. God's Grace supports us, enables us, comforts us and holds on to us through all our trials and troubles, including our death. Our true inner self is held in the eternal care of God, now and always.

Olivia

I have known Christians in other parts of the world, as well as many in the UK, whose faith has given them sustaining strength at times of pain, sorrow, deep disappointment or fear. In them, I have seen the Grace of God at work. They have been a living witness to the reality of Christian hope, in their struggle and suffering. I know only a few who have come through deliberate, brutal suffering inflicted by others, like the persecution in Smyrna, into what could be described as the 'victory' of God's grace. Olivia is one.

Olivia is living in the UK now, nursing, and providing some financial support for members of her family back at home, who may not otherwise survive. She told me that she was only fourteen years old when some tribal/political henchmen came to her Zimbabwean rural village. They ordered members of her extended family to stand around in a circle, at the front of her uncle's mud-built home. In African extended families, an uncle is regarded as a second father. Therefore, she was very distressed to see her beloved uncle, a good man, being dragged into the middle of the group. The man directing the operation shouted some instruction and his gang cut off her uncle's hands. He shouted again and they cut off his arms. She was screaming and crying as they repeated this barbarous process on both legs and, finally, his head. They shouted a warning to the people and left.

Olivia said that for months and months, she was haunted by terrible images of her uncle's head rolling on the ground, of family members trying to gather up the parts of his body so that he could have a decent burial and of the whole family in agonised shock, wailing in inexpressible sorrow.

Several years later, whilst Olivia was training as a nurse, she was sent to a big hospital in Harare to care for patients in a psychiatric ward. After a week or so, she recognised one of the patients. He was the very man who had directed the savage execution of her uncle. Olivia couldn't prevent herself shaking, as all the fear and pain welled up within her again. At first, she could not go near him, as the trauma and grief was still very much alive and now erupting from where it had been buried in her memory. Later, recognising the depth of his depression, his constant crying and hopelessness, she sat down beside this broken man. She came again the next day, and the next, to sit near, week after week. She held his hand to comfort him. Olivia prayed with him and talked to him about God's love and God's forgiveness. None of this was easy for her but, in time, she was even able to forgive him for her pain. When she left the hospital, she gave him her only bible, although she could not afford to replace it until she came to England, as a qualified nurse.

I think that Olivia was wearing the 'crown of life'.

For those who suffer

Lord and loving God, you see all suffering, misery, despair, persecution and injustice in this world. Your cross tells us that you share people's pain today and that you struggle with those who suffer. Hear our prayer for the poor and oppressed, for those burdened by war, fear, grief and sorrow or racked with guilt for their own folly and for the hurt they have caused. Fill us with compassion. Enable us to be part of the means by which your comfort may be received and by which faith, hope, justice and peace may come, by your grace. Amen.

The Question of Suffering

Many of us pray for people at times of suffering and disaster when our natural inclination is to want them to be relieved. If a sick loved one recovers or people come safely through flood or fire, we give thanks to God.

The sincere faith of some leads them to ask God to intervene to bring healing and deliverance, when there is pain and tragedy. The New Testament not only includes the healing miracles of Jesus but also His instructions to the disciples to 'heal the sick' (Mat 10 v 8, Luke 9 v 2 and 10 v 9). The deep conviction that Christians today share the ministry passed to the disciples would encourage us to trust God, believing that He will heal. He will save people from physical disaster and suffering, as well as from spiritual death.

Some other people would say, 'What is the point of believing in God, if He can't change things…. if He has no power to stop suffering and disaster or chooses not to? What is the point of God's existence?' The letter to the Christians in Smyrna says that if you are faithful and trust in Christ then, in even the most disastrous suffering, God will be there giving comfort, inner strength, courage, peace of mind and the gift of life eternal. He will give inner victory, healing in spirit, even joy and assurance of His presence and promise … although suffering may continue till death. Christians are aware that God does not frequently intervene to save people from physical or mental suffering but are convinced that it is right to ask God for courage, inner healing and peace?

Reflection

Many faithful Christians know that God does not usually intervene to save us from sickness and disaster. They have accepted that as reality, even though they may share with God their longing for physical healing. Nevertheless, they pray for their loved one to be in the hands of God, for inner healing, assurance and eternal peace.

- Is that enough? What do you think?

- Will God intervene and take away pain and torment, if we pray?

- What is borne out by the experience of Christians who trust in God?

- Are people who do not expect God to cure illness among those of 'little faith'?

- Can Christians genuinely hold to both possibilities, that 'healing of the body' is the work of God's hand, as well as healing of the inner life?

- What is real and reliable? What do you believe? Why?

Pergamum

The Acropolis and an example of its decorations

Pergamum Theatre

Acropolis columns

Roman statue just beyond the gate

The Red Basilica

The internal area where a church was constructed

Pillar bearing the Asclepion mythology

Asclepion
Healing Centre

Tunnels & facilities for healing

Chapter 4

Pergamum

About twenty kilometres in from the west coast, from a huge rocky vantage point, the fine city of Pergamum looked down upon green hilly countryside. It's quite a climb to reach the acropolis but, if you were to go, try to choose April or May when the grassland wears a glorious mantle of vivid, wild, red poppies which, gleaming in the sun, seem to welcome you from all directions. Recalling that it takes quite an effort to reach the top, makes me wonder, with regret, if perhaps I had sometimes been too eager to get there hastily, without adequate thought for one or two members of the group in their eighties! However, no one was ever left behind and they always seemed to regard the exertion as well worth while ... once we arrived.

The city reached its peak during the second century BC, rivalling Alexandria as a place of science and scholarship. Pliny (AD 61-112), a Roman Lawyer and magistrate, who wrote hundreds of letters to significant people of his time, said that "Pergamum was by far the most famous city in Asia". Strabo, famous Greek philosopher and historian, said more or less the same. Many people think that the last King of Pergamum, Attalus 3rd, had taken leave of his senses when he bequeathed the entire kingdom to Rome in 133 BC., as that hastened Roman dominance in Asia Minor. It became the capital of the province and that status lasted for four hundred years.

The Acropolis

The magnificent buildings of the fortified acropolis had been clad in sparkling white stone and marble. There were palaces, fountains and a bustling agora (market place). Pergamum was a great religious centre with its major Sanctuary of Athena and temples dedicated to Trajan, Serapis and Dionysus. Asclepius, the god of healing, was also honoured in the town. The best known place of worship here was the great altar dedicated to Zeus, which was constructed in about 180 BC. Smoke from the sacrifices would have been rising every day, as a constant stream of worshippers came to the city. The altar was discovered in 1875, when Carl Humann, a German engineer, was clearing rubble to build a road. Fragments of frieze were uncovered by one of his workmen. He then ensured that work proceeded carefully and the beautiful Zeus Altar came to light. The monumental frieze from the altar, depicting a battle between the gods and the giants, was taken to the Pergamum Museum in Berlin and, although there have been a number of cries for its return, it has remained there to this day.

The Library

Eumenes 2nd established the famous Library of Pergamum about the same time as the Zeus Altar was being erected. Its two hundred thousand books were rivalling the supremacy of the great library in Alexandria, Egypt. The papyrus rolls were made from bulrushes that grew near the River Nile. It is thought that the supply of papyrus was deliberately cut off to preserve the fame of Egypt's coveted literary esteem and to curb the development of Pergamum's library. The people of Pergamum, however, were not going to be beaten. They developed a new way of producing their books. They began writing on thin animal skin, known as 'Pergamum paper', from which the word 'parchment' was derived. Because the skins dried and became too brittle to roll, they cut the parchment into rectangular pieces and linked them as pages: the codex was invented....Brilliant!

The Theatre

Pergamum was built in the Hellenistic period but later taken over by the Romans in 133 BC. It's therefore no surprise to find that the theatre had been constructed by the Greeks and adapted, only a little, by the Romans. The engineering is remarkable – places for ten thousand people in eighty tiers, built into the natural contours of the hillside. This was typical of Greek theatres, as Greeks did not have the knowledge and skill to build arches. The Romans introduced arches into the architecture of established cities all across Anatolia, as they extended and improved them. You can recognise the work of skilful builders, in the Roman craftsmanship at the city entrance. As you come in, the evenly cut stone, finely laid, can be seen in the wall on your right, whereas in the wall on the left, the blocks had been more roughly hewn by Greek builders and are not of even proportions.

"Hello, hello!", "Where are you from?", "What is your name?" Cheery questions seemed to come from all directions as a group of Turkish school children mingled among the members of our group of 'pilgrims', on a visit to the theatre. They were anxious to make contact with the visitors. A young man said that he'd like to sing to us. He went to the stage area below and sang, demonstrating the magnificent quality of the acoustics. One only has to speak from where he was standing to be heard in ten thousands seats. Oh, I forgot to mention the rapturous applause for the song.

The Asclepion

From the Acropolis on the hill, the sacred way leads down towards the Asclepion (or Asclepium). It is an amazing healing centre dedicated to Asclepius, the god of healing. The sanctuary and healing ministry was set up here in the 4th century BC and was still attracting record numbers in the Roman period. Ancient mythology honoured Asclepius, the son of Apollo, who was a famous physician. He became so successful that he could even 'restore the dead to life'. However, this created resentment from Hades who kicked up a fuss to Zeus who, in turn, sent a thunderbolt to strike Asclepius. The emblem of Asclepius was a staff, with a snake encircling it, a symbol that's still used for medicine today.

Various medical treatments were developed here – mud baths, hydrotherapy, physiological exercises, drugs, herbal remedies and treatments for psychological disorders. The scent of pine could be calming when walking among the trees. Patients could bathe in or drink water from the spring. There were cool tunnels where people who were feeling disturbed could hear the comforting sound of gently flowing water or listen to the priests chanting soothingly and whispering encouragingly, through grills in the tunnel walls.

Galen, the most eminent 2nd century physician (129 – 199 AD), was born in Pergamum. After medical training in Smyrna, he worked at the Pergamum healing centre. His understanding of the human body became the foundation of medical theory and practice for fourteen hundred years.

The 'logo' of the healing centre, seen on a column, represents an ancient medical myth. As you look at it, imagine that you are looking at a bowl of milk from above. It had been left for a sick old man who was returning home, without cure. As he approached it, he saw two snakes heading into the bowl. You can see them represented on the column. Knowing that the snakes were deadly and their venom poisonous, he decided that, being old and sick, he might as well take the drink and die. So he drank ... but the 'fatal venom' in the milk cured him, making its medical benefits known. Snakes, which have the ability to renew themselves, were sacred to Asclepius.

The Red Basilica

On the edge of Bergarma, today's name for this busy town, are the ruins of a colossal red brick hall. It was built during Hadrian's reign (117 – 138 AD) as a Roman Temple to the Egyptian bull god Serapis and possibly dedicated to Isis and Harpocrates as well. Later, in the Byzantine period, it was converted to a basilica and renamed Red Court. It seems that, some years later, the building was neglected and probably suffered earthquake damage. Using part of what remained, a church was later constructed in the central area. Probably, some of the Christians who gathered there for worship were descendants of those to whom the letter was addressed in the Book of Revelation.

Letter to the Church at Pergamum
Truth - Revelation 2 v 12 – 17

> "You are holding fast to my name. You did not deny your faith in me." Revelation 2 v 13

Christ is calling the church to truth. He commends the Christians at Pergamum because they did not renounce their faith, despite the compelling pressures upon them. They were, however, reprimanded for allowing false prophets to contaminate the fellowship of the church with their distortions of the truth. Truth is as much the mark of the living church, as love is, although there are times when it is difficult to hold the two together. As Christians, at times, we may be so resolved to love that, unwittingly, we relax our grip on right and wrong in the life of the church. On the other hand, in our zealous pursuit of truth, we can become harsh. Truth can be hard-hearted if not tempered by love and love can become simply sentiment if not tempered by truth. As Christians, we want to avoid allowing truth to degenerate into a matter of personal opinion and become entirely subjective. We would also want to avoid becoming so confident that our understanding of truth is divinely authentic and other interpretations are mistaken. This could lead us to adopt dogmatic, arrogant and judgemental attitudes which have no place among the fruit of the Spirit.

Post Truth

We are now in period of history which is being regarded as a 'post truth era'. The Oxford Dictionary declared 'post-truth' as the

word of the year in 2016. It refers to fabricated or distorted information which is argued passionately, to win supporters. To some extent, it has become a general characteristic of our age to 'cherry pick' certain facts and ignore others, to sustain a point of view. Some who communicate in this way, even refer to providing 'alternative facts' and publicly dismiss news they don't welcome, as 'fake news'. Collins Dictionary selected 'Fake News' as the word of the year in 2017. This term is used also to describe news with unreliable foundation. 'Post truth' is now heard too frequently from the lips and in the 'spin', of some politicians and journalists. Sometimes journalists are accused of 'never letting the facts get in the way of a good story'. The impact of so called 'good stories' of distorted truth can heap embarrassment and shame upon others.

Post-truth is a style of communication in which facts become less important than an appeal to the emotions or to common desires, ideas, misunderstandings and prejudices. It has been used in advertising for years, sometimes promising good health, happiness, good looks, social success, popularity - all in the latest tube of toothpaste! Perhaps, occasionally, in the church, we can slip into making promises that Christ never made.

When faced with complex issues in our generation, it may be hard for Christians to be certain about factual truth. We have to take account of new information almost every day. Recent scientific knowledge and changes in social attitudes seem to contradict many things that we received from the past as 'truth'. Understanding every part of the Bible as literal, historical record can undermine the meaning and spiritual content within the scripture, and miss the deeper truth. For the most part, Christ used stories to communicate the truth about God, about the world and about us. Frequently he said, "The Kingdom of God is *like* ...." rather than offering definitive, propositional statements. The New Testament word for 'truth' is usually 'aletheia'. New Testament scholars tell us that a better translation would be 'reality' rather than 'truth'. The biblical understanding of truth is that truth is active. It is about what we do and what God does, not simply about what we think or say. It is who we are, in reality, and who God is.

Jesus said, "I am ... the truth" John 14 v 6.

He said, "....I came into the world to testify to the truth." John 18 v 37.

He is our touchstone for truth. In Him is the essence of truth. In relationship with Christ, we begin to discern the truth for living, truth about love, justice, compassion, hope, grace and goodness. Frederich Nietzche, a great German philosopher and declared atheist, suggested that the whole of western thought is based on our understanding that 'Truth is divine'. He said,

> "Even we knowers of today, we godless antimetaphysicians, still
> take our fire from the flame lit by the 2,000 year old Christian belief
> that truth is divine."

That conviction was probably well established in western thought in his day, towards the end of the nineteenth century and well into the twentieth, but to what extent is that same flame lighting our fire in twenty first century conviction?

Antipas

2 v 12 refers to the message coming from 'the one who has a sharp two-edged sword'. It is speaking of Christ who is bringing the Word of God. In each letter, the nature of His Word to the church is clearly 'two edged' – a word of 'praise' and a word of 'judgement'.

2 v 13 "I know where you live" reminds me of warnings that sometimes came my way when I was an energetic boy getting caught, because I was up to mischief. In this verse, it is a word of understanding. God knows the situations in which we live. This letter acknowledges that He was well aware of the way in which the faith of many Christians in Pergamum was being harshly tested by pressures from Rome and by the lives and attitudes of many in the cosmopolitan society around them.

"You are living where Satan has his throne." Is this a recognition that what they were struggling against had sprung from the source of evil? Is it a way of describing the corruption and depravity which had become 'enthroned' in some parts of city life and culture? Was this a nick-name for the great altar of Zeus that dominated the town or a jibe at emperor worship? We cannot know. We can know, however, that the writer was not imagining a red devil with horns and hooves but an immensely powerful and utterly unscrupulous influence in their lives. They could not escape its impact as it infiltrated the community.

This understanding is not far from the powerful and complex strands of culture, politics, economics and social morality which are deeply bound together in our own society. We cannot be free from its influence and the church is not immune to its effect. Christians in Pergamum, sustained by God and each other, had remained true, even with the threat of torture and death hanging over them. This had already become reality for Antipas, a 'faithful witness' (martyr), 'who was put to death in your city'. We know nothing else about Antipas although, like others, he may have been called to appear before the Roman proconsul who was, by this time, almost a chief priest of the Imperial cults.

Pergamum dedicated a temple to Augustus as early as 29BC. There had been no provincial temple prior to this, built to honour an emperor. From that time, the Empire became more fanatical and zealous about total allegiance to Rome. There was a law requiring every citizen to go to the temple of the emperor, once each year, to swear allegiance to the emperor as 'Lord'. An official certificate was issued, allowing citizens to worship any god they wanted. But how could a faithful Christian publicly declare that the emperor is his Lord?

Domitian was quite mad when he came to power as emperor in 81 AD. He first killed his brother and then initiated a vigorous persecution of Christians and of Roman senators, including numerous innocents whom he blamed for earthquakes and other natural disasters. He sent Christians to the lions and to the gladiators but, to give him greater amusement in the arena, he compelled dwarfs and women to be gladiators and fight to their death. It is no surprise to know that his rule came to an end around 97 AD, with his assassination.

This sounds incredibly barbaric, and it was. While we may not have had first-hand experience of persecution, we sometimes need a reminder that it is reality for many Christians around the world, who are suffering barbarity. Only this week, early in 2017, I have become aware of a statement from 'Release International', which monitors and supports persecuted Christians, in up to thirty countries. It indicates that Christians are facing an increasing array of violent persecutors around the world: "These include the brutal Islamic State in the Middle East, heavily armed militants in Nigeria and Hindu extremists in India". Rt. Rev. Prof. Peter Stephen's adds, "Not since the early Church have Christians suffered greater persecution than today." There are references to attacks on churches, arrests, slaughter with knives, discrimination in legal systems and to Christians suffering in North Korea, China, many countries across Africa and Asia, Pakistan, Iraq and Iran. He continues, "It is inexcusable that most western governments, including the British, have been indifferent to the plight of persecuted Christians seeking refuge."

2 v 14 &15 The letter refers to Balaam and Barak to illustrate the detrimental influence that the Nicolaitans were having on the church. The Nicolaitans seemed to think that there was nothing wrong with 'the ways of the world' and were urging Christians to compromise, to keep the peace and avoid conflict in society, to adjust to the morality of the community and avoid trouble, as this would help to make the gospel more acceptable. The Book of Numbers chapters 22 – 24 tell us about Balaam. He was a prophet summoned by Balak, King of Moab, to curse the Israelite tribes and restrain them from crossing the River Jordan. This was because the king feared their possible violence and that their vast numbers would take over the land, overwhelming his people. Despite the huge reward offered by Balak,

Balaam failed, as each time he tried to curse them he found that, guided by God, he could speak only blessings. Jude verse 11 and 2 Peter 2 v 14 – 15 suggest that Balaam then persuaded Balak to entice his own Moabite women to seduce Israelite men, to take them to idolatrous festivals and corrupt them. Scripture leads us to believe that thousands were involved. The letter implies that the Nicolaitans were seducing the church.

2 v 16 The church is called to repent and to overcome what is false and corrupt, with the warning that Christ Himself will soon speak powerfully from among them.

2 v 17 Before God's final promise in this letter in words of inspiration and encouragement, the clarion call of the letter is repeated, urging Christians to listen to God's word to the churches. The message is not for the church at Pergamum alone but will speak to all churches ... and we can safely take it to mean, for all time.

We are familiar with the symbolism of 'manna' from Exodus chapter 16. God's gift of food saved the Hebrew people from starving in the wilderness. They continued to eat manna 'for forty years (v 35), until they reached the land of Canaan'. The Hebrew people still remember God's gift of deliverance and recite its history at the Passover each year. Christians associate manna with 'the bread of life', which Jesus talked about in John's Gospel chapter 6. Its meaning is linked with the Last Supper and with Holy Communion in the church.

The symbolism of the promised gift of a white stone, on which is written a new name, is not quite so easy. I am grateful to the compilers of a variety of commentaries who have introduced me to various possibilities. I cannot even remember which suggestions came from which Biblical scholars, although I greatly appreciate what they have taught me! I'll share some of their insights with you:

i. The Greek Games, that were established in the Hellenistic period, had become part of the way of life and continued under the Romans. A 'tessera' (a small square tile) was given as a token of outstanding victory. Frequently, this would have been a white stone bearing a significant inscription. It gave the victor free entry to many important events and places. Perhaps a Christian can be like a victorious athlete whose prize enables him/her to enter fully into fellowship with God and share in the 'victory won by Christ.'

ii.   Successful, popular gladiators were among the celebrities of Anatolia. If they survived to old age, they could be retired and therefore not expected to fight again. At that point, they were awarded a tessera inscribed with letters, to indicate that they had proved their value and their days of battling were at an end. A faithful Christian, who had 'fought the good fight,' would be honoured by God with peace and rest from the struggles of life.

iii.   The jury in the courts of law indicated the verdict with stones. Black stones for 'guilty', thus condemning the person under judgement and white stones for 'not guilty', setting him free. The stones went into a large metal bowl. If there were more white stones than black, the prisoner was given his liberty. A faithful Christian, being justified by Christ, is acquitted of his guilt and receives freedom given by God.

iv.   Some people today wear St. Christopher on a chain around their neck. For many, it's a decoration but for others, a sign of protection given by the saint when travelling. In Pergamum and well beyond, many people would carry a piece of jewellery, an ornament or a charm, possibly valuable, made of diamond, silver or gold. On the other hand, it would often be only a small smooth stone, the value of which would have been in its significance. It usually bore the name of a god, which was known only to the owner. To know the name of a personal god implied that you had some influence over the god. John would not have been suggesting that Christians had control over God but he would have been aware of how powerful such superstitions were among the people. His words suggest that you have power if you know the one, true, living God, then you share in the power of His grace, through our Lord Jesus.

We cannot know which of these thoughts John had in mind, as he dictated this letter to the church in Pergamum. Perhaps none of them, although each one gives us a little insight into the possible significance of the message.

Throughout the Book of Revelation, significance is given to the use of "white" to describe the outstanding purity of God. The author uses a Greek word that indicates 'whiter than white', that is overwhelming, radiant white. Later in the Book of Revelation, there are references to 'white raiment', 'white robes', 'white linen' and the 'great white throne of God'. There is a similar approach to the description of some things as 'new'. Here the Greek word means exceptionally new, unique, previously unknown newness. In this verse, the reference is to a 'new name', and later we find 'new Jerusalem', 'a new song', 'new heaven and new earth' and 'God will make all things new'.

The letter to the Church at Pergamum concludes in this verse with the profound assurance of God's promise - to give sustaining nourishment to the spirit of those 'who win victory' over all the manipulative pressures, threats and temptations of living in that city. Such victory is regarded as being a reflection of God's glory and of purity in their lives. This can be known only to those who know Him and have the name of Christ written on their hearts. It's a promise of transformation and renewal, of new selfhood, new character and new hope which anticipates 'a new creation'. Charles Wesley echoes the message in his hymn "O for a heart to praise my God", which concludes –

> "Write Thy new name upon my heart,
> Thy new best name of Love."

Reflection

- Do you think that 'truth' has become a casualty in the Church, in our desire to be open - minded and caring towards others or would you say that Christians can too easily sacrifice love to preserve uncompromising commitment to truth ?

- Has 'fake news' and 'post truth' information been fed into our society as though it is genuine truth?

- To what extent do you think 'fake news' is harmful or is it just another way to communicate conviction, alongside scientific argument, economic argument or argument about what is practically possible?

- Are powerful, complex strands of culture, politics, economics and social morality subtly bound together in our society, in ways that could be described as evil and therefore working against God's will?

- How aware are we of Christians around the world who are persecuted because of their faith in Christ or because of actions they pursue that arise from their faith?

- Thousands enjoy watching sport today, supporting their football team, being glued to Wimbledon on TV or obsessed by the Olympics ... and revelling in the latest victory.

What victories, in personal lives, in society, in the nation and in the world, do you think God would want Christians to be winning today?

A touch of Turkish Humour

You may enjoy an old Turkish joke on the theme of 'Truth'.

A neighbour called on a man to ask if he could borrow his donkey. "Oh, I am sorry," said the man. "I don't have a donkey."
Then a donkey brayed loudly from behind the house.
"I thought you just said that you don't have a donkey?" said the neighbour.
The man replied, "Look, I am your good neighbour! Are you going to believe me or a donkey?"

Thyatira

Remains of a Byzantine church

Coins of Thyatira

A few decorative ruins of Thyatira

Early evening
shadows over a
small part of
ancient Thyatira

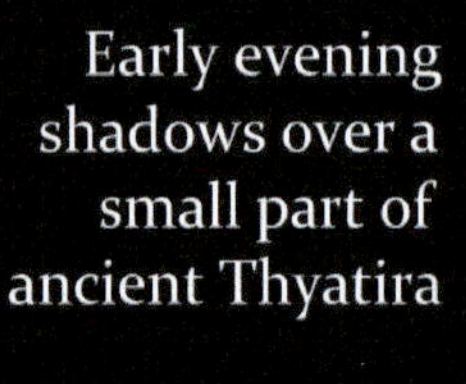

Fallen arches, in
Akhisar, from among
the protected ruins of
Thyatira

Skills, from among
the Craft Guilds of
1st century Thyatira,
like pottery and
copper work, are still
to be seen today

From the
contemporary
market stalls
of Akhisar

Chapter 5

Thyatira

Patience!

My last journey to Thyatira became an unplanned, enforced practical exercise in patience, endurance, forbearance and keeping cool! Not only for me but for the whole group with me. To begin with, an early start on this first full day was not popular, following a late arrival at our Izmir hotel the night before. A big festival had jammed the streets with cars and coaches and crowds were spilling into the roads. Our coach had had to creep along and we were very late. Our first day was a trip to Pergamum (Bergama) 62 miles away. The roads were busy again and progress was slow. A good number soon dozed off, trying to recover from the tiring flight, the day before. When we arrived and had shaken ourselves, we shared a full and interesting morning.

Had it not been for our programme, Pergamum would probably have been enough for the group. Nevertheless, by mid-afternoon we were on our way to Akhisar, about 50 miles further, to visit Thyatira but, would you believe it ... road works! That virtually brought us to a standstill for over an hour. I think some were ready to get out and walk the rest of the way. There were, of course, great sighs of relief when we eventually arrived and made our way to the archaeological site, to get an 'on the spot' idea of the Church in Thyatira ... but it was all locked up! We were too late and members of the group were far from pleased. I wasn't overjoyed myself. Some were almost ready to get on the next flight home. Now it was a matter of sufferance, resignation and fortitude, rather than patience. We certainly could not have been counted among Christians in

Thyatira who were commended for their patience, in the letter addressed to this town in Revelation (2 v 19). We found a way, however, to make contact with the site manager, who kindly returned after opening hours and allowed us to see that small remaining section of ancient Thyatira, which included the ruins of a church.

Perhaps, in the end, this visit was a practical lesson in generosity, understanding and goodwill shown to us by the site manager. We were exceedingly grateful to him. Afterwards, no sooner were we on the coach than some of the group went out like a light, during the long trip back to base.

The City

Not a lot of this ancient city is visible today, as most of it is covered by the modern town of Akhisar. Archaeologists and historians visit because this is the site of one of the Seven Churches of Asia addressed in the Book of Revelation. The younger Pliny tells us that the town was founded by the Lydians, probably around the fifth century BC. It was then re-established in the third century BC as a military fort, when Macedonian troops were stationed there. From 190 BC, Pergamum took control and used Thyatira as a strategic component in its own protection, and in defence of Sardis. Josephus, the famous first century Jewish historian, notes that a Jewish colony may have been established here to help create a balanced community. Later, it developed into a small but successful commercial city. The lower portions of a few columns remain. These were part of a colonnaded street that would have been lined with shops and market stalls, attracting many visitors from east and west to come to the town for business.

The outer walls from a temple, possibly dedicated to Apollo, remain and some walls of a large church. However, Thyatira had no religious prominence in its day. There were no major shrines or palaces, although there was a female oracle called the Sanbathe. When the town ceased to be a military base, it no longer had any political significance and so the community here was not facing major threat or extensive persecution of

Christians. In his letters, Pliny refers to this town as 'a place of no importance', despite Thyatira having been chosen by a number of trade guilds to be the home of their headquarters. There were copper smiths, clothiers and tanners, potters, dyers and weavers. There were guilds for the woollen trade, for bakers and skilled workers with bronze. It was also a good site for the slave dealers. To select this place would have made strategic sense for trade, because the city was on the main road from Izmir to Bursa and ran through the valley of the River Lycus. For centuries, this route was vital for communications. All these things worked together to create thriving commercial success, which made quite a number of people in this town rather wealthy.

Coins

Tyrimnus was a local god but it seems that Apollo, the sun god, was supreme among the gods of Thyatira. Images of the gods appeared on the ancient coins of the town. As emperor worship increased during the Roman period and was included among the rituals of the city, the image on the coins frequently represented the emperor as 'Apollo incarnate'. When John's letter arrived, these first century Thyatiran coins were in circulation among the traders, the wider community of the town and the Christians. It's quite likely that the images on the coins would have reminded Jesus' followers of His words about 'coins and Caesar' (Matt 22 v 19-21, Mark 12 v 13-17), especially as the emperor was claiming to be a god, demanding worship and insisting on a sworn oath of allegiance from every citizen.

Lydia

In Acts 16 v 13 – 15, St. Luke recalls meeting Lydia from Thyatira. He describes her as 'a seller of purple cloth'. Those who travelled to sell good quality cloth, especially rich purple cloth that was usually worn only by the upper strands of society, would probably have built up a good bank balance. Lydia met St Paul just outside Philippi, where she listened to his preaching. She already worshipped God but now she became a believing Christian and was baptised. Lydia invited Paul and Luke, together with Timothy, to stay in her home. I imagine that could have led to some long and late discussions about aspects of faith that would have deepened Lydia's spirituality and understanding. I wonder if she returned to Thyatira and helped to build up the church. Perhaps, as an elderly woman, she was among those who heard the words of Christ, through St. John's letter in Revelation –

"I know your works - your love, your faith, service and your patience.
I know that your last works are greater than your first." (2 v 19)

"I will give you the morning star." (2 v 28)

Letter to the Church at Thyatira
Godliness - Revelation 2 v 18 – 29

"I have this against you: you tolerate that woman Jezebel".
Revelation 2 v 20

2 v 18 This is the longest of the seven letters. It presents its message as 'words from the Son of God', perhaps in contrast to the edicts which came from the 'incarnate sun god Apollo', 'son of Zeus'. In describing Christ, the author could be using familiar images from life in this town, as the people would have been accustomed to seeing flames and fire from the famed metal works.... and 'burnished bronze' would quickly convey something highly valued, gently gleaming and greatly praised. The Greek word translated as 'burnished bronze' is not found anywhere else in the New Testament. The image also seems to have Daniel 10 v 6 in mind.

2 v 19 The opening words are of warm commendation of the Christians in Thyatira: 'Love, faithfulness, service and patient endurance'. Four great Christian qualities were being put into action. It seems to be clear that faith was expressed in practice, as the text refers to

'deeds' and to 'service'. It goes on to say: 'Now you are doing more than you did before'. Isn't that typical of the church? There's always more to do and it's those who are already committed, who are most likely to ensure that something more is done. When Paul wrote to Christians in Thessalonica, he expressed his 'pride and joy' … because your faith is growing abundantly, and the love of one for another is increasing.' (2 Thes. 1 v 3). Spiritual growth, strengthening Christian fellowship and practical involvement in service to others, all belong together.

Jezebel

2 v 20 Verses 18 and 19 were good news but now- 'You tolerate that woman, Jezebel, who calls herself a prophet and is beguiling my servants to practice fornication and to eat food sacrificed to idols'. The Church at Thyatira had been praised for the qualities of its members but it seems that those attributes did not include 'holiness'.

They were not all godly people.

The Jezebel of 1 Kings chapt. 9 had been dead for years. This reference, therefore, is obviously a symbolic way of describing powerful, corrupting influence, from within the church, which was leading God's people, in Thyatira, astray and distorting Christian teaching. Jezebel, wife of King Ahab, had been responsible for the death of Naboth, God's faithful prophet. She had enticed the King and, through him, the nation of Israel away from God and towards idols and immorality. The use of her name here must be attached to powerful influence of a similar kind, in the church at Thyatira. We are all human, weak and subject to failure but 'Jezebel's work' seems to have been consistent, thorough and deliberate.To what or to whom does the name 'Jezebel' refer?

i. Was she a church leader who'd had depraved influence on significant numbers of people and had moved part of the church community in her direction? If so, perhaps she had called herself a 'messenger from God'. Her detrimental impact on the Church reminded John, as he composed this letter, of the way in which Old Testament Jezebel had led God's people astray. Was John hoping that Thyatirans would learn from their scripture?

ii. Could this have been a reference to the Oracle – the woman fortune teller in the town? There was still a very strong Greek element in Anatolian culture. Greek Oracles resided at many of the temples and shrines of Asia Minor. Like the Oracle at Delphi, they had a dominant influence in daily life.

iii. The Nicolaitans had become well established at most of the churches in western Anatolia. Perhaps this reference to Jezebel represented the effect they were having in Thyatira. The compromises they encouraged and the morality they introduced could well have been the cause of troubles in the church.

iv. The Roman attitude was generally to regard any god as one among many. They would offer sacrifice and worship at the temple to whichever god seemed most appropriate for the need of the moment. Perhaps this influence in the town had been brought into the church, encouraging some Christians to mix their faith with other religions. The behaviour under judgement, in this letter, could have been the outcome of syncretism in the church?

Terrorist Jezebels!

The distortion of Christian lifestyle and belief within the church, in Thyatira, stirs my sympathy for devout Muslims today.

The Nicolaitans and the 'Jezebel' of Thyatira were active in the church. They were among the leadership. They selected portions of Christian faith which they interpreted in ways that led Christians away from Christian living. They promoted their misinterpretation of God's Grace as 'giving freedom to do anything', and if that 'anything' could be regarded as sinful, they argued that it would provide an even greater opportunity for God to demonstrate His grace and forgiveness. They therefore presented this as good Christian witness. Consequently, Christians were led into overindulgent sexual practices and idolatrous worship, both of which were entirely contrary to the church's true teaching but were presented by Nicolaitans as part of the faith.

Many devout Muslims, today, are distressed by shame being brought upon them, by the impact of the so called 'Muslim State' using similar methods – extracting isolated verses from the Koran and from historic records of Islamic leaders. 'Muslim State' sympathisers somehow manage to work from within some mosques, in Muslim communities and online, persuading other Muslims that these distorted interpretations reveal the true hopes and objectives of Islam. In so doing, young, disaffected, idealistic Muslims are being led into violent and destructive acts which are contrary to true Islam. The terrorist atrocities that emerge are frequently blamed on the Muslim faith, by some in wider society. True, peace-loving Muslims get 'accused'. Sadly, we could too easily identify periods in Christian history when similar tactics have been used from within the church.

Commercial Jezebel?

2 v 20 (cont.) Is it possible that the commercial life of this town was personified in Jezebel? The main route from east to west came through the town and kept it buzzing with business. Trade guilds dominated the life of Thyatira. If you wanted to be successful in business, you had to join the guilds and be part of the business culture. To isolate yourself from the guilds would be to give up your chance of commercial prosperity. But why would any business man or woman want to steer clear of the guilds? The reason was because of the close association between the guilds and the pagan temples. The guild banquets were held regularly in the temples. The opening ceremonies included offering sacrifice to the god of the temple, and the meat which had been offered to the idol would be part of the banquet meal. There would be excessive eating and

drinking, which would usually end up in drunken revelry and loose morality. Members of the church were involved in business. The Christian trader, therefore, had to choose between failing in business or compromising. Business was how the town survived. It seems likely, therefore, that Jezebel and the Nicolaitans persuaded many to relax their standards to get on in the world, to be less rigid in ethical and moral principles, to meet society half way and to identify with the majority of the Thyatiran community– in order to make good money.

The outcome would have been that, although the church was flourishing, growing in numbers and becoming more 'successful', beneath the surface, it was disintegrating – losing its true centre and its Godly character. Its true witness and purpose was weakening; the reflection of the nature of Christ in its life must have been fading away.

21st Century Jezebel?

Could it be said that Jezebel is alive and well in society today? I begin to wonder, when at times almost every news bulletin seems to have Trade at the top of the agenda, alongside the economy and wealth creation. To some extent, that is inevitable, as our national leaders have a responsibility to secure the economy for the future: but at what price? For many in politics, business and private life, 'making money' seems to be of highest priority, overriding all other matters concerned with human well-being.

Trying to answer the sixty-five thousand dollar question on quiz shows used to be like aiming for the moon but now the prizes and lottery winnings are astronomical. Salaries of top executives can be three hundred times the income of their workers. In 2016, it was announced that a company annual report would be confirming an agreement of a £70 million salary for the Chief Executive. The 'out of this world' expenditure on weddings blows my mind. I've just read of a wedding costing £29 million. The highest on record, so far, is the wedding of

Prince Charles and Princess Diana at £85 million. You can buy yourself a Lamborghini car for three and a half million or a much cheaper Ferrari F60, for just under two million. Yet many of the millionaires who can think in these figures keep their major resources in foreign banks, to avoid their Inland Revenue liabilities that would help to support our hospitals, schools and social care.

Some companies with widespread, successful business in the UK keep their financial headquarters out of the country to 

avoid taxation. They find legal routes for this practice and, in so doing, they fail to make just contributions to the costs of the nation, including the support of thousands of their own customers, who provide their income.

There are times when politicians appear to be more eager to establish major trade deals with other nations, than they are concerned about the lack of human rights and the oppression of the citizens within those countries. Some deals are made without due regard for the undiplomatic and even pugilistic attitudes of the leaders of those nations, in their grandstand declarations.

Government spokesmen and women make dramatic speeches about representing all strands of society, about securing adequate support for the elderly, ensuring that all children will have a first class education, providing major resources to enable everyone to receive the best health care in the world, training sufficient nurses, teachers and skilled workers for the demands of society, eradicating child poverty, securing higher incomes for the poor ... The rhetoric vibrates with seductive appeal to win votes, to win power. Many of the policies, however, when taken together, seem to allow resources to flow towards wealthier, successful sections of society, leaving many of the poorest and the most dependent in a weaker position, and those in the middle, over-working to survive.

I have no right to be judgemental. My own collection of failings is as bulky as anyone's. The 2017 Brit Award winner, 'Rag 'n' Bone Man', speaks for us all: presidents, prime ministers, politicians, principal executives, popes, priests, preachers, pastors and all people, in his song "I'm only human after all". I am not suggesting that it is possible to live in this world without some compromise, misjudgement or self-interest (that seems to be, part of 'being human'), but an overwhelming desire for wealth, without moral scrutiny, can rapidly undermine the stability of a nation and erode the values by which a nation claims to live. That's what urges me to ask if there is some deeply engrained power of 'Jezebel' alluring and corrupting the world today and sometimes sneaking into the church?

2 v 21 "I gave her time to repent but she refuses" A reminder that we are not forced to give in. Our obstinate wills are not shattered by force. We are *invited* by Christ, who longs for us to respond.

2 v 22 – 23 It is not easy to understand to what these verses refer. The imagery and the message suggest punishment and revenge, for not repenting, but that would contradict our understanding of Christ's patience and grace. The Gospel appeal is without pressure and coercion. It seems more likely that this is a recognition and, therefore, a stern warning of the inevitable outcome, if they go on in this way. If they do not change their ways, the drunkenness would most likely lead to liver disease, psychological disorder, brain damage, suffering and death. It would almost certainly also lead to unhappiness, broken relationships, social conflict, brawls and murders. These are consequences that 'Jezebel's people' would bring upon themselves.

2 v 24 When there is a scandal, it doesn't take long for the facts to be exaggerated by gossip but this writer is seeking to keep things in proportion. It would be wrong to think that the whole church had been defiled. Many had done their best to live godly lives and had not followed 'Jezebel'.

2 v 25 The church was therefore told to 'hold fast to what you have.' What great advice! At times, when things go wrong, we easily dwell

only upon the disappointment and grief for what has been lost but here we are being called to focus on what we still have, and to treasure it.

2 v 26 Christ's promise is that those who hold on to their faith, resist evil persuasion and seek to live godly lives will share in His Kingdom. The promise is that, despite the chaos and confusion, God is still God and, by faith, we shall share His sovereign rule.

2 v 27 – 28 It would seem likely that problems had not only hit the church in Thyatira but also the wider society. It is clear that the author knew this town and understood its problems. Perhaps he was aware that moral decay in the society was leading to disaster. If social cohesion was crumbling, moral life deteriorating and law and order losing its grip, then those who were holding on to what is right and good would eventually be needed. When the nations become like 'smashed pottery' (v 28), godly leaders would be required to govern the nations (v 27) according to God's will.

In these thoughts, there is a challenge to us to participate in national and local politics and to consider seeking office in those areas, or in other forms of community leadership. It is true, in our generation, that Christian men and women are needed to help govern the nations. Together with others, who treasure truth and integrity, they could contribute to honest communication with the public and work with compassion, seeking to understand need, at every level of society. Our responsibility would then be to encourage and support policies based on values that resonate with the gospel, for the benefit of all people.

The letter concludes with the promise: 'I will give them the morning star'. There has been a lot of discussion about the interpretation of this symbol. The author of Revelation interprets it for us in chapter 22 v 16, where Jesus says, "I am the bright morning star." God's highest and best gift of all is Himself, given to us clearly and vividly in Jesus Christ and always available and present in Spirit.

Reflection

- What do you think of the Church in Thyatira? Who or what do you think was 'Jezebel'?

- Who or what could you identify as 'Jezebel' in our society, in our churches or our personal lives?

- Repentance requires a change in direction. If you think repentance (2 v 21) is appropriate for some of the objectives and practices which are deeply engrained in our own society, which practices would you think of and how can a change of direction be possible?

- In the media and in our daily lives, how much credit, praise and support is given to those who resist corruption in business and politics and who steer a course of truth and justice in public life? (2 v 24 -25 & v 27).

- What action can Christians take that would help to guide the course of public life towards more Godly goals?

Sardis

Church built on the edge of the ruins of the Temple of Artemis
and dated by archaeologists as from before the year 400

Synagogue of Sardis

Two photographs of the outer courtyard but note the Christian Icthus symbol scratched into the paving in the lower picture

Ornamental marble facings on the inside of the Synagogue walls following the renovations and extension, around 300AD, to cater for up to a 1,000 worshippers

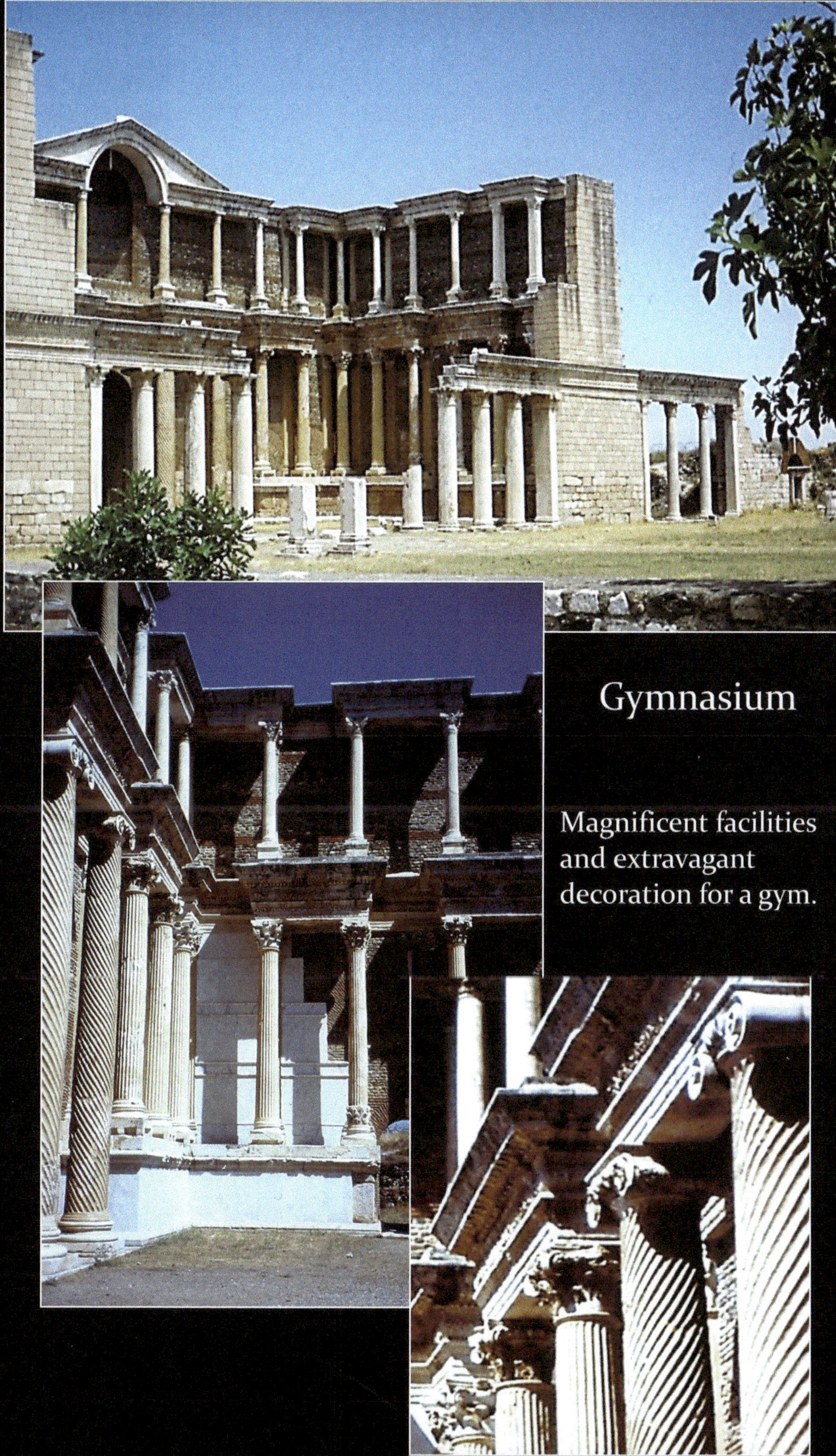

Gymnasium

Magnificent facilities
and extravagant
decoration for a gym.

Sardis Gymnasium
Bathing Pool
The steps led into
the pool which is
now filled in

A row of Sardis shops

Part of the plumbing
in one shop

A large sink made
from stone slabs
engraved with
crosses in another

Chapter 6

Sardis

The City of Sardis, capital of the Lydian Kingdom, commercial, political and cultural centre of western Anatolia, a wealthy and successful city was surrounded by most beautiful countryside. The city was built among mountains, sandstone hills and green slopes. Its roots may have stretched back as far as the thirteenth century BC. It became the capital of the Lydian Kingdom, which was widely regarded as among the most eminent kingdoms in the world. The Lydians produced a seven string lyre, bringing diversity and development to the music scene. They introduced gold and silver coinage and invented the game of dice for the world of entertainment.

In 546 BC, Cyrus, King of Persia, conquered Sardis. His success has been attributed to his camels. The tale tells us that, seeing the Lydian army of King Croesus lined up on their horses ready to defend Sardis, Cyrus, who was aware that horses hated the sight and smell of camels, mounted his soldiers on camels to attack. The Lydian horses turned and fled, leaving the Phonesian 'Camel Corps' to deal with the few foot soldiers of Sardis, before taking the city. Later came the Greeks, who had spread across Asia Minor after Alexander the Great's invasion in 334 BC., followed by Roman infiltration from around 129 BC. Throughout all this, the city continued to thrive. It was an earthquake, in AD 17, that caused the greatest damage.

The Temple

Like most of the cities the acropolis, the residential area for the officials of the town and the municipal buildings, were constructed on a high plateau. The main temple, dedicated to Artemis, was on lower land nearby. The ruins of the temple are impressive against the backdrop of the green landscape, Mount Tmolus and brilliant blue sky. A few lower sections of the original seventy-eight columns which had surrounded the temple area, still remain. A couple have been restored to their full height. There were a number of small buildings around the temple but very little of their ruins are to be seen. The construction of this quite magnificent building was in about 334BC. Restoration and enlargement, following later earthquake damage, continued up to 150 AD but was not completed by the time it was abandoned in the fourth century.

For years, the temple building was empty and lifeless, serving only to provide building materials that were being commandeered for other projects. The ruins still stand lifeless today, although I do recall one visit during which the temple court area unexpectedly sprang to life. A visiting group of children, in their maroon and grey school uniforms, streamed onto the site. Some of the girls spontaneously broke into dance, just to amuse themselves. Others soon joined the line, all laughing and singing. I presumed it must be a popular song as the rhythm kept them all in step, more or less, as the dance spread across the temple floor.

A group of American archaeologists unearthed this temple in 1910. They also discovered some Lydian tombs from the seventh century BC. Further exploration, from 1958 onwards, led to the restoration of the synagogue ruins, a gymnasium and quite a long row of shops. More recently, archaeologists have found the city's gold refinery nearby.

The Church

It looks to me as though, as soon as the temple was vacant, local Christians made good use of bricks and stone from the outer buildings. A small fourth century church has been partially restored on the site, nestling at one corner of the great temple. It had no fine, tall columns nor the splendour of the Temple but I find it quite inspirational. The lower part of the outer wall is still in place. The collapsed dome has been put together, at ground level, inside the wall. I have often taken groups into the double apse, where you can look out to the hills and the sky through a triple arched window. There we have read John's letter from Revelation, remembering that this little place of worship was built by a group whose Christian forebears, just a couple of hundred years before, must have taken to heart God's message to the Church in Sardis ... 'Wake up and strengthen what you have,' and 'I declare openly before my Father, that you belong to me'.

Gymnasium

Perhaps I should avoid standing too close to ancient Greek and Roman male statues, as they could easily make me look a bit puny. The statues give the impression that all the men were handsome, confident and muscle-bound. They certainly kept themselves fit and strong, in case they were summoned to war, competing in the games or simply keeping healthy. Even so, I have a feeling that there were also a lot of posers who, not only celebrated the body's beauty and strength, but also loved to arouse admiration and desire among their fans ... What's changed?

The renewed emphasis on health and fitness today is to be welcomed but there seems to be a powerful expectation compelling some to go far beyond this. I'm thinking about the inappropriate preoccupation with body image. Perhaps this requirement is being imposed upon us by the 'perfect image' portrayed in magazines and by some celebrities, film stars, fashion models and sports personalities, and bolstered by the skilful advertising of the cosmetics industry, as well as by some of the messages and images found on social media. Botox, facelifts, liposuction and other forms of cosmetic surgery are big business and in demand by many who think that their natural looks are not acceptable. Some young men spend a fortune on gymnasiums to build up their biceps, even resorting to drugs to achieve a fashionable physique. Some young women would never respond to their front door bell without their full make-up and hair 'do' and have even been heard to say, "I hate the way I look."

A few years ago, when I was speaking at a youth convention in southern California, I was with a fine crowd of eighteen year olds, at a retreat centre among rocks and pine trees, amidst awesome natural surroundings, up in Mount San Bernardino. Each morning, I was surprised to see that all the girls came to breakfast, even at the earliest hour, with their hair brushed and beautifully arranged, with their faces fully made up and well dressed in bright and fashionable outfits. They looked stunning of course. I do realise that they were having breakfast with the boys, and I am glad that people take care of their health and appearance but I found myself wishing hard that they could appreciate the beauty of their own, and each other's, natural attractiveness ... not only in how they look but in their whole person.

Sardis had fabulous facilities for fitness and, no doubt, the regulars would have been familiar with the Greek/Roman instructions to oil their bodies well before exercise, to follow recommended routines and to resist making the obnoxious grunts of 'muscle men'. They may have followed the advice of Galen (from the health centre at Pergamum) to 'build up your strength by climbing the ropes while a gym buddy tries to hold you down'.

The large Gymnasium complex, restored in recent years, enables us to see what a plush place it was. Three sides were colonnaded and the somewhat stunning façade is evident today. There were numerous rooms, a wrestling pit and swimming pool. The baths included facilities for steam, massage and hot and cold treatment.

Synagogue

Sardis was the Hebrew capital of Anatolia, so a synagogue to hold a thousand people would have been necessary. The reconstructed ruins, from the third century AD, convey its final size and splendour. The superb ornamental marble facing on the inside walls are colourful and impressive. Mosaics had covered most of the floors. At one end a semi-circular apse incorporated three rows of marble seats, probably for the elders. It's likely that this feature influenced the architecture of Christian church buildings. Archaeologists suggest that, at a later stage, the Synagogue was used as a Christian church. Carved into the pavement of the Synagogue forecourt, a bit of Christian graffiti is still clearly visible.

It's a circular 'ichthus', the testimony of an unknown Christian vandal who was declaring that 'Jesus Christ is the Son of God and Saviour'.

Other signs of Life

The main road of Sardis, south of the Synagogue, was lined with a parade of shops. Their lower walls have been unearthed and the identity of some shops is apparent. There was a hardware store and 'Jacob's paint shop'. One shop now has a large, tall sink in one  corner, supported by two slabs with crosses carved into the stone. It is thought that this shop became a Christian baptistry. Decoration and pagan inscriptions on the slabs have had the crosses superimposed upon them. A length of a Royal Road, from Susa to Sardis, has recently been uncovered. Beyond this road, there are a few other important features of the old town life – ruins of the stadium, a theatre, the market and a house from which many bronze products were excavated. It may be that other aspects of life in Sardis will be uncovered in time, as much more of the city remains unexplored.

Letter to the Church in Sardis

Kosher – Revelation 3 v 1 - 6

"You have a reputation of being alive, but you are dead."
Revelation 3 v 1

"What a lively church you have in Sardis!"
"You have such talented and generous people."
"Your church is always on the go with something good."
"Your reputation goes before you – it always has."

It is quite likely that the successful Sardis church was admired by some. Perhaps they even envied its good reputation, its socially distinguished members and their generosity ... but this letter suggests that it was becoming a spiritual graveyard. How could that possibly happen to a church? And what a shock this letter must have been.

3 v 1 'You have a name of being alive, but you are dead.' Towards the end of the first century, when this letter was 'despatched' to Sardis, it was still a successful and wealthy town, although its greatest days were in the past. A number of strategic roads came to the town, making it a good place for commerce. It was a centre for the woollen trade. The Roman Law Courts were based here but the town could not rise to the success that was enjoyed during its period as capital of the Kingdom. It must have been hard for the city not to cling to its old reputation as the capital. The AD17 earthquake had demolished many fine buildings and left the people devastated. Emperor Tiberius cancelled all taxes to the Empire for five years and made a donation equivalent to around ten million pounds today, to assist the rebuilding. Sardis was, therefore, restored with little effort from the people. It's as though they didn't need to fight for their future or work to build up their life again. It is suggested that the city became lazy and that the lack of energy and vision in the town crept into the church.

The church in Sardis was not facing an influx of Nicolaitans and false teaching. It was neither living with persecution nor suffering the fear and grief that was haunting Christians in some other towns. This church was not facing severe protest and opposition within the town, as churches might do when standing up for what is right and just, and openly declaring faith in Christ. The letter reprimands Christians of Sardis for maintaining a false front. There was a massive gap between their reputation and the reality.

3 v 2 God does not expect us to be perfect or He would not have come in Christ to bring forgiveness and redemption. The word really means 'not complete' rather than 'perfect'. Their actions were good but they were not filled with God's purposes: they were empty actions,

without spiritual meaning and, therefore, not complete in the sight of God.

1 Samuel 16 v 7 puts the idea more vividly when God says -

'They look at the outward appearance, but the Lord looks on the heart.'

Isaiah 29 v 13 also gives a helpful explanation when Isaiah brings God's word

'These people draw near with their mouth, and honour me with their lips, while their hearts are far from me'.

There is no condemnation in the judgements of this letter. There were probably many good things in the life of the church of Sardis but without full recognition by the people that they were ultimately accountable to God. This church was challenged because looks can deceive. The church was not what it seemed to be. It was not entirely genuine. Perhaps it did not match up to what it claimed to be. The popular phrases of the large Jewish population in Sardis were bound to have 'rubbed off' onto other people. I am pretty sure, therefore, that they would understand the message fully – 'You have the reputation of being alive but you are dead' – you are not Kosher Christians in Sardis.

Be Genuine

Jesus spoke critically to those who prayed long elaborate prayers, flamboyantly donated gifts or fasted to attract attention. He disapproved of their vain attempts to gain the reputation of being outstandingly good religious people. He spoke directly to leaders and teachers who were not Kosher.

"Alas for you scribes and Pharisees, you utter frauds! What miserable fakes you are … You clean the outside of the cup and the dish while the inside is full of greed and self-indulgence … You

> hypocritical scribes and Pharisees! You are like white-washed
> tombs, which look fine on the outside but inside are full of dead
> bones and all kinds of rottenness. For you appear like good men on
> the outside – but inside you are a mass of pretence and
> wickedness."
> Matthew 23 v 23, 25, 27 – 28 (J.B.Phillips)

The word used for an actor performing for an audience was 'hupokrite'. It came into common use to describe a fraud.

3 v 4 Refers to the fact that we can become morally and spiritually soiled. Herodotus, Greek historian, described in detail the ways in which society in Sardis had declined morally and spiritually. Perhaps it was inevitable that, to some extent, the church, being part of that society, went the same way .... and possibly it is inevitable for us.

As I put these words on paper, I am acutely aware of the challenge this presents to us in the church and the western world today. I am also aware that our human nature is weak and vulnerable. We are a confusion of contradictions, rationally and emotionally. You'll remember St Paul's words -

> 'My own behaviour baffles me. For I find myself not doing what I
> really want to do, but doing what I really loathe.'
> Romans 7 v 15 (J.B.Phillips)

'Hypocrite' is not an appropriate word to describe those who strive but fall short. Otherwise, every one of us is clearly a hypocrite. That judgment alone, upon ourselves or on others, excludes the Grace of God, which is the centre and focal point of the Christian Gospel – ie. the forgiving, renewing, empowering, transforming, strengthening, encouraging, uplifting, overwhelming, never ending loving-kindness of God made real for us in Jesus Christ.

Wake up and Live

3 v2 'Wake up! Strengthen what remains and is on the point of death.'

3 v3 'Remember what you received and heard. Obey it, and repent.'

Not everyone in Sardis had lost their faith and vitality, though the letter urged them to 'wake up'. Some had fallen asleep but not all. What would be the point of calling on the 'dead' to wake up? John knew there was still life in the church of Sardis. Let us not be fooled by appearances as, in every dying congregation, there are many hoping for God's challenge and renewal. 'Make strong what remains.' Even if only a few remained faithful in Sardis, they needed to be strengthened because God intended to use them. The word for 'strengthen' was used frequently in the early church, when seeking to give encouragement to nurture and build up the life and faith of the people. Verse 3 urged the Christians in Sardis to remember what they had heard and what they had been taught from the start. That was, of course, the Good News of Jesus Christ. They were also prompted to remember that what they had been given was the power of God's Holy Spirit. The Spirit gave life to the church: love, peace, joy, purpose and direction, together with the preaching of God's word and the power of His presence in their lives. These things gave distinctive witness to God's reality.

3 v 4 God's Promise was that 'they will walk with me, dressed in white, for they are worthy'. Those who resisted the corrupting influences of Sardis would be considered worthy. Those who had weakened but had then overcome, been forgiven and renewed would be alongside them. White robes were understood to represent purity or victory. Later, in Revelation 7 v 14 and 22, John expands this point. He says that we can wash our robes in the blood of the lamb and they will be white. The language and the images are strong but the meaning would have been clear to the readers of the time – that they could be purified through the death of Jesus on the cross.

3 v 5 The letter concludes with a vivid reminder of God's eternal promise to the faithful –

> '… I will not blot your name out of the book of life. I will confess your name before my Father …'

I suppose that the Book of Life is a little like our understanding of a Book of Remembrance, a Roll of Honour or a War Memorial, where we enter or engrave names to ensure that they are not forgotten. In scripture, however, this telling image takes the idea further. Our memorials preserve the names of those who have died, whereas the Book of Life records the names of those who live. It is a book of eternal life, indicating those whose names have been written on God's heart and therefore will be held by Him for ever. Jesus encouraged his disciples to be glad that their names were 'written in heaven.' (Luke 10 v 20)

With that symbolism in mind, we could conclude that some of the people involved in the Church of Sardis could have had their names well up on the church roll and yet not be included on God's roll. This would not have been because God rejected them but because they had excluded themselves. Nevertheless, this letter could have spurred them on to wake up, to be strengthened in their faith and in the church fellowship, to hold on to the heart of the Gospel, to remember that life comes from the Spirit and to repent.

Reflection

- It seems that the muscle-men of Sardis may have been as obsessed with their body image as increasing numbers of young men are today, as well as young women. Why is it happening?

- If you regard it as a concern, how could young people be encouraged to maintain health and fitness without promoting the current obsession with their body image?

- 'You have the reputation of being alive but you are dead.' Could that criticism of the Church in Sardis be directed to the church today? If so, or even if you think 'not quite', what leads you to that view?

- Some churches are very busy. To what extent are the busy programmes promoting – true community, healthy relationships, care for others, concern for the world, joy, service to those in need, justice, mercy, knowledge of God, Christian hope, peace of mind and peace in the world, Christian fellowship, gentle evangelism and genuine worship?

- Is it true that churches sometimes dwell too much on their reputation from the past, rather than on their contemporary life and mission?

- We are all aware that we are not perfect people and that we do not have perfect churches. As the New Testament word that is translated as 'perfect' really means 'not complete' what are the ways in which your church is not complete?

- The Christians in Sardis were urged to 'strengthen what they have'. Identify the good things in your Christian living and in your churches that could be strengthened, and thank God for them.

- In your private reflection, mull over the words of St. Paul (Rom 7 v 15): 'My behaviour baffles me. For I find myself not doing what I really want to do but doing what I really loathe.' Be aware of ways in which this may apply to your life.

- Think about people whose names you consider must be included in the 'Book of Life'. What are your reasons?

Philadelphia

'Three huge, strong, sturdy pillars have
remained' .... This is one of them

'I will make you a pillar in
the Temple of my God'
Revelation 3 v 12

Philadelphia was in the
midst of rural villages, as
the modern town of
Alasehir is still

Some Christian texts
unearthed by
archaeologists have
still not been fully
deciphered

Chapter 7

Philadelphia

A Christian Site

The modern town of Alasehir covers most of ancient Philadelphia. Consequently there is not much left to be seen. Portions of the rough stone walls of the city remain on the north-eastern side. There are parts of a small theatre and significant remains of a brick built Byzantine church from about 600 AD, that was extended in 11th century. Three very sturdy pillars are still in place, supporting the lower portion of the arches which once rose above them - but little else. Some eleventh century frescoes are to be seen although, being exposed to the elements for centuries, they have greatly deteriorated. Nevertheless, they indicate that this building was in use for five hundred years of worship.

The New Testament church here was small but it grew strong. By the Byzantine period, Philadelphia was the seat of the bishop. It remained the home of the bishop until the nineteenth century, by then bishop of the Greek Orthodox Church. There are small numbers of Christians in Philadelphia today. It was an unexpected delight when, on one occasion, about a dozen local Christians came to meet our group. They encircled one of the great pillars and sang for joy ... so, of course, we all joined in. We were a bit cautious, at first, because that was really forbidden, as the sites were officially secular museums and no public display of religion was allowed. But breaking the rules made it all the more enjoyable. (As we got away with it!)

The City

From the hill where the acropolis once stood, including temples, council chambers and palaces, there's a good view over the modern town. It is still in the midst of rural villages, as the ancient city was. In 189 BC, Macedonian soldiers were instructed to camp on a hill where there'd been a Lydian settlement for centuries. The soldiers stayed and the town grew. The hill overlooks two valleys and the Royal Persian Road runs by, along the borders of Mysia, Lydia and Phrygia, providing important trade routes. The site was on the eastern edge of Greek culture in Asia which, by this time, was well established in the west. In stationing the soldiers, King Attalus II of Pergamum founded Philadelphia. As the king had been devoted to his brother and predecessor, Eumenes, he named the town 'Philadelphia' – 'city of brotherly love.' The city's early coins carried images of the two brothers.

Strabo referred to Philadelphia as 'a city full of earthquakes', which is why many inhabitants spent much of their life in huts, in the surrounding rural area. They could quickly escape to them for safety. William Ramsay, Scottish archaeologist and New Testament scholar, believes that the reason for founding the city was to spread Greek culture and language into Phrygia and Lydia. Within thirty years, Greek was the language of Lydia and the Lydian language was fading away. In AD 17 and again in AD 23, major earthquakes hit the area and much of the city had to be rebuilt.

It's disappointing that so much of the ancient city is buried under the modern town of Alasehir, as history suggests that it had some fabulous buildings. The Emperor Tiberius provided vast amounts of money for restoration, which enabled buildings of outstanding architecture to be constructed. Monuments were built in his honour. Later, Caligula and Vespasian made similar contributions and were also venerated within the town. Before Christianity arrived, the gods of Olympus had pride of place in the worship of Philadelphia, although Dionysus, god of the grape harvest, was probably closer to the hearts of the people. This was a grape growing area and Philadelphia was renowned in the region for its superb grapes and wines, and still is today. It has now added the harvesting of cotton and liquorice to its fame. The archaeologists tell us that various inscriptions refer to thanksgiving and confession to Dionysus, as well as recording his extremes of punishment.

Letter to the Church in Philadelphia
Open Doors – Revelation 3 v 7 - 13

"I have placed before you an open door." Revelation 3 v 8

3 v 7 The message to the Christians in Philadelphia is from 'the holy one and true one'. John is conveying the message of Jesus Christ. Christ is holy as God is holy. John has no greater reality to share with his Christian companions in Philadelphia. His message begins by assuring them of its dependability, its trustworthiness, its truth. It is the message of Christ and truly from God who, above all else, is reality. We have mentioned before that the word 'truth' (aletheia) would be more accurately translated 'reality'. Jesus said, "I am the truth." In Him we find the dependable reality of God, truth about the world and truth about ourselves.

3 v 8 'I know your works ... You have kept my word and not denied my name.'

3 v 10 'Because you have kept my word of patient endurance.' The message is full of praise and encouragement. Most of the letters include judgement but not this one. Christians in Philadelphia had been facing disruption, insecurity, earthquakes and injuries, false claims, public pressure, persecution and grief, but they had held on to their faith and had stood their ground in witness and patient endurance.

Earlier, when thinking about persecution in the arena in Smyrna, we mentioned that it was the execution of Christians from Philadelphia that stirred up the crowd and gave rise to their baying for the blood of Polycarp. Many Christians from Philadelphia suffered in this way. Their families, friends and fellow Christians faced grief and fear, as they looked on, but it was said that none gave in. They kept their Christian faith. I find myself challenged by Christians who hold on to their faith and witness, when their lives are at stake. Could I do the same? Nothing could have been more appropriate in this letter than admiration, praise and encouragement. Their pain and courage humbles me.

Witness in the Arena

They were hollering and screaming, stamping feet and sounding horns. It was a tremendous din and all coming from five to six thousand teenage young people who packed the auditorium. Together with another five thousand or so, they had gathered in London, in the mid 1980's, for a weekend of celebration, music and drama, discussion, testimony and worship. The shouts and cheers were to welcome Terry Waite, Envoy to the Archbishop of Canterbury, as he was greeted on stage at the Royal Albert Hall. That wonderful building is quite reminiscent of a Roman theatre but it was his words during the interview that brings the event back to mind. After a little light chatter, I asked him about his role, in negotiating the release of hostages in risky places. He outlined, briefly, the positive outcome from sensitive consultations in Iran, Libya and Lebanon. That prompted me to ask if he had found himself in fearful danger. You could have heard a pin drop in that huge hall, as he described one occasion, when he was grabbed and a gun held firmly to his head. He was defenceless and realised that it could be the end.

As we drew the conversation to a close I asked if there was any thought he would like to leave with the young people. He replied –

> 'While I was sitting in the box up there, before the time to come on, I saw a banner held high by a youth group from Lymm, in Cheshire. I grew up in a village nearby. My mother lives there now. In that small English village I was given opportunity, through my church, to develop what small abilities and gifts I had. So I want to say to you,

please remember this, that although the world is confusing and
difficult and full of conflict, take what you have been given by God -
take what you have been given seriously. Allow those things to
flower and develop, and you'll be surprised at the way in which God
will open up the future for you. Don't be put off by people who say
you can do nothing. If you have a little bit of faith, in God and in
yourself, as the Bible puts it very simply, mountains can be moved.'

That prompted another eruption of multi-decibel delight in applause and
cheers from the arena to the highest balcony, in response to his
message of witness, affirmation and encouragement. He was assuring
the young people that God will open up the future, urging them to seize
the opportunities and he was gently fostering their faith. His words seem
to resonate with the major themes in John's letter to the Christians in
Philadelphia. The spiritual significance and practical meaning, however,
hits home with greater impact in the arena of service to which Terry
Waite returned. Within months, he was off to Lebanon in the hope of
negotiating with Islamic Jihad for the release of hostages. Having been
at gun point before, he was aware of taking enormous risks. The
attempts to get into negotiation led to his being captured by Hezbollah in
1987 and held for five years. The first four years were in solitary
confinement. I can't imagine how I would have survived being locked up
alone, year after year. I think I'd have gone mad. There certainly were
some terrible times when Terry felt he was going over the edge. To my
mind isolation was more than enough torture but he was frequently
blindfolded, beaten, subjected to mock executions and chained to a
radiator. His life and witness, throughout such torment and pain, speak
powerfully of the faithfulness and courage being spoken of in John's
letter to persecuted Christians in Philadelphia. Such faithfulness and
courage is not found solely in the circumstances or fresh faith of the first
century Christians in Philadelphia but also in the loyalty, integrity,
practical commitment, trust and faith in God seen equally in the lives of
many Christians today.

Opportunity

3 v 8 'See I have set before you an open door which no one is able to shut.' St Paul also uses this image. When he was writing to the Corinthian church about preaching, teaching and building up the churches in and around Ephesus he described it this way –

> 'A wide door for effective work has been opened to me...'
> (1 Corinthians 16 v 9)

He wrote to the church in Colossae saying –

> 'Pray for us that God will open to us a door for the word.'
> (Colossians 4 v 3)

When Paul and Barnabas returned to Antioch he descirbed –

> '...how God had opened a door of faith for Gentiles.'
> (Acts 14 v 27)

John was convinced that God had opened a door for Christian mission in Philadelphia. He may have thought that the busy life of the town unlocked opportunities for witness, as visitors came from many nations for the temple festivals. Others came to the markets for grapes or wine. This could have provided opportunities for faithful Christians to mingle, to be hospitable, to care and to talk to visitors about Christ. John could have been thinking of the strategic position of this city which was ideal for Christian witness to spread beyond its borders. The city shared borders with three provinces enabling communication to be easier than it would otherwise have been. The Greek language had already spread into Lydia and Phrygia. Was God calling Philadelphian Christians to start travelling with the gospel message? The town was on the road from Smyrna on the west coast right through into the east. Tradesmen, travellers, armies and festival-followers journeyed on that road. The door was open.

Jesus had, of course, referred to Himself as 'the door' (John 10 v7 and v 9). This is the heart of the matter not only for the church in Philadelphia but for every person. He is our 'open door' to God, to know what God is like, to be close to God, to know that we are loved by God, to relate to God, to live with God, to share God's action. In every age, the church should keep watching for God-given opportunities for mission, service, spiritual growth, practical ministry and actions of justice, compassion, reconciliation, peace-making and care for the poor and vulnerable. The tricky bit is in keeping alert to recognise an open door, to ensure that our action is an appropriate response to the opportunities that come our way and to find the will to get on with it.

3 v 8 'I know that you have little power'. This may be recognition that the people were tired out from dodging the damage and disruption from earthquakes and exhausted by persecution and grief. It could be reference to the fact that, at this stage, the church in Philadelphia was small and did not have strength in numbers for mounting major mission initiatives. Like them, we always have difficulties to overcome.

Pillars in God's Temple

3 v 11 Many in the early church anticipated the return of Christ in their life time. 'I am coming soon; hold fast to what you have, so that no one can seize your crown.' John frequently urges Christians in the seven churches to hold on to what they have. Advice to the Church in Philadelphia sounds like good advice for all Christians in any age. Instead of worrying about what we don't have; what we fail to understand or can't believe; what gifts we lack or opportunities we desire, we are being urged to – 'Hold on to what you have!'

3 v 12 If you do remain faithful and true – 'I will make you a pillar in the temple of my God; you will never go out of it.' When writing to the Galatian church, Paul described Peter, James and John as pillars of the church (Galatians 2 v 9). In our local churches and chapels today, those who work hard for God and the people, and especially if

they have sustained that service over many years, are often described in that way, as though the church would fall down without them. Sometimes, their families suggest that God went a little too far by adding 'and you'll never leave it', when already they complain, "You might as well take your bed to that church!" John is not, of course, speaking of any church building. He refers to the temple, because the people were accustomed to seeing huge columns in the pagan temples, supporting great stone friezes, pediments and heavy roofs. It's a powerful image of the strength found by the faithful to support and sustain others in being Christ's church.

I mentioned that there is not much to see of the remains of Philadelphia but I find that the simplicity of what you can see has profound meaning. Three huge, strong, sturdy pillars have remained standing for about fourteen hundred years. The rest of the building has gone. The pillars have been shaken by major earthquakes and survived plundering and wars but they are still standing. They are a strong, solid reminder of God's revelation to faithful Christians in the church in Philadelphia, where God's promise could not have been clearer – "I will make you a pillar in the temple of my God and you will never go out of it."

'You will never leave it' or 'You will never go out' picks up another common experience of the people. Earthquakes and tremours came frequently. Those who lived within the city were frequently having to pack up and leave in a hurry, just in case their house came tumbling down or because it had already. They would go right out of the town, to ensure that they and their families would be safe. The promise to Christians in Philadelphia was that, although many things could shake their faith, if they remained true, nothing could bring down the pillars of Christ's church and cause them to run. God's promise to the faithful was that they would be made 'a pillar in God's temple'. Then the promise took another step forward – 'I will write on you the name of my God'…. and then another – 'and my own new name.'

Perhaps John was recalling the fact that, in the pagan temples, a pillar was set up for each faithful, long serving, priest when he died, with the expectation that it would stay there for ever. His name would be written upon it and would remain as a witness to his life and example. This could serve as an illustration to show that the witness of a faithful Christian does not end with his/her death but, as a pillar in Christ's church, continues to support and influence the faith of others. The pillars of the temples also carried the names of the gods. So faithful followers were being assured that they were pillars in God's own temple and His name was written upon them. One other idea may also be referred to in this image. It was customary to tattoo the name of the master onto the arm of a slave so that, if a rogue tried to steal a slave, it was clear that he wasn't available. If a slave ran away, being marked with the name of the 'one to whom he belonged', he could be found. Perhaps the illustration is affirming that it would be crystal clear that the Christian belongs to Christ.

Before the town was established by Attalus, the Lydian name for the settlement was Calletebus but, with its new foundation, it was given a new name – Philadelphia. Following a major earthquake AD 17, when Tiberius generously enabled the city to be rebuilt, in gratitude it was again re-named – Neocaesarea (New City of Caesar). Later, the town had reason to be grateful to Emperor Vespasian and it was given yet another a new name – Flavia, as the Emperor's family name was Flavius. The new names didn't last very long and the city returned to the name of Philadelphia. The people of Philadelphia were accustomed to being given a new name but the new name of Christ was written upon the Christian's heart. It was an indication of a new nature in Christ and, for the faithful Christian, that was indelible. It would never be erased. It was God's eternal promise.

Reflection

- Are there 'open doors' for Christian witness and service in your life or in the life of your Church?

- What difficulties and hindrances do Christians face today in witness and service? How can they be overcome?

- Describe ways in which you have seen faithfulness and courage in other Christians?

- What are the strong, sturdy pillars of Christian faith for you?

- Who do you think of as a pillar of the Christian community in your life; giving support, inspiration encouragement, loving care & leadership among God's people?

Laodicea

Syria Street

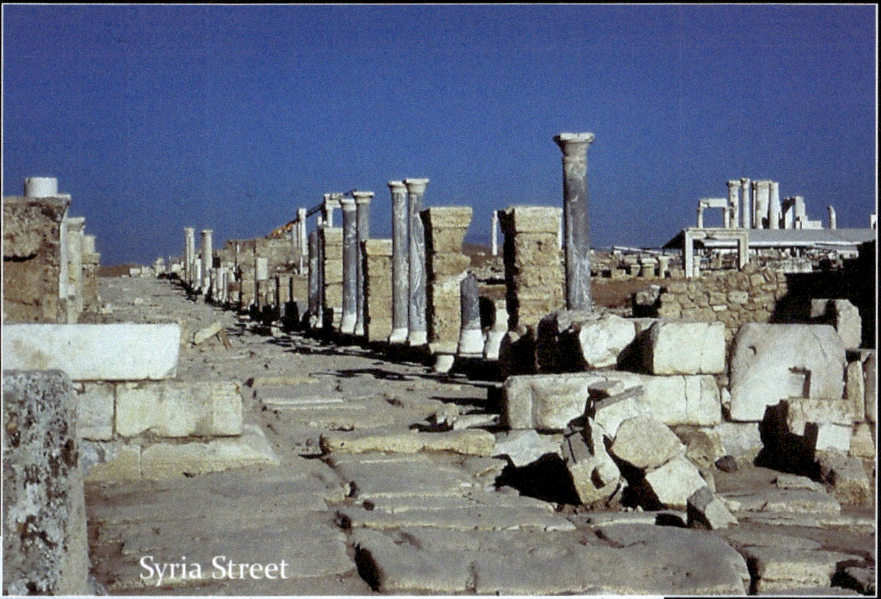

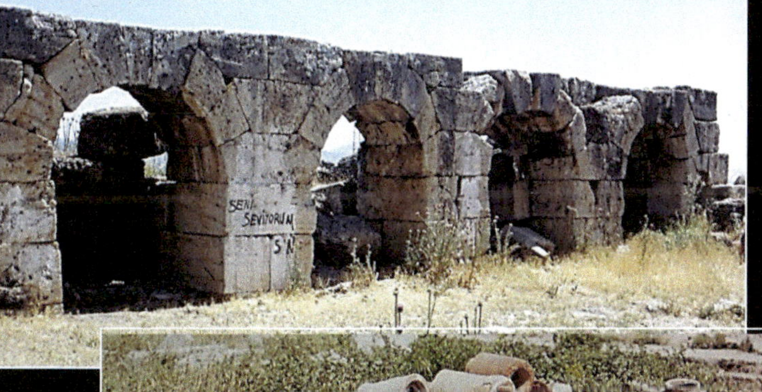

Aquaduct carrying water 7k from Hierapolis

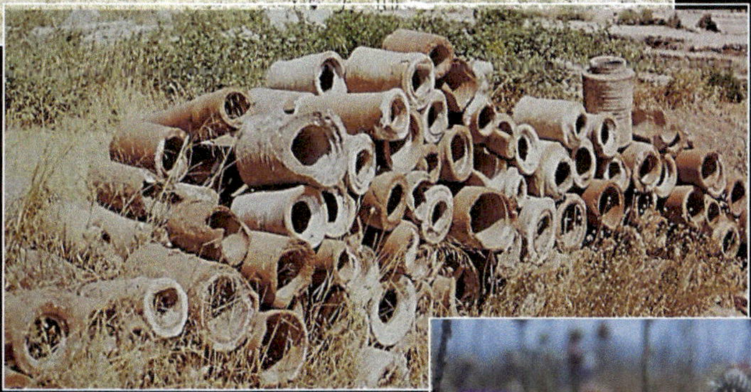

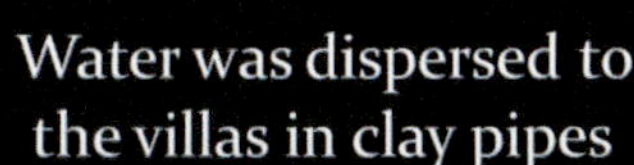

Water was dispersed to the villas in clay pipes

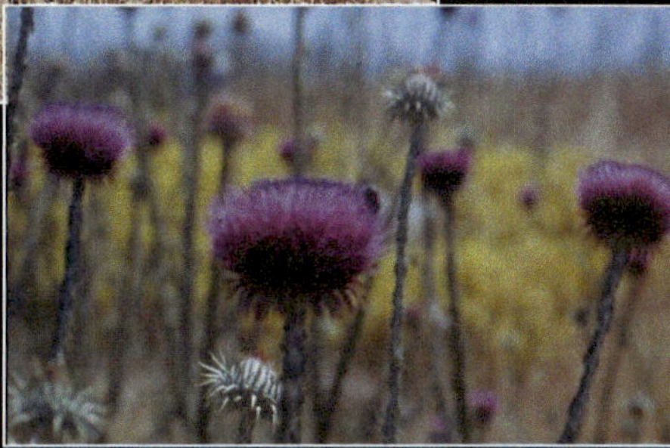

Hierapolis

Extensive necropolis – tombs of all shapes and sizes

Triple – arched gate to the main street. A small church built just inside.
The remains of it can be seen at the bottom right of the picture.

Statues, a colonnade and shops lined the main street of Hierapolis

The Roman baths, when vacated for new ones, became a Christian church

Pamukkale

Hot springs have been flowing for about 14,000 years, forming pools, like terraces down the hill

Stalactites around the pools

You can bathe in the sacred pool of the Temple of Apollo, where the columns fell

Laodicea

Archaeological Site

I warned the group, on my last visit to Laodicea, that we'd need to walk through an expanse of uneven scrubland to reach the ruins, although they may find that it would be made more pleasant by the big, beautiful, purple, wild thistles spread among the grasses. It had been like that on every previous visit. I was, therefore, surprised when the coach pulled into a new carpark and we approached modern entrance buildings, as we walked across a splendid stone block surface to the posh ticket office. In the last few years a great deal of work has been done at many of the sites, to make them more attractive and comfortable for visitors and, at the same time, new excavations have brought to light more of the ancient cities. We walked along Syria Street which, previously, had been completely buried. Recent excavations, rather than simply scattered ruins, now enable visitors to imagine this large busy town.

Syria Street had been a bustling shopping thorough-fair, bordered by colonnades and pedestals, in a city described by Hadrian as 'the metropolis of Asia'. There was a sizable Greek theatre at the end of the street. Other visible remains include an odeum, temples, supports for a bridge, a church, baths, a gymnasium, a large stadium, many scattered sarcophagi, a cistern and an aqueduct plus pipes that brought water into the city. The Ephesus gate was the grand entrance from the west but another triple gate remains almost completely buried. Most of the streets and buildings were unexcavated but who knows what may have been unearthed by the time you read this.

The town was originally called Diospolis (City of Zeus) and then Rhodas but the city of Laodicea was established by the Seleucid King Antiochus

II, at around 250 BC, in honour of his wife Laodice. Research supports the view that Laodicea was destroyed by an earthquake and never rebuilt, although it has also been suggested that it was left desolate after the invasion of the Turks and Mongols in the 13th to 14th century. It is certainly true that the ruins were undisturbed for centuries. The modern town of Denizli, nearby, grew up by the Lycus River.

Daily Life

The life of Laodicea was greatly influenced by its strategic position on a major road from Ephesus in the west, good communication with Hierapolis, a few miles to the north, and a road out to Syria, in the east. Other roads into the city added to its perfect location for trade and for defence. After 133 BC, when Rome took over the governance of the area, it became a military outpost for the Empire. Imagine a typical day in the town –

The town wakes up to the sun rising over the elegant buildings, plush mansions and lush gardens, despite the limitations of the water supply. The streets are soon busy with people rushing to their work, to the temples or to the markets. It wouldn't be long before many would be bargaining for the famous woollen products and cotton cloths. This town was renowned for the vivid fashionable colours of its fabrics. Merchants are arriving from far and wide. Lucrative business deals are soon underway and big money is changing hands or being deposited at the banks.

Queues would be forming at the medical centre, as there was always a demand for its specialist eye ointment. It had recently been transferred from a temple thirteen miles west of the town and the people were delighted. In the afternoon, you'd probably hear roars from the stadium as the crowds cheered their favourites, while, in the evening, you might hear screams from the theatre, as gladiators fight to their death. That's entertainment for you!

The synagogues were often buzzing as many Jews lived in Laodicea; Christians had little active opposition. There was an overall sense of security in the town. You may see a few of the poorer people but, generally, they were not very visible. Perhaps the only thing to be wary of was the foul-tasting water coming into the city on the aqueduct. Roman soldiers, when they finish their duties, would often be sitting in the town squares with tankards in their hands, watching the sun go down, whilst aristocratic households would provide their guests with flagons of wine, sumptuous meals and music, before retiring for a restful night.

Letter to the Church in Laodicea

Passion – Revelation 3 v 14 - 22

> "You are neither cold nor hot … I am about to spit you out of my mouth!"
> Revelation 3 v 15 – 16

3 v14 A message 'from the Amen' sounds a bit strange but the text is self-explanatory, as It continues, 'who is trustworthy and true'. The sentence is an affirmation of utter reliability. In St John's gospel, where Jesus says several times, "Truly, truly, I say to you," the Greek text reads, "Amen, amen, I say to you". Amen is 'truth'. Christ is truth and you can wholly and completely depend on the truth of this message from Him.

3 v 15 –16 'I know that you are neither cold nor hot. How I wish you were either one or the other! But because you are lukewarm, neither hot nor cold, I am going to spit you out of my mouth.'

The aqueduct in Laodicea brought water from Hierapolis, seven kilometres away. It rose from the hot springs with a temperature of between 35 and 100 degrees centigrade, and still does today. It travelled along the aqueduct, through stone pipes into the city to be stored in water towers, before being dispersed to the villas in clay pipes. By that time, the water had cooled somewhat. As it cooled, the calcium carbonate minerals from the hot springs had begun to solidify in the lukewarm liquid. Incrustations are evident today on several of the stone arches of the aqueduct, where the stonework had sprung a few leaks, and on the water towers. A mouthful of that water would have been enough to make anyone spit it out. It seems that John was using a nasty, unpalatable, everyday experience to drive home the force of the message. Straight for the jugular! 'I'm going to spit you out of my mouth.'

This is the only letter with no praise for the church. It is entirely judgement and criticism of a church that was losing its way. Verse 15 jumps in at the deep end. The Church in Laodicea was not being rebuked because of heresy or corruption. The focus of the letter is on its spirit. The letter declares that they had no passion. Its people were neither hot nor cold.

Perhaps this letter could speak directly to us today. No church would want to become insular or lukewarm but sometimes we don't realise what's happening to us. There are probably times when most of us need to guard against a lack of passion, losing our zeal, weakening in active commitment and being without a burning desire for others to find faith in Jesus Christ. This letter is addressing matters of the heart.

John Wesley, in his sermon on the 'Almost Christian' described himself as active in doing good but empty –

> 'Many of you can testify that I went for many years as far as an almost-Christian can go. I avoided evil like the plague, I used my time to the full and seized every opportunity of doing good. I used all the public and private forms of worship. God is my witness that I did all this sincerely, having a real desire to serve Him and to do His will in everything. I wanted to run my best in the race of faith, and win eternal life for myself. Yet the Holy Spirit has convinced me that all the time I was only an almost-Christian.'

Wesley was only able to say, "Now I am a Christian" when his experience in a Society meeting in Aldersgate Street, London, compelled him to write –

Journal 24th May 1738
'I felt my heart strangely warmed. I felt that I trusted in Christ and Christ alone for my salvation. And an assurance was given to me that He had taken away my sins, even mine.'

The letter to the Church at Laodicea is not requiring us to become hot-gospel fanatics but it is an invitation and encouragement for us to seek passion in our faith – for it to be in our heart and mind. It is a calling to be thoughtful, enquiring, energetic, courageous, active Christians in soul and body, and totally committed to Christ.

Complacent and Self-satisfied

3 v 17 ' For you say, "I am rich, I have prospered and I need nothing." You do not realise that you are wretched, pitiable, poor, blind, and naked.'

In material terms, society in Laodicea was wealthy. It's likely that most people could have said, "Really, I have all I want. I don't need anything more." Following an earthquake in 60 AD, the town was rebuilt from its own resources. There was no need to appeal to Rome. Contentment can too easily become complacency, which blinds us to our true spiritual condition. Equally, pride and success can lead us to believe that there is nothing we need. Like us today, Christians in Laodicea absorbed attitudes from their society, and their church had become half-hearted, instead of wholehearted and fervent in spirit.

Inhabitants of this wealthy city and major banking centre were told that they were 'poor'. A community famous for its medical centre, ophthalmic expertise and eye ointment were notified that they were 'blind'. Promoters of the most magnificent cloth, at the most popular fashion hub in Asia, were informed that they were 'naked.'

3 v 18 You could have found everything you need in the market place of Laodicea so, continuing with the symbolism of the market in this letter, the readers were advised that Christ is the best supplier for

their needs. If you are spiritually poor, He has gold. If you are spiritually naked, He has clothes. If you are spiritually blind, then even the renowned Medical School of Laodicea would not be able to provide the right ointment for healing but Christ can.

3 v 19 Christ reassures them of His love. They may be able to manage without the subsidy of Caesar but they will not find what is needed without the Grace of God – the active loving–kindness of God. Then the letter invited them to repent ie. to turn away from complacency by turning towards God. That is the one thing that Christ cannot do for us. Repentance has to be our own. We must do the turning - and He is waiting.

3 v 20 This verse immediately brings to mind Holman Hunt's famous paintings of Christ 'The Light of the World'. He stands at the door knocking and ready for it to be opened from within. It points to Christ's personal appeal to the Church and to each of us. His offer of Christian passion, power in mind and spirit, the warmth of His 'inner presence' and, therefore, communion with Him. In painting this scene in words, in which Christ offers to come in and eat with us, the writer has deliberately chosen to use the word 'deipneo', which has been translated variously as 'eat', 'dine' or 'sup'. It is not, 'I'll call in for coffee' but, 'We'll share the main meal of the day - substantial nourishment, plenty of time together, and true fellowship.'

3 v 21 John concludes his final letter to the Churches of Asia Minor with a word of reassurance. To be in communion with Christ is to be in communion with God and to share God's glory – which is represented as - 'sitting with Christ on His throne'.

Reflection

- What do *we* regard as genuine passion in our own faith and in the life of the church today?

- Could the message to Laodicea, "You are neither hot nor cold", apply to us and to our church today? In what ways? Why and where does it come from?

- In our comparatively wealthy lives in the church today – how poor are we?

- In our fashion conscious generation – how naked are we?

- In our ophthalmic wonderland of lenses, implants, eye surgery and medication, as well as closed circuit television, security cameras, computer screens, Skype and an increasing variety of portable, visual telephones – how blind are we?

- If you were brought before a court on a charge of 'being a Christian,' would there be enough evidence to convict you?

- Even though Holman Hunt's painting is dated, it is still greatly treasured by many, as it represents Christ, the Light of the World, knocking on the door of our lives. If you were artistic, and perhaps you are, what would be an appropriate picture to represent the message of His painting to the modern world? What is that message?

Hierapolis: Pamukkale

Colossians 4 v 12 - 17

Hierapolis is not even listed in the 783 pages of my best concordance, not once among its more than 200,000 references. It gets only one mention in the New Testament (Col.4 v 13). However, that is a good reminder to me, that the early church was growing in many places we know little about and perhaps have never heard of. The Christian faith was taking root in places other than those to which the New Testament writers have directed our thoughts. One good reason that makes this town well worth remembering is that a first century leader of the church, here, made a most significant contribution to New Testament scholarship.

Papias (AD 60 – 131) was Bishop of Hierapolis. Irenaeus, a second century theologian and Bishop of Lyons, tells us that Papias was a disciple of John and a companion of Polycarp. Quotations from his five books are included in the records of Eusebius (third century historian and Bishop of Caesarea). From this source we learn that Mark recorded the words of the apostle Peter –

"He set down accurately, though not in order,
everything that he remembered of the words and
actions of the Lord."

This has been vital in our understanding of the eyewitness origin of the material of St. Mark's Gospel and in recognising that it was the earliest. These words, and a few more sentences of Papias enable us to see how many verses of St. Mark were used by St. Luke, who added more, and by St. Matthew, who produced quite a different arrangement of the material, as well as adding to it.

Exploring The Ruins

Until recently, a visitor's introduction to the city would have been quite a long walk up hill, through an extensive necropolis, to the higher plateau on which Hierapolis was built. Tombs of all shapes and sizes line the road - dozens and dozens of them. Some are architecturally splendid, which is an indication of the wealth and success of the city. The earliest inscription to emerge dates the founding of Hierapolis, by Eumanes II, in the latter years of the second century BC, although it seems likely that there was a settlement here earlier. By New Testament times, it had a population of about a hundred thousand and had become an industrial centre.

The city attracted visitors from far and wide to the healing waters of Pamukkale. In Roman times, the spa and the natural springs were very popular. The 'new' Roman baths form part of the museum now and the old baths, when vacated in favour of the luxurious, upmarket replacement, became a church for Christians. Many of the ruined buildings lie where they were toppled by one of the many earthquakes. You can quickly find yourself surrounded by the remains of numerous ancient buildings. That is a note-worthy achievement considering that it was 1957 before archaeological exploration began.

Before an Italian team started excavating the site, there was nothing but a shabby shed by the sacred pool. Now you can see a triple-arched Byzantine gate and an earlier Roman gate, in better condition. It was built to honour Emperor Domitian and originally had two storeys. There's the main street, which would have been lined with shops. A church was built onto the inside of the wall, at the gate.

The fine Roman theatre is a little way up the hill. The wall behind the stage was still intact until it collapsed, early in this century. It was being restored last time I was there. That wall, decorated with statues and stone work, is the 'scena', which gave its name to our modern term 'scenery'. Simulated sea battles were performed in the orchestra area in the fourth century, as it was sealed and could be flooded for that purpose.

St. Philip

Just north of the theatre, on the side of a hill, the Martyrium of St. Philip came to light, a few years ago. The octagonal building surrounded a double cross, inside a square. It was almost certainly a fifth century construction. It is believed to mark the spot where the apostle Philip was tied upside down and left hanging from a tree, until he starved to death. His grave has still not been located.

The ruins of a few churches can be seen, as well as the remains of several temples built to honour Artemis, Poiseidon, Men, Cybele, Pluto and Apollo. From time to time, noxious fumes are still discharged from the Plutorium, beneath the temple of Apollo, where there was a shrine honouring the god of the underworld. In Roman times, Hierapolis was a very popular spa town. Visitors came to seek comfort and healing for gall bladder and kidney diseases. Other hot springs in Turkey have a reputation for being beneficial to people suffering from other diseases. There are over a hundred spas and springs in Turkey and the waters of each one have been analysed to identify their specific minerals and beneficial effects.

You can still bathe in the spa water of the 'sacred pool', next to the temple of Apollo. Marble Corinthian columns still lie in the pool, where they fell at the time of the earthquake. It's a great experience - crystal clear water, wonderfully warm, blue heavens above and a feeling of swimming into history.

Gratitude

I have become increasingly aware of the enormous debt we owe to the expertise, persistence and hard work of archaeologists. Our eyes have been opened to an incalculable amount of knowledge of history, culture, architecture, philosophy, spirituality and daily life of past generations, through their almost fanatical, enquiring minds and their hard slog digging. I thank God for them.

If you like, I'll add to that another little bit of Turkish humour – about archaeologists.

At an archaeologist's convention in Turkey, a visiting participant from another part of the globe boasted, "In an excavation in our country, we discovered telephone cables twenty five meters down, which confirms for us that our ancestors were clever enough to have used telephones centuries ago."

A Turkish archaeologist replied, "In an excavation here in our country, we dug fifty meters down and found nothing ... which clearly confirms that centuries ago, our ancestors were using wireless telephones."

Pamukkale

The Turkish name Pamukkale means 'cotton castle'. It is an appropriate description of the white terraces that tumble down the hill just beyond the springs. Hierapolis is built on a high plateau but at this point the mountain drops away to lower ground. Here are the springs that provide water, via an aqueduct, for Laodicea. We mentioned that the mineral content of the water tasted awful by the time it reached Laodicea but here the mineral deposits are glorious. Water from the springs has been flowing for some fourteen thousand years, spreading out to leave its calcium deposit over a vast area, forming an astonishing white mountain. From the viewing area, now set up at an ideal distance below, it looks like snow. Adding to its stunning beauty, pools have formed in the travertine, like terraces down the hillside, and quite spectacular stalactites have crystalized around the pools. I have never seen anything like this place. When I catch even a glimpse of the expanse of this white mountain against the backdrop of a glorious blue sky, and watch the sparkling water dancing its way in various directions towards the beautifully crafted pools of still, calm, water, it lifts my heart.

On my early visits, we could paddle in the pools but now, with increasing popularity and many more visitors, measures have been taken to preserve the white surface, limiting where you can walk. Nevertheless, it is still worth taking off your shoes and socks to walk down the hill, in the gullies where water flows, and enjoy the warmth on your feet. In the nearby hotels, you can wallow in the warm spring water at your leisure.

The Church in Hierapolis

Colossians 4 v 12 – 18

4 v 12-13 It is clear that Epaphras, who was imprisoned with Paul when this letter was written, was a faithful leader in the church at Colossae. He seems to have been their minister. Paul assures the people of their minister's prayers and his hopes for their maturing life and faith. Paul then recognises the hard work Epaphras had put into his ministry among those people … but not only in Colossae. Paul's words of praise were testimony to the ministry of Epaphras in the three churches, in Colossae, Laodicea and Hierapolis. It seems most likely that Epaphras had a major role in the foundation of the three churches and in nurture and oversight of the three Christian communities.

4 v 14 Paul sends greeting from Luke and from Demas. We know that Luke travelled with Paul and stayed with him to the end (Timothy 4 v 11). Demas was mentioned in the letter to Philemon as a companion in their mission but, in Timothy 4 v10, we learn that he did not manage to stay on course to the end.

4 v 15 A note of special greeting was added for Christians in Laodicea and for Nymphas (male) or Nympha (female). From the text, we cannot be quite sure which is right. It seems that he/she was leading the church which met regularly in his/her home. There are several

other references in the New Testament to Christians meeting for worship in the homes of Christian leaders. There were no church buildings, in the earliest years, and there are no records of how many such groups there may have been but these homes were the cradles of the universal church.

4 v 16 The implication of the concluding words of this verse is that Paul wrote a letter to the church in Laodicea. If that is so no record of it exists. It may be true, of course, that Paul wrote a number of other letters of which no evidence has emerged. The earliest rumours of there being a copy of a letter from Paul to Laodicea were in the fourth century. Jerome, fourth to fifth century biblical scholar, concluded that the copy was forged. His view has been upheld by the majority of academics since. The Oxford Dictionary of the Christian Church considers that his scholarship was unsurpassed in the early church. Some scholars suggest that Paul may have been referring to his letter to the Ephesians which, it is thought, he expected to be sent on a circuit around the churches in Asia Minor.

4 v 17-18 This letter concludes with a final word of encouragement to spur on Archippus (who became the first Bishop in Laodicea) to complete the mission he had undertaken. It would seem that Paul's final greeting was in his own hand, probably distorted by the restriction of his chains. His words act as a reminder to the Colossians and to Archipus that he was bound and therefore prevented from continuing his mission, and that the responsibility and privilege now fell upon them (and us). Finally, a very brief prayerful word from Paul, asking for God's grace to be with them.

Reflection

- Some Christians think of St. Matthew's Gospel as the first. What difference does it make when you know that St. Mark's was the earliest, recording the words of St. Peter?

- Can you spot some of the clues in St. Mark's Gospel that tell us that his words have come from someone who was present? (eg. 'immediately', 'the grass was green', 'they were astonished', 'Jesus sighed' ...)

- At some points, the account of an event in one Gospel is not quite the same as the account of the same event in another Gospel. Does this give you cause to question the authenticity of scripture or does it confirm that Gospels are proclamations and not biographies? How do you support your thoughts about this?

- Are people surprised to know that the first gospel came mainly from the Apostle Peter, recorded by John Mark, written when Peter was alive, and not made up many years later, as some critics say?

Colossae

The city of Colossae was a few miles from Laodicea. It had close links with its neighbour and with Hierapolis. The three cities grew up near to the River Lycus, though were established in different centuries.

There was also close cooperation between the churches in the three towns.

The site of Colossae remains completely unexcavated and so there is very little to see. There is nothing left of the acropolis on the hilltop. There are some cave rooms and graves carved into the rocks nearby, as well as some indications of a theatre, but that is all. Colossae was a unique and important site in the ancient world and for the early Christian church. That's why I don't want to exclude reference to it. The town was fifteen miles east of Denizli, in the ancient Lycus Valley. It was situated on the historic military and commercial routes connecting south-west Anatolia to the east. Xenophon, a Greek historian from the 4th century BC, records that Colossae was one of the six major cities of Phrygia. Xerxes and his troops stopped there in 481 BC, and Cyrus of Persia, in 401 BC. They were the best years for Colossae. Working with Laodicea in the woollen trade enabled the city to flourish. Pliny the Elder described Colossae as one of the famous cities. It declined as Hierapolis and Laodicea prospered and developed but its major downfall came with the earthquake of AD 60. Although Colossae was destroyed, people lived there until the eighth century, by which time they had been worn down by Arab attacks.

There are suggestions that St Paul may have visited Colossae but most sources are inclined to think that is not so (Col. 1 v 4). Epaphras, perhaps together with other followers of Paul, laid the foundations of the Christian community in the city. Paul wrote to the Church in Colossae with care and commitment, even though he had probably never met the people. He expressed his delight and thanksgiving for them and for the true Christian faith they had embraced. Questions have been raised about the authorship of the letter, as the grammar doesn't fit well with Paul's, though that could be because a scribe did the writing, while Paul expressed his thoughts. Colossians 4 v 3 tells us that Paul was imprisoned when he wrote (in about 62 AD). In the letter, we learn that it was to be taken to Colossae by Tychicus, accompanied by Onesimus, who came from Colossae (Col. 4 v 9). By that time Epaphras was also imprisoned.

Paul's Letter to the Christians at Colossae

Paul wrote to combat false teaching which had infiltrated the Church at Colossae. He argued against the notion that, to have fellowship with God, they must worship some spiritual rulers and authorities and be obedient to certain food laws. He did so by simply setting out the true Christian gospel. The revival of circumcision suggests that there were numbers of Jews in the church. Emerging syncretism and immorality would not have been acceptable to true Christians or true Jews, which implies that other 'pagan' influences were threatening the true church. He warned them that the practices being adopted by some would distance them from God. Only Christ brings salvation and hope for the world.

The beginning of Gnostic philosophy was infiltrating the church. That was the belief that all material things are essentially and eternally evil and that God was interested only in spiritual things, as spiritual things were good. It followed, therefore, that God was not creator of tangible, physical things but of the spiritual only. The creator of all physical things was ignorant of God, distant from God and hostile to Him. The letter was written to make it clear that this is not the truth about God, and to enable the reader to realise that we know the Creator in Jesus Christ the Son of God. In Colossians 1 v15-17, Paul explains that all things were created through Christ and that all things spiritual and material hold together in Him.

'Christ is both the first principle and the upholding principle of the whole scheme of creation.' (1v17)
(J.B. Philipps : The New Testament in Modern English)

Paul declares that Christ is supreme and that He is the source and centre of all things. In Him is the fullness of God the Creator and sustainer. All things have stability, meaning and purpose in Him. Paul's words bring to mind Paul Tillich's phrase : 'The ground of our being'.

Tillich was re-thinking God as the depth and centre of all life. I am not suggesting that he and St. Paul were on quite the same lines but both speak of God in the depth of reality. The Apostle seems to be locating Christ in the depth of all human life and in the depth of all creation.

> 'Truth is deep and not shallow, suffering is depth and not height. ...
> There is a depth in God and a depth out of which the Psalmist cries
> to God.'
> (Paul Tillich 'Shaking the Foundations' p60)

The Gnostics argued that as all matter is evil, Christ must be a spiritual phantom and not a real, tangible living being, and that His salvation was only for the spirit. But St. Paul witnessed to the reality of Christ who died on a cross for the salvation of all creation. Gnostics believed that we could do anything we like with our body and with the physical world. It was all evil and could not be saved, so what did it matter? Paul's teaching expresses God's love and care for the world and its people - for all parts of His creation. Jesus demonstrated a way of life that calls us to moral responsibility towards others and for the world around us. In a few words, Paul summarised the incredible depth and breadth of Christ's person and ministry and the impact of His saving grace.

1 v 15 – 20 outlines the nature and the work of Christ, magnificently. This is probably the highest expression of Paul's understanding of the person of Christ in the New Testament. For us, this is radical, profound and enriching faith, so I imagine that it must have opened the eyes of Christians in Colossae. It is well worth reading. Paul invited his readers to understand 'new life in Christ' and to live it, in the power of the Risen Christ.

Reflection

- In Col. 1 v15 – 20 St Paul is explaining that Christ is the first principle and the upholding principle of the whole scheme of creation and that all things spiritual and material hold together in him. In your view, what does this mean?

- Do you think of God in the heights or in the depths?

- Some Christians think that God's primary interest is in our spiritual life, some others think that He cares most about the way we live and take care of the world, while still others think he cares equally about both. What do you think? Why?

- If you were preaching, what would you say about 'Let the peace of Christ rule in your hearts'? (Col 3 v 15)

- When thinking about the Church in Hierapolis, we read Paul's letter to the Colossians Chapter 4v 12-18. In v 12-13, Paul expressed generous praise for Epaphras. How often do we praise and thank our ministers for their leadership and service - or others who give leadership to the church?

- If Christians meet together in a home (Col 4v15), can it be regarded as a proper church? What are the essential characteristics of a proper Christian church?

Aegean Coast

Troy & Troas

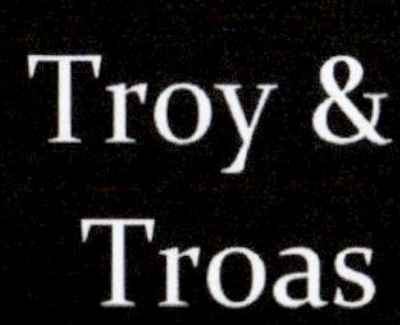

Troas Roman bath and gymnasium

Among the ruins of Alexandria Troas

Apollo on a Troas coin

Priene

Columns from the
Fourth century BC
Temple of Athena

Rectangular formation
used for the Odeum
and a grid system for
the streets

From ruins of the bishop's church

Miletus

Miletus Theatre expanded to seat 15,000

The Harbour Master's Head Quarters

One of the four harbour monuments has survived

Didyma

Madusa greets visitors to the
Temple of Apollo at Didyma

The skill of stone
masons is evident in
the temple precincts

Their work expressed
reverence towards a
variety of deities and
mythical creatures

Some columns lie where they
have been since they collapsed
in the 4th century

108 columns surrounded the vast Temple - bigger than a football
pitch, each one elaborately decorated at its base.

Two great pillars can be seen soaring into the sky but the icthus symbol, carved on the paving between them, tells of the witness and increase of Christian faith

Chapter 9

The Aegean Coast

Troy & Troas

The Trojan Tale

The region of Troas covered the area of the promontory that reaches into the Aegean Sea, south of the Dardanelles Straits, on the north-west coast of Turkey. The principal cities of Troas were Assus, Troy and Alexandria Troas. As St Paul made several visits to Troas, it is among the cities that figure in the New Testament. However, thanks to Homer and his sensational legend of the Greek invasion, Troy, a few miles from Troas, became one of the best known of all cities in Greek history.

The wooden horse now at the entrance to the Trojan site is, quite obviously, an attraction for tourists, some of whom face disappointment when they discover that the Trojan horse was probably never one with four legs. Historians tell us that 'horse' was a name given to the battering ram. One lady I met on site, a historian, was getting very cross indeed with people who were taking photographs of 'that wooden thing', as she thought it was 'totally misleading to visitors'. I'm sure she was right. Nevertheless, in this case, I far prefer Homer's famous story, in his great poem the Iliad, to history's use of common or garden battering rams. You will know about the Greek invaders hiding in a wooden horse, until the Trojan soldiers hauled it into the city, before facing a severe penalty for their military naivety.

Shattering our fantasy further, archaeologists have raised serious questions about the whole notion of the Trojan war being fought here. In the rubble around the ancient walls, very few weapons have been found – no arsenals or armouries, no communal graves, none of the evidence one would have expected to find, to verify the site of an ancient battle. A puzzle remains, because history tells us that the invasions of the Greeks continued for ten years, during which time the Trojan soldiers managed to fight them off, but how did it end?

The Archaeological Site

The site is small and there is not very much to see, although what remains is most significant. Excavations have revealed thirty levels of habitation, the earliest being a bronze-age settlement from about 3,000 BC. Nine levels at the site remain visible to visitors. At various levels, you can see the walls of houses, mosaics and temple foundations. The period of the Greek invasions is thought to be at six or seven levels deep. There is evidence on the site of a theatre and of city gates, even though a considerable amount of stone-work has been taken away and used for other buildings.

Heinrich Schliemann, while excavating Troy in 1873, stumbled across treasure that he identified as the treasure of King Priam. Trevor Bryce, researcher from the University of Queensland, in his book 'The Trojans and their Neighbours', described the treasure as vessels of gold, silver and bronze, thousands of gold rings, other jewellery and some weapons. Some of these treasures are now in the Museum of Archaeology in Istanbul and some at the Canakkale Museum. Other items of the gold and silver jewellery have found their way into the Pushkin Museum, in Moscow, and The Hermitage, in St. Petersburg. Later researchers believe that the treasures were not found in one hoard but gathered from across the site, and are not from the era of King Priam, who was King of Troy during the years of the Trojan wars.

Alexandria Troas

The Greek City of Troas was founded by Antigonus, a general of Alexander the Great, in about 310 BC. Originally, it was named 'Antigonia Troas', later to be renamed 'Alexandria Troas' and dedicated to Alexander the Great. A good man-made harbour was engineered in Roman times and a colony of Roman soldiers stationed there. The harbour developed into a busy sea port and the town became a successful commercial centre. Strabo, the Greek historian, regarded Troas as 'a renowned city'. At one time, Constantine considered making this town the capital of the Eastern Roman Empire. There's little to show now of this major port with its fine buildings. The ruins are overgrown with thistles and shrubbery but there are remnants of the city baths, a theatre, a stadium, necropolis, gymnasium, a temple and parts of the city wall.

St Paul in Troas

Anxiety in Troas – 2 Corinthians 2 v 12 - 13

When Paul was writing to the Corinthians, he described his brief stay in Troas. Luke recalls the greater significance of that visit in Acts16 (below). Paul was anxiously waiting for Titus, who was visiting Corinth. It seems that he was expecting him and was getting quite worried because Titus had taken a letter to the Corinthian Church, on his behalf. The letter was quite a stern response to difficulties there and Paul wanted to know the outcome. While he was waiting, he took the opportunity to preach and found that the Good News was well received. Following the obstacles he had faced in the previous few days, mentioned below, it felt as though a door had opened wide. He didn't stay long, however, as God was calling him to Macedonia.

Calling in Troas – Acts 16 v 6 – 10

v 6 – 7 Paul and Sylas travelled through Phrygia and Galatia but they were prevented from preaching. We are not sure why but they accepted it as within the will of God's Spirit. They had intended to go through Bithynia but, as that was not possible, they went on to Troas. What was standing in their way? They knew that it was God's will to take the gospel message to the people of those places. Were they hindered by Roman opposition or bad weather? Did something lead them to an inner conviction that caused them to change their plans?

Do you see a change in v 6 - 7? St Luke wrote the Acts of the Apostles. Previously, he had been describing what 'they' did, now in verses six and seven, he refers to 'we' and he continues in that way to the end of Acts. It seems that Luke had joined them. He was the doctor. Did he arrive because Paul was not well enough to preach or travel into Bithynia? We don't know the nature of his 'thorn in the flesh'. It is entirely speculation but physical weakness may have been the hindrance.

v 8 – 10 That night, in Troas, Paul had a dream or a vision of a Macedonian man urging him to, "Come over to Macedonia and help us." He regarded this as a call from God. It would be a most significant step for Paul to cross the sea to Philippi, as he would then be spreading the Gospel into Europe. To 'marry the east to the west' had been a goal of Alexander the Great. Now, as Paul was called to take the Gospel from east to west, he would be used by God to move towards such unity in the name of Christ.

Who was the man?

It is just possible that this Macedonian was St. Luke. Eusebius, 3rd Century historian, says that 'Luke was a long-standing companion of St. Paul'. That suggests that they met in their younger days. Perhaps Luke's training as a doctor was at the medical centre in Tarsus, Paul's home town, where they could have met and become friends. Little seems to be known about the medical school in Tarsus, perhaps because the university there gained widespread fame and status for philosophy, thus overshadowing other disciplines. A few prominent medics, however, left us clues to its reputation. Luke could have come to Troas from Macedonia and appealed to his friend, Paul.

There's also the thought that the man in St. Paul's dream could have been Alexander the Great. The city of Troas was dedicated to him. He had dreamed of uniting the east and the west and now St. Paul was contemplating crossing the Aegean to Philippi, a decision that, in time, had enormous impact on Christianity, which became largely a European faith.

We do not know if Paul was aware of a specific, identifiable need in Macedonia that may have prompted his dream or if it arose from his sense of urgency for God's mission. We can see in the rest of the chapter, however, that personal need in Macedonia was being met as events unfolded. On the first day, Lydia from Thyatira, who sold purple cloth, was among the people met by Paul. We came across her earlier, in Thyatira. She already worshipped God and yet her spiritual need continued. The Gospel message touched her life, at her point of need. The next day, God spoke to the heart and mind of a slave girl, and then to a jailer who was led into faith and joy. There were probably many more we know nothing about.

Every day, there are some people around us, in spiritual need, crippled by fear, worry or failure and guilt. There are those who are weighed down by work pressures, relationship troubles, money worries, addiction problems, depression and other debilitating circumstances. Many churches respond generously to appeals when there's a tragedy in the world. They collect for 'food banks' and support projects for disadvantaged children or for refugees, and rightly so. I am passionate about Christians making a positive, practical response to such need. But we would be both foolish and faithless, if we did not also respond to inner need, spiritual anguish and the desire for peace and hope. Practical help is needed but so is the healing, strengthening, life-changing love of God in Jesus Christ. That's a vital part of our mission.

Reflection

- Action for justice and response to practical need are essential expressions of the gospel but we have said that we would be 'foolish and faithless', if we were not to respond to inner need, spiritual anguish and the desire for peace and hope. How are you able to take part in that vital aspect of Christian mission, even in a small way?

- How does your church tackle this work, in balance with practical service and action for justice?

- How should we express this area of Christian evangelism in our contemporary context?

A Young man dropped off – Acts 20 v 7 - 12

20 v 7-9 St Luke describes a gathering in Troas, when St. Paul returned from Macedonia. In the evening, Paul was speaking in a crowded upstairs room. The atmosphere was warm from oil lamps. It was well into the night and the people were listening intently. A young man, Eutychus, who was sitting on a window ledge, struggled to keep awake, but couldn't. He not only fell asleep but he fell from the window, three storeys high, to the ground.

20 v 10 When Paul ran down, the crowd expected the young man to be dead. Luke recalls that Paul threw himself on Eutychus, hugging him. I wonder if the fall had knocked the breath out of him and Paul was reviving him. 'Be calm, he's still alive!" shouted Paul.

20 v 10-12 When the excitement was over, the crowd returned to the upstairs room and Paul broke bread. Was this a late supper to keep them going or was it a 'breaking of bread' - Holy Communion – Eucharist. Eucharist is the Greek word for 'thanksgiving'. Did they share in thanksgiving for the life, death and Resurrection of Jesus ... and thanksgiving that Eutychus was alive?

If I could imagine myself in Paul's position, I think that, at this point, I might have said, "Now it's so late, let's call it a day," (or perhaps 'let's call it a night!') but they picked up where they'd left off. Paul was still speaking at daybreak. He would be leaving that morning, to meet leaders from the Church in Ephesus at Miletus, and so they wanted to use every moment to talk about their faith and their mission.

Paul forgot his coat!

2 Timothy 4 v 13 After Paul's release from Rome, he called at Troas again, following an interval of six or seven years. However, he was re-arrested and had to leave Troas in a hurry, to be returned to Rome. In the rush, he must have left his cloak and some books. Carpus had been taking care of them but, in his letter to Timothy, Paul was hoping that Timothy would bring them with him to Rome.

Priene

There is no mention of Priene in the New Testament, although it is likely that Christianity had reached its people in New Testament times. By the fourth century, it was the seat of the Bishop. It's an old city, originally established on the coast, as a sea port. It was the custom to build a port on the coast and the port city a short distance inland, on higher ground. There is no sign of the early coastal town now, as the silt, relentlessly 'transported' by the River Menderes, has changed the shape of the coastline beyond recognition. The harbour has been filled in the same way as at Miletus, twenty miles or so further south, and the bay between them is no more. To make a brief visit to the archaeological site of the city, now about ten miles in from the sea, is well worth a walk up the hill.

The city was rebuilt on higher land in 350 BC, on what looks like a shelf at the foot of spectacular Mount Mycale. The mountain provides an impressive backdrop to the remaining columns of the Temple of Athena. The construction of the temple started in the fourth century BC. Its completion, in 334 BC, was financed by Alexander the Great, who lived in Priene for some time. Other shrines were dedicated to Zeus, Demeter and some Egyptian gods. The town was expertly designed on a grid system, with streets that intersected at right angles. Its architecture was predominantly Greek, although later given a face- lift by the Romans. The council chamber (Odeum), which could seat 640 people, was, unusually, built in a rectangular formation, with a wooden roof to provide good cover. The fine Greek theatre, built into the hill, thought to be about the best Hellenistic theatre in the world, would have seated about five thousand people. Five elaborate marble seats were installed at the front for dignitaries. Two unexpected features of the theatre are the base of a water clock, at the west side of the orchestra area, and an altar dedicated to Dionysus, on the other side.

There had been a stadium, which had had seats on one side only, as the other side was too near to the cliff edge. The gymnasium had been in a safer place. In the ruins of the bishop's church, near to the theatre, you can see the base of the altar and steps to the pulpit. The Bishop resided in Priene throughout the Byzantine period. I think that the Christian Gospel may have been brought to the town in the first century, as it seems likely that the port was still in use. We know, from Acts 20, that Paul sailed into Miletus harbour, which is a little further south, and that the two harbours silted up during the same period. Ports were, of course, places where travellers were coming and going, and some of them were followers of Christ. The Gospel message would come and go with them. Christian faith may, therefore, have been brought to Priene by boat.

Miletus

At first glance, the ruins of Miletus do not look very inviting but it had been an important commercial, intellectual, and political centre, as well as a major port. As you approach, the solid looking theatre, built into the hillside, dominates the landscape. A Byzantine fortress overlooks the theatre, from higher up the hill. Most of the remaining ruins of the town are on lower land behind the theatre, around what was once the area of four sheltered harbours. Despite the fact that the sea is now five or six miles away, that low land still gets soggy from time to time.

The earliest settlement here was between 1,600 and 1,200 BC. It became known as a city of philosophers, including Thales, who is thought to have founded Greek philosophy, geometry and astronomy. He resided here from 640 to 546 BC. The inventor of the sun dial, Anaximander, had links with Miletus, as did Hippodamus, who was behind the move to build towns on a grid system. Aspasia, champion of women's rights, was raised here in the 5th century BC. Consequently, Miletus had some outstanding fathers and mothers to brag about.

Miletus developed into a city at around 480 BC and, in 334 BC, was captured by Alexander the Great. Miletus was about the busiest port on the Aegean. Commercial traffic between productive centres further inland, travelled via the River Menderes and the port of Miletus. Merchant ships sailed to and from the port, to Italy, Greece and Egypt. The Menderes, that stretches for three hundred and sixty three miles, is the longest river in the Aegean region. It carried great quantities of silt that filled the harbour and 'removed' the city from the sea. (You may know that Menderes River introduced a new word to the English language - 'meander'. Its name means 'a winding course' that wanders to and fro.)

Inevitably, success led to growth in population, which reached more than 100,000. That prompted the authorities to increase the capacity of the theatre but it didn't expand beyond 15,000. On the fifth row, there is an engraved notice to say that the row was to be reserved for 'God fearing

Jews'. Other ruins include the city council chamber, market places, a stadium, a synagogue, the Roman Baths of Faustina, with walls fifteen meters high, the harbour master's HQ , a temple dedicated to Serapis and a fifth century AD basilica church. Near the harbour, was the Delphinium where Apollo was worshipped as a Dolphin, to protect sailors. Two stone lions still guard the harbours and part of one of the harbour monuments has survived ... could it possibly be the actual mooring from which St. Paul sailed away?

There were a few other temples or shrines but the main religious centre for Miletus was the great Temple of Apollo, some miles further south at Didyma.

Proper Poorly in Miletus

2 Timothy 4 v 20

Writing from prison in Rome about his return from the third mission journey, Paul mentioned that he had had to leave Trophimus at Miletus, as he was too unwell to travel. Trophimus had been with Paul and seven other friends, when travelling through Macedonia to Troas (Acts 20 v 4), and arrived before the all-night meeting. As Trophimus had been delayed, recovering in Miletus, it is not clear how he and Paul reached Jerusalem at the same time, as suggested in Acts 21 v 29. We know little about Trophimus but if he is the man praised by Paul, in 2 Corinthians 8 v 18, as some scholars think, he was highly regarded within the church.

Prayerful Parting

Acts 20 v 13 - 38

20 v 13 Paul walked across the headland from Troas to meet the ship at Assos. The journey would have been slower by sea. This would have given him time to visit a few Christian communities, on the way, as he did when the ship docked each night on the journey to Miletus, as mentioned in the next few verses. In the Troas region, as

elsewhere, the priority Paul gave to pastoral care for others becomes a challenge to us – to every Christian. He walked over twenty miles to spend time with people – strengthening relationships, encouraging their faith and, you can be sure, praying with them.

20 v 14 – 17 The ship took time to navigate the rocky west coast, especially round the tip of Cape Lectum. Paul boarded at Assos and they sailed through the narrow strait between Samos and Trogyllium towards Miletus, where they docked. Luke explained that they didn't stop at Ephesus, because Paul was anxious to reach Jerusalem by Pentecost. However, as he wanted to see the church leaders from Ephesus, he sent a message asking them to meet him at Miletus. The journey from Ephesus to Miletus would have taken a few days, as there are at least thirty to forty miles between them. Even so, the time of their arrival still enabled them to have several hours with Paul, before his ship sailed.

If you haven't read Luke's account of his conversation with the elders from Ephesus and their parting, may I encourage you to think it through with emotional and spiritual sensitivity. It is a detailed and moving account. (v 17 to 38)

20 v 18-20 You may wonder if Paul was boasting about his work in Ephesus. Didn't they know he had given all he could in preaching and caring? Rather than bragging, it seems more likely that he was seeking their confirmation and support, in the face of mounting opposition. He was anticipating trouble in Jerusalem, where something of a character assassination was undermining his message and building up opposition to him. That approach is being adopted too frequently in contemporary times, when opponents of public figures prefer to denigrate them, rather than engage in honest debate about their message. In order to defend the Gospel message, Paul was appealing to the knowledge of the Ephesian leaders, who had a wealth of first-hand experience of his ministry.

The mission they shared in Ephesus included some hard times, 'humility' and 'tears'. Paul was clearly a capable, intelligent, spiritually mature person. He was emotionally strong and frequently tender-hearted. The more you read of his life and of his writing in the New Testament, the more you can sense that he felt the pain of people and earnestly longed to share the healing grace of God.

20 v 22 By this verse, we know that Paul was ready to surrender himself. For him, his life or death was not the issue, the Gospel was. He was committed to following the One who had laid down his life, which meant, if necessary, Paul was ready to do the same. He urged them to follow his way of life (v33 – 35), modelled on the example of Christ – 'It is more blessed to give than receive'. We might add, 'Love one another as I have loved you.'

Paul encouraged the leaders in Ephesus to 'keep watch' for themselves, for each other and for the church. He warned them that 'wolves may come', though we don't know whether he was thinking of the Jews, the Romans, the Nicolaitans or even some of the local people (v 30). Paul reminded them to help the weak and to collect for the poor. He commended them to God's care, to God's Grace – to God's overflowing and strength-giving loving kindness.

20 v 36-38 Paul knelt with his companions from Ephesus, probably on the flagstone area by the harbourmaster's headquarters or by the harbour monument near to the ship, and they prayed. They were embracing and crying as they said goodbye. Their sorrow was deep, because they knew that they would not meet again. For three years, Paul had been their pastor, teacher, spiritual guide and church leader. They had shared danger and joy. For even longer, he had been guiding them in God's mission and now they must continue without him. The scene speaks volumes of love, grief, gratitude and of the bonds of God's Spirit. I imagine that, having said all that could be said, they walked with him to the ship in silence.

Praying with St Paul

To hear Paul praying for the Christians in Ephesus, read Ephesians 3 v 14 – 19 and perhaps join with him in praying that prayer for your church and for the people you care about. Also pray for church leaders and those who carry public office.

Reflection

- Is pastoral visiting a 'waste of time'? Why or why not?

- Visiting socially is good but what is different about a pastoral visit?

- How is this role shared in your church?

- Should every Christian have a pastoral role of some kind or should only those with appropriate gifts and training take it on?

- In Acts 20 v 18 - 20 was Paul boasting about his ministry or rightly defending his record and seeking support?

- What do you think of the modern approach by some, of undermining and seeking to discredit a spokesperson, rather than honestly debating what that person is sincerely advocating?

Didyma

T he Temple of Apollo at Didyma must have been a spectacular, overwhelming, revered, sacred place. It was the primary and ceremonial temple for Miletus, even though there were a few other temples in that town. Didyma was several miles from Miletus but the sacred way led ceremonial processions from the town to the temple. If you arrived there today, you'd be greeted by two magnificent, huge Medusa heads. They were added to the frieze above the columns, by the Romans, late in the life of the Temple, during the second century AD.

Perhaps I should have mentioned, well before now, that the Romans loved colour. The internal walls of the villas would have been tastefully adorned with attractive patterns and pictures, in vivid technicolour. The elaborate, decorative pediments, capitals and friezes of many temples would also have been artistically painted in a rich variety of colour.

The Structure

Didyma Temple was the third largest Hellenistic structure in the world - 360 ft. long and 167 ft. wide - bigger than a football pitch. The Temple of Artemis in Ephesus and the Temple on Samos were just a little bigger. Statues of lions and priests stood around the temple and 108 gigantic columns surrounded its courtyard. You would feel dwarfed beside them. It takes seven or eight people with outstretched arms to encircle one column. The base of the columns are superbly sculptured, like the decorative stone work of the walls. Some columns lie where they have been since the building collapsed, in the early fourth century AD. They had been built to a great height, which must have been quite a feat of engineering. Sand banks were built up to enable each stone section of a column to be put in place. More sand was added to build a higher ramp to the next level, for another heavy section to be added ... and so on, until the column reached its full stature. When the capitals and friezes had been mounted above the columns, the fluting was begun, by cutting the stone from the top downwards. The sand was removed, stage by stage, as the stonemasons descended.

The History

Historians have discovered reference to a sanctuary having been on this spot, beside a sacred spring, since 1900 BC. Some early buildings excavated here were probably facilities for people whose work was concerned with the temple. Didyma was not a city. It was a sanctuary for the people of Miletus, but open to all.

A bronze statue of Apollo was set up in the inner sanctuary of the temple in 500 BC. It was later confiscated by the Persians as spoils of battle in 494 BC and, although Alexander the Great managed to retrieve it, no one knows what happened to it. By 6 BC, this Apollo Temple was ranked high in religious importance in Anatolia. Herodotus tells us that King Necho of Egypt presented his armour to the temple, as a thank offering for his success in battle. The battle is thought to have been the battle of Megiddo, where Josiah lost his life. (2 Kings 23 v 29)

After some decline, the Greeks rebuilt the temple under orders from Alexander the Great. The Romans continued building but they were very slow. After six hundred years, it was still incomplete. Many lives were lost in the construction and conditions were poor for the labourers. In fact, they went on strike until the priests were willing to negotiate terms.

The fame of Didyma, a temple of prophecy, was maintained by hundreds who sought advice from the oracle. This oracle rivalled the oracle of Delphi. The spread of Christianity challenged the fame of Delphi and of

Didyma. Christian graffiti, carved into the top step between two great columns at Didyma temple entrance, remains as a small, yet clear, Christian witness. It is the circular ichthus symbol, declaring that 'Jesus Christ is Son of God and Saviour'. However, resistance to the early church was mounting. Advice was sought from the oracle by Diocletian (284–305 AD), on how to combat the increasing popularity of Christianity. Later, Christian chapels nearby were destroyed by order of Emperor Julian (361–363 AD). 385 AD was the year that Theodosius brought consultation with oracles to an end, by law, and the Temple fell into disuse. In the Byzantine period, Theodosius II financed the building of a church, in the courtyard of the temple, which served local Christians magnificently for years, until a 15th century earthquake brought the use of this site to an end.

Aegean meets the Mediterranean
Natural harbour at Fethye and an imposing 4th century BC Lycian tomb overlooking the town
Refreshing hot mud baths on the River Dalyan
Lycian tombs high above Caunus, on River Dalyan, since 400 BC

Patara

where St Paul, &
others sailing from
the Aegean to the
Mediterranean, sort
a larger vessel

Lycian tomb by the triple
arched entrance to Patara

Lycian pillar tombs at
Xanthus
A few miles in from
the coast

Myra

..... it's backcloth honeycombed with tombs

St Nicholas

The Church of St Nicholas

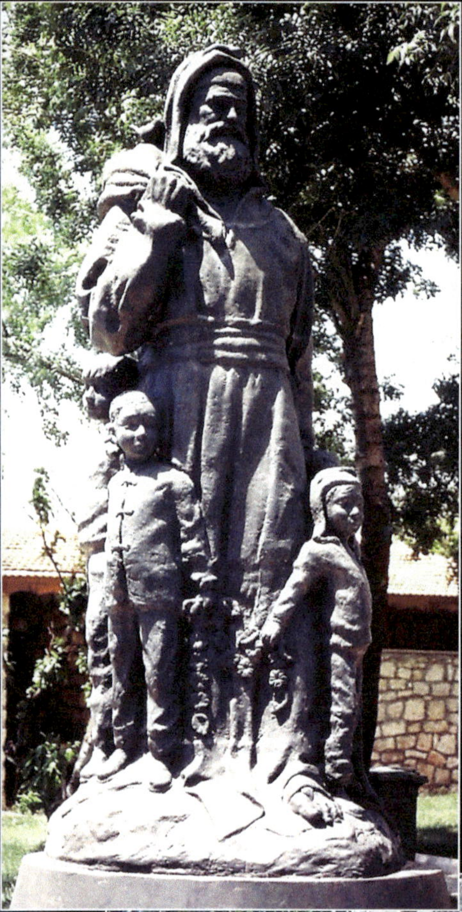

UNESCO statue of Santa with children from around the world

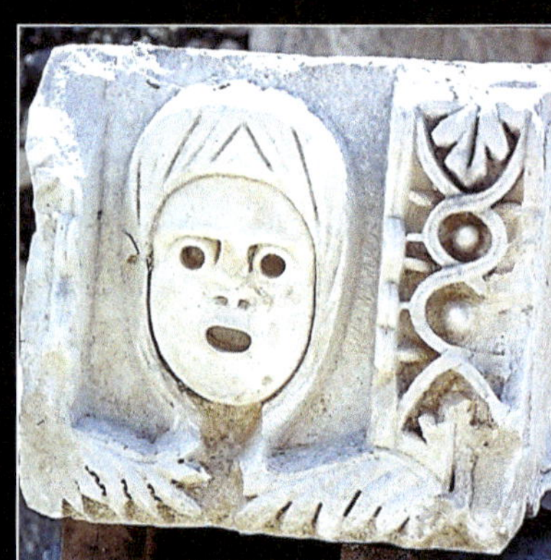

One of the stone masks at the theatre entrance

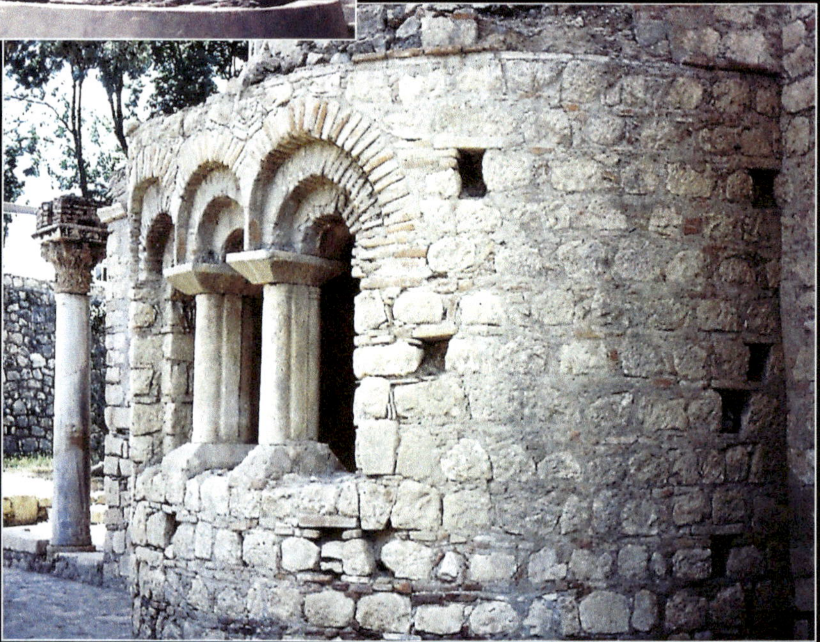

The church was built in 3rd century AD and restored by

Attalia

Hadrian's gate in honour of his visit in 130 AD

The Yivli minaret is Antalya's Symbol. The mosque was originally a Byzantine church until 1230

Perge

A canal system ran through the main street to cool the city

Remains of two towers at the entrance, built in the 4th century AD. Innner gate was built by Greeks in 3rd century BC

Chapter 10

The Aegean meets the Mediterranean

The Coast

When sailing southerly from Kusadasi and around the south-west corner of Turkey, where the Aegean meets the Mediterranean Sea, the coastal scenery looks magnificent. The shores are rugged and rocky, with miles of clean sand and beautiful bays. It's where you find calm clear waters of the richest blue or deepest green. It is not surprising that this area has become so popular with holiday makers. St Paul would have seen this coast looking as stunning as we see it, although without the hotels and sunshades. The Lycian tombs (400 BC), carved like Greek temples high on the rock face, where the River Dalyan flows into the Aegean Sea, were there centuries before Paul sailed this route. They were built as resting places for the gentry of the ancient city of Caunus, which was on the level ground far below the rock face.

The people of Caunus had an enviable view as they looked out to extensive, tranquil waterways, where the river widened before meeting the sea. The natural breeding ground of loggerhead turtles is nearby. It has been so for thousands of years. At times, you can see them resting on the beaches. It's just possible that St Paul spotted them too. In 1987, at the age of 77, Dr. David Bellamy, popular botanist, TV personality, author and campaigner gave high profile to a project to save the turtles from the tourists. The end of the long beach is now protected at breeding time, to preserve the eggs laid there by the turtles. Dr. Bellamy reminded the world that the sea turtle has been around for ninety five million years. He said that having been brought up in a strong Baptist home, he knew that he had a responsibility to speak out about them and take action.

In antiquity, the River Dalyan was known as the River Indus. It is more than one hundred miles long. You can take a hot mud bath half a mile or so inland along the river, where the liquid mud is maintained at a temperature of about 40 degrees C. This has been enjoyed for many centuries, particularly because the mud is renowned for its medical benefits – for soothing rheumatics and helping with some gynaecological conditions. Rumour has it that to bathe in the mud will make you look ten years younger but it didn't work for me. Nevertheless, it's a great experience. We have no idea, of course, if St Paul had a dip.

The sheltered bays and natural harbours, where luxury sailing boats and launches moor today, were the places where travellers sailing around the coast would stop to change vessels. A sizeable ship was needed to cross the Mediterranean, whereas a smaller boat was generally safe for the Aegean coast. We know that it was necessary for Paul and his team to stop at a few of these harbours, as the New Testament records.

Telmessus

As far as we know, this ancient city was not a place where St. Paul took a break. It was destroyed by earthquakes in 1856 and again in 1957. The modern town of Fethye was built over the ruins, around some of the loveliest bays on the coast. Archaeologists have turned up evidence indicating that Lycians lived here from as early as 1400 BC. The understanding of Herodotus was that they originally came from Crete. Their imposing tombs, fourth century BC, with Ionic columns and triangular pediments, overlook the town. A little below are the ruins of a castle built by the Knights of St. John, from Rhodes. The Crusaders had a significant role in the town from the 12th to 14th century. There had been an influential Christian community in Fethye from the early days of the church. This congregation was even represented at the fourth Ecumenical Council at Chalcedon in 451 AD.

Patara

When Paul was travelling, the seaport of Patara was a good all-weather port, at the mouth of the River Xanthus, on the south west corner of Turkey. It was one of the harbours where he transferred to a larger vessel to cope with the Mediterranean Sea. Plagues of malarial mosquitoes, severe earthquakes, in AD 142 and again in AD 240, and the silting up of the harbour brought this major port to the end of its active life.

The ruins are visible but, I found, not easily accessible, as the grass and shrubs are quite overgrown. Until the fifteenth century, pilgrims travelling to Jerusalem would include Patara in their itinerary but there are few visitors now. There is a triumphal triple-arched gate from AD100 at the entrance to the harbour and a fourth century BC Lycian sarcophagus tomb beside it. The remains of Hadrian's grain store tell us that it was once a large, imposing building. I found ruins of small temples and a theatre, among the undergrowth, Roman baths and a 6th century church. History speaks of a significant temple of Apollo, with its own oracle, but its whereabouts have not been discovered. Strabo regarded a son of Apollo and a daughter of Xanthus as founders of this harbour town.

Homer mentions that a hero of the Trojan wars lived in Patara. Could that be a reference to Alexander the Great, as he lived here for a while? Brutus, who led campaigns against the Lycians in 42 BC, also lived here at some time, as well as Ptolemy II. The best known son of Patara was probably St. Nicholas, who was born here in 300 AD. He became the Bishop of Myra and the legendary Santa Claus. We'll think more about him when we reach Myra.

St Paul and Patara
Acts 21 v 1 – 15

21 v 1 On the homeward stretch of Paul's third missionary journey, after leaving Miletus, he was anxious to reach Jerusalem by Pentecost. They stopped overnight at Cos, then at Rhodes and the third night at Patara. We don't know how long they waited but they found a ship bound for Phoenicia for the next part of the journey.

Whilst exploring the site at Patara, I made my way under the hanging branches of trees and found some ruins of the dockside. There were three small docking bays. One was quite complete and filled with muddy water. It was about the right size for a small boat, perhaps of about thirty foot. I thought it was just possible that this was the very place where coastal boats may have been moored, when travellers like Paul and Luke needed to change to a larger vessel, to sail across the Mediterranean. My imagination may have been working overtime but it made sense.

21 v 2-7 After passing Cyprus, the ship landed at Tyre, in Syria, to unload. Paul and his companions made contact with a group of local Christians who hosted them for a week. The locals did their best to encourage Paul not to go to Jerusalem. They believed that would be against the will of the Holy Spirit but, as Paul was determined, the families gathered on the beach to pray with him before he and Luke set sail again.

21 v 7-9 Another group of Christians greeted Paul and Luke at Ptolemais and they stayed with them for a day. The next stop was Caesarea, where they were welcomed into the home of Philip the evangelist. It seems to have been true, from the earliest days, that wherever there were Christians there were friends. Hospitality was understood as a ministry and to receive it was a blessing and gift from God.

21 v 10-12 Luke has told us, in v 9, that Philip had four unmarried daughters with a gift of prophecy and then, in v 10, that Agabus

arrived from Judaea and enacted a prophetic message from the Holy Spirit. He took Paul's belt and bound his own hands and feet to warn Paul of his likely arrest and shackling, in Jerusalem. They begged him not to go.

21 v 13-15 You can hear Paul's anguish as you read his reply. Their pleas were a hindrance to him, at a time when he needed their love and support. Following his Master, Paul was prepared to face whatever may confront him, even death. Reluctantly, they gave up trying to persuade him and they prayed, "The Lord's will be done." After a few days' break, Paul and Luke set sail for Jerusalem.

Xanthus

The port of Patara, one of the largest and best on the Mediterranean, served the ancient city of Xanthus. Like other port cities, Xanthus had been five or so miles in from the coast and high above the river, near to the modern settlement of Kinik. Xanthus had been the capital of the province of Lycia. Herodotus tells of a fierce attack on the city by the Persians, in about 540 BC. It reached a point where the Lycians were aware that they didn't stand a chance. Anticipating defeat and fearing the treatment that could be suffered by their wives and children, Lycian soldiers gathered their families, together with their slaves and possessions, and locked them in the inner fortress, before going out to fight to their death. As they left the city, they set fire to the fortress and no one survived. The city faced another brutal attack in 42 BC, by the Romans led by Brutus.

Many of the monuments from Xanthus were taken to the British museum, in 1840. Others are in the archaeological museum in Istanbul. Excellent plaster replicas are in place on site, making it possible to see some of the ruins, as they would have been. You can see walls from houses and shops, a Roman arch, a significant Roman theatre and hippodrome and a Lycian acropolis. Among the remains of a Byzantine monastery, there's a pillar, erected in the

5th century BC, that's covered with Lycian inscriptions, most of them still un-deciphered. The pillar tombs, which have a rectangular stone sarcophagus on top of a rectangular pillar, are the oldest style of Lycian tombs and seen only in Xanthus.

When St. Paul and St. Luke stopped at Patara, to find a ship to help them on their journey to Jerusalem, we don't know whether they remained at the port, Patara, or went into the port city of Xanthus to talk with others about Christ. It would be unlike Paul to have missed such an opportunity. It seems that there could have been a Christian community here from the first century. By the 4th century, the church had established a monastery and during the Byzantine period Xanthos became the seat of the Bishop.

The City of Myra and St. Nicholas

The city of Myra is mentioned only once in the New Testament (Acts 27 v 5 – 6). Paul was a prisoner being escorted to Rome by Centurion Julius, in AD 60 – 61. Luke and Aristarchus went with him as companions. Their ship docked at the port of Myra which, in Paul's day was on the sea. Here the centurion found a ship from Alexandria, moored at Myra's sea port, on its way to Italy. They were able to join this ship to continue the journey.

The ruins of ancient Myra are now on the River Myros, as the sea has receded from the port. Remains of the replacement port, Andriake, can be seen nearer to the sea. The ruins include a watch tower and another of Hadrian's grain stores, as well as some bits of port buildings. During the holiday season, small boats will take you to see the submerged Lycian or Byzantine city of Kekova. Alternatively, you could enjoy the lovely beach or have a beautiful walk beside the river, into the old town. Myra was built against a striking rocky backcloth, honeycombed by a network of tombs cut into the rock, stretching high on the cliff face. As you approach, they look rather like elaborate, baroque, multi-storey dwellings. Below the tombs, are the well preserved remains of a fine Roman theatre. In the forecourt of the theatre, impressive stone masks have made me smile. The figure of Tyche, goddess of fortune, is near to the steps that would have led to the upper seats. Much of the ancient city, as yet unexcavated, is buried beneath the modern town of Demre/Kale.

St. Nicholas

Although we shall return to St. Paul's visit to Myra, most visitors go for St. Nicholas, rather than St. Paul. Nicholas was born in Patara, in AD 300. Later, he became the third Bishop of Myra. Records of the first Great Ecumenical Council, in AD 325, hosted by Constantine in Nicea, indicate that Bishop Nicholas was an active participant. He was devoted to the poor, persecuted under Diocletian and imprisoned for his faith.

Legend tells us that Nicholas found a way to deliver three small bags of gold, in secret, to provide dowries for three desperately poor sisters, saving them from prostitution. This is said to have given rise to the giving of gifts on the eve of 6th December. It has also been linked to the use of three gold balls as the pawnbroker's symbol. Another legend, about three boys, who were believed to have been murdered and buried in a barrel of salt, tells how St. Nicholas restored them to life.

Nicholas was buried in a tomb just outside the ancient city. Some suggest that the tomb was in his own church. Others believe that a chapel was built over the tomb, a little later. The foundations of that chapel are part of the Church of St. Nicholas today and the broken sarcophagus remains there. By the sixth century, a larger church replaced the original building, on the same site. It was damaged during Arab invasions in AD 809 but fully restored in the 19th and 20th centuries. Italian sailors and three priests broke into the sarcophagus in 1087 and carried away most of the saint's bones to the Church of San Nicola, Bari, in Italy. It seems likely to me, that it was Italian influence that adapted his name to 'Santa Claus'. We have grown accustomed to recognising that 'Santa Maria' is St. Mary. It is not difficult to see how

Santa Nicholas could have been abbreviated to 'Santa Nich'las' and then 'Santa Chlas' or 'Santa Claus'. How he became known as Father Christmas in England, Pere Noel in France and Grandfather Frost in Russia, I have no idea.

On 6th December each year a service of worship is held at the Church of St. Nicholas, in his honour and, on that day, the Turkish Government sponsors a St. Nicholas symposium.

Early in the 11th century, there was a custom in England of appointing a boy bishop each year, on St. Nicholas Day, 6th December. He was paraded around to bless people and officiated at some ceremonies. The practice was abolished during the reign of Elizabeth 1st, in the 16th century. St. Nicholas became the patron saint of Greece and Russia. He has been regarded as a protector of scholars, sailors, merchants and children. He has been loved all over the world, particularly because of his care for the poor and for people in need.

In the millennium year 2,000, a Russian sculptor, Gregory Pototsky, created a bronze statue of St. Nicholas. It was mounted on a pedestal in the town square and later, in 2005, moved to the church, because the town Mayor had decided to replace it with a plastic Santa. Also in the millennium year, another statue of Santa was set up beside the church by UNESCO. It depicts children of the world gathered around him, representing Santa Claus in the image with which we are more accustomed - but less like the real St. Nick.

Passion for the Poor

Christmas is a great time. I love it but I am saddened by the way in which the distinctive witness of St. Nicholas has been virtually lost, in our western representation of Santa Claus. I am thinking of his passion for the poor. At Christmas, many people make generous contributions to charities that provide invaluable service to vulnerable people. The tradition of giving gifts is thriving. Nevertheless, we are well aware that most of our giving is to our close family and friends. Massive amounts of money are spent on food and drink, new clothes, new furniture and new cars. Amazing displays of Christmas lights decorate houses and gardens, public buildings and town centres. This vast expense is mainly for our own amusement and our jolly Santa Claus has been put at the helm, egging us on.

What's happened to Santa's passion for the poor and those in need? St. Paul frequently emphasised this dimension of Christian discipleship. The life and teaching of Jesus leads us into a ministry of seeking to restore human dignity, self-respect and worth, to those who are marginalised and undervalued. It stands out a mile in His attitude and actions towards Samaritans, lepers, women, children, sinners, outcasts and the poor. His Spirit shaped the life and example of St. Nicholas. Why then, have we almost allowed this to slip out of the character of Bishop Nicholas and become content with a message like "Ho! Ho! Ho!"?

The Adventures of St. Luke

Extracts from his travel journal – Acts 27 v 1 - 44

This would have been an appropriate title for Acts chapter 27. It moves at a pace, is littered with detail and is full of apprehension and excitement. Perhaps it would be helpful, however, to recall the events recorded by Luke, preceding this chapter. You'll remember that Paul had been anxious to reach Jerusalem but, on his arrival, the warm welcome was quickly overtaken by trouble. He was arrested in the Temple and accused of turning people against Israel and the Law of Moses. A confusion of chaotic events followed, described by St. Luke in Acts chapters 21 to 26. In my next chapter, in the section entitled 'In his own words', we'll follow St. Paul telling the full story, in which we'll be reminded of the plotting and intrigue that brought him before King Agrippa. His defence was a simple but powerful testimony of his life.

Festus interrupted, declaring that Paul must be mad, although Agrippa could find no legal fault. Nevertheless, as Paul had appealed to Caesar, he had to be sent on to Rome. Guarded by a kind centurion, Julius, Paul sailed to Myra, where they looked for a ship bound for Italy.

27 v 1-4 We meet Julius, the Roman officer whose charge was to take Paul and other prisoners safely to Rome. By v 3, we begin to see what kind of man he was, when he allowed Paul the freedom to visit friends and, in v 43, when he saved Paul and the other prisoners from being killed by the soldiers. Verse 2 raises a question for us: "Did Aristarchus register as Paul's servant?" Otherwise, he would not have been allowed to travel with him. If so, what loyalty!

27 v 5-6 The ship bound for Italy was probably carrying grain and had stopped to load up at Myra. That explains the huge grain stores at several Mediterranean ports like Myra and Patara.

27 v 9-12 Paul gave advice, as he had a great deal of travelling experience but, of course, the officer preferred to be guided by the ship's captain … and they sailed into trouble. Luke's reference to the Day of Fasting (Day of Atonement) tells us that they were well into October, as Atonement was celebrated in the middle of that month. St. Paul was warning of danger, because it was inadvisable to sail the Mediterranean beyond September.

27 v 13-20 The breeze from the south was overtaken by strong wind from the north east. Having struggled to keep control, they finally had to give up. The ship was being driven off course by the storm. Navigation was impossible without sun or stars and they feared for their lives. Grain ships were large, heavy vessels, driven by one huge sail, which transferred the full force of the gale to the mast, putting great strain on the ship's timbers. Making every effort they could to prevent the ship from breaking up, they passed ropes under the ship (a dangerous operation) and secured them to the deck to hold the wooden structure together.

27 v21-31 Everyone panicked as danger was increasing. The severity of the storm made them all afraid, although Paul spoke of his trust in God. He warned of peril but, imploring them to have faith in God, he assured the ship's company that all would be safe.

27 v33-44 Paul urged them to eat and build up their strength, ready to face the ordeal. Through the storm, they were able to see that they were approaching land but their worst fears were realised as the ship ran aground and began to break in pieces. Fearing that they would face penalties if they lost the prisoners, the soldiers prepared to kill them, until the centurion stepped in to prevent it. He was anxious to save Paul. The ship continued to be battered until it was wrecked. Some swam to the shore, while others clung to planks of wood. Eventually, they all reached the beach of a more sheltered bay. Later, the bay became known as St. Paul's Bay which, today, is a popular holiday spot.

The delay in Malta extended through the winter, until the seas were safe again and a ship from Alexandria was available for the next stage of the journey. That gave Paul, and probably Luke and Aristarchus, opportunity to share their Christian faith, to preach the gospel and to care for people around the island. A Christian community took root.

Reflection

- In v 23 to v 26 (which are about being saved from the sea) do you think that Paul or Luke is looking back in a spirit of gratitude for coming through danger or that God stepped in to save them?

- God's will is always for the safety of all people but if he chose, at this point, to intervene to save Paul, why did God not also save the Titanic or innocent people suffering from drought and famine?

- Should Christians do more to reclaim St. Nicholas, from the distortions that represent him as a great champion of consumerism and patron saint of parties?

- Would it be better if Christians resisted being swept along, by the modern trend of heavy spending at Christmas? Especially considering the amount we spend on our families and friends, decorations, food and drink etc., Should we, instead, seek to reinstate generosity towards poorer people across the world, especially at this time of the year? Where would we begin?

Attalia

E ast of Myra, on the Mediterranean coast, at the most inland point of the Gulf of Antalya, was the ancient city of Attalia. There's only one reference to it in the New Testament. (Acts 14 v 25). St Paul, together with Barnabas and Mark, sailed from Attalia harbour to Antioch, on their return from the first missionary journey in AD 48. Little of the ancient town is visible today, as it has grown into the attractive, popular and busy tourist resort of Antalya, on the 'Turkish Riviera'. It's in a beautiful setting, skirted on the west side by the Taurus Mountains that glide down to the sparkling Mediterranean. The lower hills, cloaked in green shrubs and backed by a great pine forest, circle around the northern suburbs. The eastern mountain range, beyond, reaches down towards the coast. In the spring, you can ski on the snowy slopes of the mountains and wallow in the warm sea, on the same day.

Hadrian's Gate

Attalia was founded by Attalus II, King of Pergamum from 159 BC. It came under Roman rule in 133 BC and prospered throughout the Roman, Byzantine and Seljuk eras. The wall, that Hadrian had built around the city, was reinforced in the 9th and 10th centuries for protection against Arab invasions. Beside the street, Cadessi Ataturk, there's a fine triple arched gateway, with elegant Corinthian columns, built to honour Emperor Hadrian, when he visited the city in AD 130. Originally, it was a two-storey construction. The town became a base for the Crusaders, during the second crusade, and came under Ottoman rule in 1390.

The Old Harbour

The rock base, on which the coastal fringe of the city is built, falls away to the sea almost vertically, providing perfect conditions for a natural harbour. The modern harbour and marina, bustling with luxury yachts and cruisers, extends beyond the original port. The old harbour walls were built by the Greeks and enlarged later by the Romans. Those walls are still in place and pretty well as they were when Paul, Barnabas and Mark disembarked.

Acts 13 v 13 -14 gives us good reason to think that Paul landed at least twice in Attalia harbour. He and his companions had sailed across the Mediterranean from Paphos in Cyprus. They were heading for Perga, which is just a few miles inland, east of Attalia. It seems inevitable that their ship came into the old harbour, even though Attalia is not mentioned here.

Kalecei

The ancient Roman town, Attalia, was built around and overlooking the Roman harbour. The old town survived for centuries, changing a little in each era and especially under Ottoman rule. Parts of the huge ancient walls are visible today, between many of the fascinating Ottoman houses, overhanging the narrow streets. It's now a busy, trendy, colourful, popular, lively and delightful place to stay. There's always a warm welcome in the comfortable boutique hotels and inns. This part of Antalya is frequently referred to as 'the old town', although officially it is Kalecei. The expansive modern city of Antalya did not begin to develop until the mid-1930's.

Archaeological Museum

The museum building was previously a 13th century mosque. Prior to that it had been a Byzantine church, built in the 7th century AD. The superb museum collection includes a 6th century pulpit, bearing a carving of Angel Gabriel. The later addition of the word 'Allah' indicates that this pulpit had also been used in the mosque. We have no record of Paul preaching in Attalia but there are a number of indicators of the church's presence here, from an early time.

Yivli Minare

The tall, photogenic, fluted minaret, near to the clock tower, stands out as Antalya's landmark. It has become the symbol of the city. The building had been a Byzantine church, before the Seljuk conquest in 1207. It was redesigned as a Seljuk mosque and medrese in 1230, under Sultan Alaeddin Keybubad. (A medrese was originally a theological school. Later, the word referred to a place of education.) The building was virtually replaced by the present mosque in 1373. Turquoise tiles once decorated the red bricks, though there's little sign of them now.

Kesik Minare

The burned out mosque, beside the old harbour, may at first seem like an inconsequential old ruin but I found it to be the most fascinating ancient building in Antalya. It was built in the 2nd century as a Roman temple. In the 5th century, it became a Byzantine church. It was damaged beyond use in the 7th century but restored and used again for Christian worship in the 9th century. Following invasions by the Seljuk Turks, in 1207, it was re-claimed as a mosque. When King Peter of Cyprus captured the city in 1361, he restored the building as a church and re-established Christian worship. However, it reverted to being a mosque under Ottoman rule. In 1851, the tower was badly damaged by fire and, since1896, it has remained a burned out ruin. What a wonderful history! It's a pity that the building didn't have a brief spell as a synagogue.

Perge

The ancient city of Perge arouses interest because it is the place where St. Paul and John Mark parted company, in AD 47 (Acts 13 v 13), and we don't really know why.

The city was four or five miles inland from Attalia and about the same distance to the east. An inscription in the ruins indicates that the city was founded by Greek soldiers, who had fought in the Tojan Wars, before settling here. Some scholars, however, maintain that there was a settlement here from an earlier time. The name 'Perge' was not Greek. In 333 BC, Alexander the Great's army came through Perge without a fight, presumably because it was largely a Greek community. The streets had been more than twenty one meters wide and lined with Ionic colonnades and rows of shops. The agora has some of its surrounding columns standing to this day. To keep the people cool in the hot summers, a canal system ran through the centre of the town. The structure is still there to be seen. The water flowed from a fountain built on the acropolis hill, falling through a series of cascading pools to a large decorative fountain, to feed the canals.

The Greek theatre was modified by the Romans, to seat 14,000. Its stage had been decorated with reliefs of Dionysus. Antalya Archaeological Museum displays a freeze from the theatre, depicting Neptune with a number sea creatures. The huge stadium, which seated 12,000, remains in quite good condition and, in the city baths, a fine example of hypocaust heating has survived. There had been a temple dedicated to Artemis but it's not been found. Records describe it as 'a marvel in size, beauty and workmanship'. South-east of the city, ruins of a Byzantine church remain on a hill. This could also have been the location of the temple.

You cannot miss the remains of two great towers at the entrance to the city. They formed the outer gate, built in the 4th century AD, as part of the outer wall. The inner gate and the defensive walls were built by the Greeks, in the 3rd century BC. This was the entrance through which St. Paul and his companions would have come into Perge. The later, outer gate led into an elliptical courtyard with a fountain. Later still, a Byzantine church was built onto the inside of the courtyard wall.

Apollonius, who became a great astronomer and mathematician, was born in Perge in 262 BC. His astronomical theories were far ahead of their time, together with his understanding of the movements of 'heavenly bodies'. He was the first mathematician to identify parabolas, ellipses and hyperbolas. Another famous inhabitant was Placia Magna. Inscriptions refer to her as the city's benefactress in the 2nd Century AD. As 'Magistrate', she held the highest office in the city, which was quite exceptional for a woman. Antalya museum is now home to her statue. Perge, a wealthy city, declined during the Byzantine period and, by the 7th Century, had been abandoned.

Mission Notes

The Parting of the Ways

Acts 13 v 13 – 14 These verses grab our attention because John Mark, who had been a loyal participant in the mission, departed at Perge, and we are left wondering why. It is also significant, that this is the first time that Paul's name comes first in Luke's record. Previously, as in 13 v 2, Saul (Paul) is listed last. The references have always been to 'Barnabas and Saul' but now Paul is emerging as the leader in the church's mission. It also happens to be the first time that he is referred to as 'Paul', the Roman version of his name, rather than 'Saul', his Jewish name. Was it decided to use the Roman name, as a more international rendering, to help identify Christian mission as universal, rather than 'belonging to the Jews'? There's no hint of rivalry from Barnabas. He humbly accepted that he was not 'number one' in God's mission.

What about John Mark? Was he a deserter?

Since Mark was a boy, his mother's house in Jerusalem had been a meeting place for Jesus and the disciples. By this time, in Acts 13, it had become a meeting place for the church. All his life, John Mark had been close to the life and work of Jesus. It seems quite natural that he would share in the outreach of the church, with Paul and Barnabas. Acts 13 v 5 tells us that 'They also had John to assist them', but by 13 v 13, John Mark had gone home.

Something had caused Paul's disapproval but, thankfully, no quarrels or criticisms of Mark have been aired by the apostles. Nevertheless, when Barnabas wanted Mark to join them again (Acts 15 v 38), Paul refused to take him. There was a sharp argument between Barnabas and Paul and they parted company. Silas went with Paul, in Mark's place, and they headed for Syria and Cilicia. Barnabas obviously had a different view of things, as he took Mark with him to strengthen the church in Cyprus.

Whatever had happened, Barnabas seems to have been more aware of this young man's potential and conviction.

That was the end of the active partnership that Paul and Barnabas had shared in God's mission, as they did not join up again. Both new partnerships were fruitful and greatly used by God, in extending Christian mission and in building and strengthening the church. We should note, however, that Paul came to appreciate and acknowledge Mark's qualities and commitment, and made that clear in his letters - see Colossians 4 v 10, Philemon v 23 and 2 Timothy 4 v 11.

Does this underline for us the fact that, in some things, Christians differ strongly in their judgements? In consequence, they may find that they cannot work side by side and yet they can continue to lead in God's mission, in different places and perhaps with different emphasis. Hopefully, they may then, in the end, reach a point of accepting and respecting each other's contribution and genuinely rejoice in the way God has used the other. The further step could then be the repairing and renewing of fellowship.

Reflection

- Paul and Barnabas parted company and, later, Paul again refused to team up with John Mark and yet they both continued faithfully in their calling. Is such conflict simply a fact of human nature to be accepted? On the other hand, as Christians often assert that the convictions we share are far more than those that divide us, should Christians learn to live with differences but stick together?

- In our contemporary context, how eager do you think Christians are to work and worship together with Christians from different cultures, traditions and different theological and social convictions?

- Given the hostility and division that's leading to violence and suffering, in our own nation and across the world, how right would it be for Christians to work and worship with people of different faiths, because of shared commitment to spiritual life, justice, service in society and peace in the world?

Aspendos

There is no reference to Aspendos in the New Testament but I did not want to bypass it without drawing attention to what is considered to be the best preserved Roman Theatre in the world. The city was on the eastern border of the ancient Kingdom of Pergamum, a few miles east of Perge. The belief that the city had been on this hilltop since the 13th century BC, and that Mopsus was its founder, has been passed down through the years. Aspendos was a thriving trading centre in New Testament times, because the River Eurymedon was still deep enough for large ships to reach the port.

Excavation has not yet been extensive, although the visible remains include a council chamber, a fountain, public baths, a stadium, a market hall and, next to the agora, the law courts. Before the end of the 2nd century, the courts had been converted into a church. The two remarkable remains are, however, the theatre and an aqueduct.

The Theatre

This is a magnificent building and virtually complete. It was built to seat about 15,000 people, although some estimate 20,000. Nowadays, several thousand more are squeezed in for the most popular contemporary performances. It is used for opera, ballet, orchestral concerts and top rock bands. I was there, once, for a Turkish opera but it really wasn't 'my cup of tea'. Nevertheless, the experience of being in a crowded Roman theatre for a live performance was well worth-while.

The 'scena' (the elaborately decorated wall at the rear of the stage) is complete, except for the statues and busts which had occupied the niches. It is three storeys high. Some of the columns and decorative stonework have survived. Part of the frieze is still in place and, centre stage, the pediment that had supported a relief of Dionysus, god of theatre. There had been a roof that sheltered performers from the hot sun, though it had been added to improve acoustics, rather than to cool those on stage. The architect for this project was Xenon, a local man, who watched over its construction, in 162 AD. An inscription tells us that the funding was a gift from two brothers, Curtius Crispinus and Curtius Auspicartus, but I have no idea who they were.

The Aqueduct

I am exceedingly impressed by the genius of engineering used in the construction of this aqueduct. It reminds me that life was moving on in Anatolia, during New Testament times. There was a good pace of progressive development that we could too easily overlook. The aqueduct was designed by Tiberius Claudius Italicus and built in AD 100. For water to travel from mountains, in the north, into the city, it was necessary, at some points, to ensure that it would flow uphill. Consequently, from a distance the aqueduct looks rather like a roller coaster, as its curves sweep up high and down again. The aqueduct includes half a mile of a gravity and siphon system, so that the momentum of water on the down-curve would carry it higher on the up-curve, into a siphoning pipe that would take it over the hump and then down again. The remains are on the road out of town, about half a mile from the theatre.

Tarsus

'St Paul's Well' This is believed to be Saul's family home

Small portions of Roman streets, once lined by columns, have been unearthed near to the city centre

Cleopatra's Gate, part of the Roman City wall
and was a major entrance to the city

One glimpse of contemporary Tarsus city centre

Antioch

St Peter's Church and mission centre. The front wall was added by the Crusaders to protect the cave.

The altar and worship area inside the cave

An active orthodox church in Hatay

Antakya/Hatay town centre today

Mosaics from
Roman villas in
the city museum

Chapter 11

Tarsus and Antioch

No Mean City – Tarsus

Acts 21 v 39

I arrived in the town centre for the first time and, stepping from the car, I spread my map on the bonnet. I suppose I was looking rather obviously like a visitor, when a Turkish young man approached to offer help. He was courteous and friendly. I wondered if, perhaps, he was hoping to earn a little money. That would have been fine with me, as he was offering to take me to places I wanted to see in the town. However, he wouldn't take a penny. I even had to persuade him to join me for a Turkish apple tea, to say thank you to him for accompanying me to all the sites connected with St. Paul. Paul tells us himself that this was his home town. "I am a Jew," he said, "… from Tarsus in Cilicia, a citizen of no mean city." (Acts 21 v39 RSV)

After a long history, believed by some to be over 6,000 years, Tarsus is still not an insignificant city. I wonder if Strabo, first century Greek historian, was exaggerating a little when he said, 'In all that relates to philosophy and general education, this city was even more illustrious than Athens or Alexandria.' It is true that the University of Tarsus had a 'worldwide' reputation as a hub of Stoic Philosophy and that a number of eminent physicians have sung the praises of Tarsus, as a renowned medical centre. Today, Tarsus has a modern, bright city centre, flourishing business life and a population of over three million. It is situated about 600 miles east of the Aegean coast and a few miles north from the Mediterranean. Not much of the city that was known to St. Paul is available for us to see, as it is buried beneath the modern town. Nevertheless, there's still a buzz in getting a feel of the place, where Saul spent his youth.

Tarsus Medical Centre

There's little direct evidence of Tarsus Medical Centre but a number of scholars pay tribute to it, in terms that refer to its high quality. Dioscorides, a famous Greek physician, dedicated his five volume medical encyclopedia to Laecarius Arius, a first century physician and pharmacologist of Tarsus. References suggest that Dioscorides had himself been a medical student in Tarsus. Galen of Pergamum, a physician and surgeon who was prominent in the Roman Empire, mentions Arius of Tarsus. First century Philon of Tarsus was yet another, who became famous for his pain-killing analgesic, adding to the reputation of this centre of medical knowledge.

Historic Headlines

- Stone tools and pottery from the Neolithic period (around 5,000 BC) have been unearthed by archaeologists in Tarsus.

- In 696 BC, Sennacherib, King of Assyria, invaded and occupied Tarsus. Isaiah tells us that he invaded Jerusalem a few years before, in 701 BC.

- In 334 BC, Alexander the Great almost died from hypothermia, when he took a swim in the freezing waters of the River Cydnus, in Tarsus.

- In 51 BC, the Roman philosopher and statesman, Cicero, was appointed as Governor of Tarsus and lived in the city.

- In 47 BC, Julius Caesar paid a visit to Tarsus. The city became the capital of the Roman province of Cilicia

- Mark Anthony came to Tarsus in 41 BC. He gave the city a reward for defending itself against the regiments of Cassius and Brutus, by awarding exemption from taxes. He also invited the Queen of Egypt to come from Alexandria, in 38 BC, to meet him in Tarsus. The story tells of Cleopatra arriving in style, being rowed along the river in her luxuriously decorated barge. Their encounter was romantically commemorated by Shakespeare.

- Tarsus became the capital of the Roman province of Cilicia in AD 65, when Pompey finally established Roman rule. The population of the city was then about 500,000. Jews, in Tarsus, were loyal to Pompey and helped maintain security in the city. Some were rewarded with Roman Citizenship. Paul's family was among them. Consequently, he inherited Roman Citizenship, by right, through his family.

- Trajan, the Roman Emperor, died in Tarsus in 117 AD. Hadrian, who was there with him, was declared Emperor.

- The Seaport on the River Cydnus, serving Tarsus, had ceased to function as a port by the fifth century AD, as the river became silted up and ships could not navigate its narrowing course. Tarsus is now about ten miles from the sea.

- The city was under Crusader occupation from the 12th to 14th century AD, like most southern cities in Anatolia. The Ottoman Turks moved in after 1516.

Relaxed Tour of Tarsus

Mustafa's English was good, which was a great help to me. We strolled around the central area of the town and he knew just where to find the few visible remnants of Roman Tarsus and places linked with St. Paul. He was a young Muslim but he had some knowledge about this man of Tarsus and he was interested to learn a little more, as we walked.

- There's an excavated portion of a Roman street, near the city centre, almost six feet below the level of the modern street. It was the first item on our itinerary.

- The street had led towards where the hippodrome had been. The foundations of the hippodrome are now beneath the grounds of Tarsus American College.

- In the garden of a primary school, a few rows of stone seats have been unearthed. They had been part of the Roman Odeon.

- The Tarsus museum had been in the old building of an early Theological school but is now housed in a new cultural centre.

- Cleopatra's Gate has been well restored. Originally, it had been part of the Roman city wall. The gate was probably known to St. Paul but there is no obvious reason why it is also called St. Paul's Gate by some.

- In a small courtyard in the back streets of Tarsus, in the Cami Cedid quarter, there's a well which is thought, by some, to mark St. Paul's family home. It is known as 'St. Paul's Well' but so is another well further out of the town. The likelihood of the Cami Cedid well having belonged to Saul's family is supported by long tradition, though there is no other evidence. It is about 120 ft. deep and seems to have an endless supply of water, which is claimed to have healing properties. An information board in the courtyard summarising his life and ministry, includes a 'portrait' of St. Paul on a brass plaque.

- St Paul's Church had become almost derelict but, probably, the restoration is fully completed by now and the church open to visitors, as a museum. The Christian community, in Tarsus, grew from the early days of Paul's preaching and gained significance in

Christian history. Three important church Councils were held here in 431, 435 and later in 1177.

Man of Tarsus

Not many men have had the profound and sustained influence on vast numbers of people, all round the world, throughout two thousand years, as Saul of Tarsus. He was a Jew, although he also had the advantages of Roman citizenship. There were a few crucial moments, when he needed to use his Roman rights for protection. Some historians say that, when Tarsus became capital of the Roman province of Cilicia, all inhabitants received Roman citizenship, which would therefore have included Paul's family. Others suggest that only some were selected, under Pompey, as mentioned above. Paul had a traditional family upbringing in Jewish culture and religion. It seems that he had a sound education, which probably enabled him to become familiar with several languages spoken in Anatolia. As was customary for boys, he was also trained in a practical skill. His ability in tent-making, one of the well-established trades of Tarsus, helped to provide an income that sustained him throughout his ministry. He was probably in his late teens or early twenties, by the time he went off to Jerusalem to study under the great Hebrew theologian, Gamaliel.

A 'publication' entitled 'Acts of Paul and Thecla', about a woman teacher, preacher and baptizer, was probably written in Smyrna around 160 AD. It included a description of Paul as a small man. It says that he was bald, had heavy eyebrows, crooked legs and a crooked nose. Not a very flattering image!

A Potted Picture of Paul

The New Testament tells us that Saul had contact with Christians, soon after Pentecost. He was rooting them out and putting them in prison. He was then overseeing the stoning of Stephen, the first Christian martyr. It was following Stephen's bold, public declaration of trust in Christ (Acts 7 v 54 – 8 v 1) that Saul was converted to Christian faith on the road to

Damascus (Acts 9 v 1 – 9). This is such common knowledge among Christians, today, that the event can easily lose its drama and surprise. It was, however, a totally unexpected reversal from his hostility and persecution. Perhaps, it would be nearer the truth to think of it as a sudden surrender, rather than a sudden conversion. He had heard brave and bold Christian witness; he had seen Stephen's humility, commitment and trust, while he was being stoned until dead; he had seen the courage of Christians he had caused to suffer in Jerusalem and, by the time he approached Damascus, he'd been walking nearly 140 miles to hunt down, torment and persecute more. Surely, he must have been reflecting and struggling with it all.

It wasn't long before Paul was, himself, publicly declaring his experience of Christ and preaching the Gospel. He had to flee for his life on a few occasions, as he aroused enraged opposition from some of the Jews. As the mission of the Apostles was getting underway in Antioch, Barnabas was aware that they needed help. He went off to Tarsus to recruit Paul and brought him back to join them (Acts 11 v 25). In AD 47, Barnabas and Paul set out on their first mission trip. By AD 57, three extensive journeys had been completed. When he returned to Jerusalem, Paul was held responsible for causing a riot and was arrested. As a Roman citizen, Paul chose to face trial in Rome. He eventually reached Rome in AD 58, where although still under arrest, he was able to preach for two years. Before the end of the first century, Clement of Rome recorded that Paul 'reached the farthest bounds of the west', which probably referred to Spain at that time. Eusebius of Caesarea confirmed that Paul continued his mission in Spain but again he was taken prisoner and returned to Rome.

At some time around AD 67, when Nero ruled the Empire, Paul was executed in Rome. The exact date is unknown. Paul's period of ministry was comparatively short and yet his passionate faith and vision left an indelible impact on the doctrine and ethics of the emerging church. His energy, determination and spiritual insight was used by God to provide a foundation and touchstone, for the ongoing theology, mission-shape and lifestyle of world wide Christian Church today.

In His Own Words

It's refreshing to read Paul's own account of his experience in the Acts of the Apostles, because Luke has made every effort to replay Paul's testimony on three occasions.

Acts 9 v 1 – 9 Saul was violently hostile to Christians in Jerusalem. When he discovered that some had escaped to Damascus to hide in the Jewish community there. He obtained written permission from the Sanhedrin to bring them back as prisoners. This practice, of pursuing and returning 'offenders', was protected by historic precedent and endorsed by Julius Caesar, in 47 BC.

It has been suggested by some scholars that, where the road slopes down from Mt. Hermon towards Damascus, travellers have quite often seen lightning from an electrical storm, as hot air from below meets cold air from the mountain. Perhaps that happened on Paul's journey. Others have thought that his experience on the road to Damascus could have been caused by epilepsy. There is no doubt, however, that for Paul this was a personal encounter with Christ, that led him to radical change.

There are usually discrepancies in the reporting of unusual happenings and so, inevitably, there's a little confusion – v 7 tells us that the men heard the voice but could not see anyone, whereas, in 22 v 9, we read that the men saw the light but did not hear the voice. Paul was left without sight for three days. He followed the instructions he was given in the vision that guided him into the city …. 'there you will be told what you are to do'.

Acts 9 v 10 – 18 In Jerusalem, Ananias, a Christian, had a vision guiding him to meet Saul. Knowing of Saul's reputation of violence towards Christians and his purpose for being in Jerusalem, Ananias thought that, perhaps, God was making a mistake. Nevertheless, being assured by God that Saul had been chosen, Ananias went to meet him and bless him, praying for God's Spirit. Saul's sight returned. He was baptized in Christ's name and they ate together.

Acts 9 v 19 – 25 In the synagogues of Damascus, Paul started preaching among the Christians he had come to take as prisoners but, unsurprisingly, the Jews could not trust him. It sounds rather unreasonable to think that Paul might have been out preaching and teaching the day following these dramatic changes but it seems that there is a time gap in Luke's account, filled in by Paul in –

Galatians 1 v 15 – 24. Paul's letter to the Galatians tells us that he first went to Arabia to prepare for the demands of God's mission ahead of him. He then returned to Damascus for three years, before going to Jerusalem, where he faced violent reactions. Fanatical opposition from Jews in Damascus led some to plot his murder. They guarded the city gates to ensure he didn't get away but Christian disciples helped him to escape over the city wall at night. As there were houses built into the wall, he could have been lowered to safety from a window. Paul was then soon heading for Jerusalem.

Acts 9 v 26 – 31 It is no surprise to find that Christians in Jerusalem, especially Jews, were not convinced that Paul was a changed man and not a spy. Barnabas courageously spoke up for Paul but the Greek-speaking Jews would not accept it. They were aware that Paul had presided over the slaughter of Stephen, who was one of them - a Hellenistic Jew. In their anger, the Jews were ready to murder Paul. Paul's supporters managed to smuggle him out to Caesarea and then pack him off to his home town of Tarsus.

Acts 21 v 27 – 36 : Much later in Jerusalem, opposition to Paul was mounting and the Asian Jews were determined to get rid of him, one way or another. They were accusing him of 'Violating the Temple', because they had seen Paul in the city with Trophimus, from Ephesus, and mistakenly thought that he had taken this gentile into the inner courts of the Temple. The penalty for doing so would have been death. Paul was a devout Jew and would not have disregarded this sacred tradition. The accusers mobbed him and chaos ensued, as Paul was being beaten up. The commander, with his guards, were soon on the scene. Paul was arrested but when the commander asked what he had done, some shouted one thing and some another. Consequently, Paul was taken to the barracks, while the mob was still screaming for his blood.

Acts 21 v 27 – 22 v 36 The soldiers had been seeking an Egyptian rebel. Until Paul spoke in cultured Greek, the commander assumed that Paul must be that man. Paul explained that he was from Tarsus, therefore an Asian Jew like his accusers, and a citizen of Rome. Once his identity had been established, Paul asked if he could speak to the mob that wanted him dead. It must have seemed a strange request but the commander gave consent. The crowd fell silent as, speaking in Hebrew, Paul explained that he was a Jew and educated as a Rabbi. He then recounted his testimony, telling them of his experience of Christ, rather than getting into argument.

Acts 22 v 6 – 21 Step by step, Paul told the people what had happened to him, since the day on the Damascus Road. They did not easily accept that his life had been changed, despite his confession of shame for overseeing the murder of Stephen. He told them of God's call and commission to go far from Jerusalem, to share the Gospel with gentiles.

Acts 22 v 22 – 30 Paul's intention to offer God's grace to gentiles without requiring them to accept the demands of the law and circumcision was outrageous to the mob. They went crazy, throwing dust in the air and waving their cloaks in protest. To get to the truth, the commander ordered that Paul should be scourged. When Paul was tied up to be whipped, he asked the centurion, who was carrying out the order, if it was legal to scourge a Roman citizen. The centurion reported this to the tribune, who was not aware of Paul's status. Cicero had decreed that it would be an offence to bind a Roman citizen, a crime to beat him, and that to kill him was as bad as murdering your own father. It seems that the commander became terrified. He called the Sanhedrin to justify the charge they had brought against Paul.

Acts 22 v 30 – 23 v 10 Paul provoked members of the Sanhedrin by addressing them as 'brothers' and not as 'rulers'. He challenged the high priest on the law and was reprimanded for insulting him. It is most unlikely that Paul was unaware that Ananias was the high priest. It is more likely that Paul was being a bit sarcastic, because he knew that a man of Ananias' poor reputation wasn't fit to be high priest. Paul's cleverest move was to suggest that the charge against him was based on the view that he was a Pharisee, who believed in resurrection of the dead. Although the Pharisees of the Council would have supported resurrection, the Sadducees argued against it. He had divided the Sanhedrin and as the argument developed, the temperature rose and a fight broke out. The meeting fell apart. The commander rescued Paul, his prisoner, and took him to the barracks.

Acts 23 v 11 – 35 Forty Jewish men vowed to starve themselves until they had assassinated Paul. They shared their plot with the elders and chief priests but Paul's nephew overheard them. With Paul's guidance, he reported it to the commander. The commander then scuppered the plans of the Sanhedrin, by arranging for a platoon of soldiers to take Paul away by early morning, to be tried before the Roman Governor, Felix, in Caesarea. The commander, Claudius Lysius, sent a message about Paul to Felix, Governor of Judea. Its contents could not have been more fair or impartial, although the outcome could have been tricky, as Felix had a reputation for being unscrupulous and out for his own ends.

Acts 24 v 1 – 27 The court met in Caesarea. Tertullus had been appointed to state the charge. It was exaggerated, distorted and largely invented. Paul defended himself before Felix, who decided that he needed to hear the commander in person. Paul was retained in prison until the commander was available. Although he had some limited freedom, imprisonment lasted for over two years. Felix sent for Paul, a few times, to enquire about his faith. It is thought that perhaps he was hoping for a bribe from Paul to release him. Two years later, Felix had been replaced by Porcius Festus, and Paul was still there.

Acts 25 v 1 – 12 When Festus visited Jerusalem, the Jewish authorities tried to persuade him that they could bring Paul from Caesarea, to face charges in Jerusalem. However, their motive was to finish him off on the way. They failed to manipulate the new Governor, who ordered that Paul should be tried in Caesarea. Festus listened to the charges but there was no evidence to support the most serious accusation, that he had defiled the sanctity of the temple. Festus was a fair man but he also needed to avoid a direct clash with the Sanhedrin, so early in his appointment. He therefore suggested that Paul should face his accusers in Jerusalem, as they had requested. Paul knew that he would not get justice in Jerusalem and, as was his right as a Roman citizen, he appealed to Caesar.

We are aware of Nero's actions against Christians, particularly in AD 64, when he blamed them and made them suffer for major fires in Rome. It, therefore, seems strange that Paul should choose to be judged by him. F.F. Bruce assures us that there was no sign of hostility from Nero in the first five years of his imperial office (AD 54 – 59). He was under the guidance of Seneca, a Stoic philosopher, and Afranius Burrus, an upright prefect of the praetorian guard. If Paul had agreed to be tried in Jerusalem he would have faced utter confusion regarding evidence to support the charges. He confirmed his decision to go to Rome.

Acts 25 v 13 - 26 v 32 King Agrippa visited Felix. He happened to be quite an authority on Jewish religion and Felix outlined this case to him, explaining that Paul's offence did not warrant death. A report of the charges and evidence would have to be submitted to Rome, because Paul had appealed to Caesar. Agrippa asked to hear Paul. Luke tells us that the next day, with a great deal of pomp and ceremony, at a gathering of military chiefs and leading men of the city, Agrippa invited Paul to speak. He spoke of his background, his identity and described his conversion. He explained that his calling was to declare how God had fulfilled the message of Moses and the prophets, through Jesus.

Festus interrupted Paul, accusing him of madness. To Paul, the salvation message of the Gospel was obviously a fulfilment of prophecy. He suggested to the King that, with all his understanding of Hebrew faith, he would agree that prophecy was being fulfilled. It seems, however, that the King was embarrassed by the confrontation and did not want to show favour to Paul's side of the case, so he dismissed Paul's suggestions with a touch of humour – "Are you so quickly persuading me to become a Christian?" (26 v 28).

Agrippa's judgement was clear. He could see no cause for execution or imprisonment. Had Paul not appealed to the Emperor, he could have been released but, having appealed, the law required that he should be sent to Rome.

Acts 27 We read about the continuation of this narrative in Chapter 11, 'The Aegean meets the Mediterranean'. Paul was then being accompanied to Rome by Centurion Julius and had to change ships at the port of Myra. (27 v1 – 4)

Radical Conversion

Two areas of contemporary thought have been coming to my mind whilst writing about Paul's Christian conversion and the incredible impact his life, his preaching and sacrificial service had across the known world, in his own lifetime and ever since. The first is the way in which it stirs my gratitude and joy, as I recall seeing some hundreds of young people, in many places around the world, coming to Christian commitment and later dedicating themselves to service. Sometimes, they have reached their conviction alongside others, at an inspiring gathering or, quite frequently, in a more private moment. When I have met some of them again, ten or twenty years later, I've learned that not everyone has stuck with it but I have also been moved by stories of some working with homeless people, others campaigning for justice, serving in Christian ministry, in evangelism or as teachers, lawyers, doctors. Still others are seeking to maintain their witness in business, engineering, building and in the daily working-world. I should add that many are also living out their faith, in family life.

My second thoughts, however, haunt me and disturb my peace of mind. 'Religious conversion' frequently hits the headlines when a theatre explodes, a metro carriage is blown apart, shoppers are gunned down by automatic weapons or a suicide bomber enters a restaurant, causing many to lose their lives, to be left maimed, to be plunged into grief or shocked into emotional distress. Those responsible are often remembered as being ordinary people before the event, recalled as a quiet school friend, an able student, a cooperative work colleague or a good neighbour. 'Religious conversion' has brought them to a radical, political conviction that has led to sacrificial terror and destruction, which is claimed to be the will of God. It is deeply troubling. This radical conversion is diametrically opposed to the conversion of St. Paul, from hostile persecution to a Gospel of the life-giving Grace of God in Jesus Christ that gripped and motivated his life.

Historical reliability of Luke's text

How do we know that St. Luke was not making up a good story when writing the Acts of the Apostles? C.K. Barrett seems to raise this question in his book, 'Luke the Historian in Recent Study' (1961). He suggests that our understanding of Luke as an accurate historian had given way to the conviction that he was a 'creative theologian', whose illustrative stories, therefore, may have been invented or reconstructed to fulfil his primary purpose of communicating the Christian Gospel. A few years before, German scholar Hans Conzelmann had introduced these thoughts and, in so doing, had initiated a debate that continued for about twenty years. The series of arguments that ensued would be too much to summarise here. I would add, however, that over the years, archaeologists have been unearthing a succession of evidence that has been found to support the accuracy of geographical, cultural and social factors referred to by Luke. Obviously, this has helped to restore some confidence in the reliability of Luke's text. A Christian preacher may give special emphasis to certain real events but she/he does not need to distort factual matters in order to be effective, nor did Luke need to in his witness to the mission of the church.

More than a century ago, Sir William Ramsey, who regarded the Acts of the Apostles as an 'untrustworthy second-century production', undertook his own archaeological explorations in Turkey (Asia Minor) to justify his view. The outcome led him to conclude, however, that St. Luke was a fellow traveller with St. Paul, author of Acts and a dependable historian, whose record of life in the early church and knowledge of geographical factors and customs of the day were sound. William Neil, Professor of Biblical Studies at Nottingham University in the 1960's, described William Ramsay's final picture of St Luke as

> '... the meticulous cicerone who guides us along the shipping routes
> of the ancient world, who is at home in the intricacies of the Roman
> provincial administration, who has a passion for geographical detail
> and may be relied on to have checked up on the dates of emperors.
> "The Truth about the Early Church' 1970

In his writing, in the Gospel and in Acts, Luke does, of course, make a significant contribution to the variety of Theology found in the New Testament. Nevertheless, his primary purpose in writing the Acts of the Apostles was clearly to witness to what God was doing in the Actions of the Apostles and in the mission of the early church, rather than to write Theology. It seems clear that Luke's Theology (i.e. knowledge of God) was in the action. The Theology of the Acts of the Apostles is in what God was doing and what the Apostles were doing, together with all who shared in first century Christian mission - travelling, preaching, teaching, healing, witnessing, sharing resources, challenging poverty and oppression, suffering persecution and constantly seeking to witness to Jesus Christ.

Reflection

- As I think about Paul's experience, I find myself reflecting with gratitude on God's grace to me. I'm thankful for the minister who invited me into Christian commitment, when I was fourteen years old, and to those who laid the foundations and nurtured my faith. I deeply regret times when I have failed to live up to that conviction and yet I am acutely aware of the way in which God's love in Christ has shaped the course of my life and sustained me through thick and thin. Do these thoughts relate to your life in any way?

- Is genuine conversion to Christ and to a Christian life, in every respect, fully possible in western society today?

- Many Christians have no conversion date or experience, because they have grown into faith step by step, throughout their lives. Others, like St. Paul, have found the direction of their lives completely changed by the love of God and have a story to tell. Do you think one of these ways is more truly Christian? What would be your evidence?

• Why do some Christian converts exaggerate their past life as though God lifted them from the gutter and saved them from addiction, degradation and degeneracy, when, in fact, it was never as bad as that?

• I think that the conversion of a whole life takes a whole lifetime, as we continually need to repent and turn again to God. What do you think?

• In contemporary, secular times, probably the majority of people do not have a passionate desire for salvation from sin or from death and hell. What then should be the focus of faith, in order to appeal to the heart and mind? Should it be 'love', truth', 'life', 'goodness', 'total acceptance', 'peace' or another Christian emphasis?

• What is true Christian conversion?

• Can we rely on the factual accuracy of the Acts of the Apostles?

Antioch

The modern city of Antakya or Hatay, 167 miles east of Tarsus, is on the Asi River, formerly the River Orontes. It is about half way between the eastern shore of the Mediterranean and the Syrian border. This border has shifted throughout history and, at times, the city has been in Syria. This is the site of the ancient town of Antioch which had a prominent role in the spread of the Gospel in New Testament times. It was the place where the followers of Jesus were first called 'Christians', in about AD 40 (Acts 11 v 26). It was the first centre of Christian mission to the gentiles, as well as to the many dispersed Jews who came to the city.

History

The Orontes River flowed from Lebanon, through the hills of Syria into Turkey, before turning west into Antioch and on to the Mediterranean. For centuries, its fertile course became the best route for traders and for armies. In his attempts to unite Europe and Asia with Greek culture, Alexander the Great took control over much of the land. Later, around 300 BC, the Seleucids established Antioch as their capital, in the Kingdom of Syria. It was the beginning of the history of this city. By AD 64, Pompey had made Antioch the capital of the Roman province of Syria. It was well on its way to becoming the third largest city in the Roman Empire, when Peter, Barnabas and Paul arrived with the Good News.

Emperor Theodosius (379 – 395 AD) was baptized a Christian when John Chrysostom, born in Antioch, came on the scene. Chrysostom was a brilliant preacher – powerful and eloquent. He was described as 'the golden mouthed'. He recorded that there were 100,000 Christians in Antioch. For the first few centuries AD, Antioch was a stable, significant and popular city. In New Testament times, it became a major centre for the life and mission of the church but by the 4th century, as Constantinople developed in importance, Antioch declined.

Simeon Stylites (390 – 459 AD)

St. Simeon has long been honoured in Antioch and the surrounding area. He was an ascetic monk who lived for 36 years on top of a stone pillar, symbolically and actually removing himself, somewhat, from the ways of the world. He founded a monastic community on a hill about forty miles east of Antioch. Simeon touched his forehead with his foot 1,244 times in succession – but don't ask me why. His austerity and passionate discipleship attracted pilgrims from far and wide, while his teaching and preaching had profound influence on the people of his day. A group of monks in Cappadocia were inspired to follow his example. His burial place was in Antioch but his grave was probably lost in a devastating earthquake, when part of the city was completely destroyed, in 526 AD. A large gathering of Christians in that area was totally wiped out. Thousands lost their lives.

In AD 540, the Persians burned down much of the city. The Byzantines established rule from AD 628 but the Arabs took over from AD 636 until 969. Almost a century later, the Seljuk Turks seized power in AD 1040, before the Crusaders besieged Antioch for seven months, finally conquering in AD 1098. From 1268, the Marmelukes gained power, and then the Ottomans from 1516. It was not until a referendum in 1939, that Antioch and the surrounding Hatay province was returned to Turkey, by a substantial majority vote.

The Christian Mission

Cosmopolitan Antioch, rather than conservative Jerusalem, was more likely to be the city from which the Christian Gospel could be spread to the world. In many of the Jewish Synagogues, the language frequently used in worship was Greek. The Hebrew moral and spiritual understanding of God was attractive to gentiles. If the understanding of some of the Jews was on the move in that direction, it seems reasonable to think that the Christian Gospel may have assisted that journey. Perhaps they were, therefore, willing to listen and respond to the preaching of Peter, Barnabas and Paul (Acts 11 v 19 – 30).

As gentiles embraced the Gospel, demands from those who wanted to keep Christianity within Judaism soon emerged. Sharp conflict arose in Antioch between Jewish Christians, on the one hand, whose conviction was that there could be no salvation without circumcision and the law, and, on the other, those who declared the Gospel message of God's grace, freely given for all. Even Peter had been cautious about the need to observe orthodox Jewish practice when he was put under severe criticism by conservative Jews who had recently arrived from Jerusalem. It was Paul's view that Peter was mistaken to hesitate about gentiles becoming Christians, without Judaism.

> 'When Cephas (Peter) came to Antioch, I (Paul) opposed him to his face, for he stood self-condemned; for until certain people (strict Jews) came from James (in Jerusalem), he used to eat with gentiles. But after they came he drew back and kept himself separate for fear of the circumcision faction.' (Galatians 2 v 11-12).

An assembly was called in Jerusalem over this matter (Acts 15 v 1 – 11). After a long debate, Paul and Barnabas reported on the work of the Spirit in Antioch, in bringing gentiles into Christian faith. The Council listened with care and were convinced that it was not necessary for Judaism to be embraced, as a condition of conversion and acceptance. A letter was prepared for Judas and Silas to take to Antioch, to welcome Gentiles into the faith of the Church. This was an incredible breakthrough in the emerging Christian theology, initiation rites and mission.

St. Peter's Mission Centre

On the road from Antioch towards Aleppo, on the left bank of the Orontes River, St. Peter found a place to begin his mission in Antioch, AD 47 – 54. His H.Q. was in a natural cavern in the rocky hillside of Mt. Staurin. It was probably the very first Christian Church. The facade, restored in recent years, was added by the Crusaders in the 13th century.

There's a large stone altar inside the cavern and, behind it on the left, an entrance to a narrow tunnel. Presumably, this was an escape route through the hill. Fragments of early Byzantine mosaics and an Armenian fresco, high on the rear wall, remain inside the cavern. Outside, there's a large relief that Peter, Paul and Barnabas must have seen almost every time they approached. Some ancient writings date it around 270 BC.

St. John Chrysostom mentions another small cave on the slopes of Mt. Silpius. It is thought to have been the place where Paul lived and worked, while he was in Antioch. There were a number of early church buildings in the city but earthquakes and development has obliterated every trace of them. Writings from AD 211 and AD 231 refer to a large house, given by a wealthy citizen, for the work and worship of the church. It included a special chair of St. Peter. Under Constantine, a huge church building was started, and completed by his son, Constantius. It was known as 'the golden church' so it may have had links with St. John Chrysostom. Unfortunately, history has left no clue about its location. All we know is that 90 bishops attended the dedication, in AD 341, and took part in the ecumenical Council that followed.

The Roman Town

The main street of Antakya, Kurtulus Cadessi, was built over a famous colonnaded street of ancient Antioch. It was probably one of the grandest roads in the Roman Empire. When constructed, around 30 BC, it was two miles long and 30ft. wide. Grandiose houses, occupied by some of the grander people, lined the street. It's disappointing that none of it is visible today.

Roman Bridge : In New Testament times, there were a number of Roman bridges that crossed the river. One is still in use at the centre of the city.

Roman Aqueduct :The remains of the aqueduct are outside the west gate. There are also some signs of the city wall, which had been built by Justinian. However, nothing remains of the theatre, the circus or the palace, which were on the west bank of the river.

Archaeological Museum : Several high quality Roman mosaic pavements have been preserved in the museum. They date from 2nd to 6th century. Some say that they are among the best in the world.

God's action in Antioch

Acts 11 v 19 – 30

Moved by the death of Stephen, Christian believers in Jerusalem preached the Gospel with energy and conviction but at the risk of persecution.

'Saul was ravaging the church by entering house after house; dragging off both men and women, he committed them to prison.'
Acts 8 v 3

For their own safety, followers of Jesus left Jerusalem. Some went to Damascus but Paul followed in hot pursuit. Others went to Cyprus and Phoenicia, and some to Antioch, where there was already a sizable Jewish community.

11 v20-21 Believers from Cyprus and Cyrene were in Antioch, where they preached to gentiles, many of whom responded in faith. This was entirely spontaneous evangelism, without institutional strategy, oversight or consent. Christian people simply shared their faith and they did so without the training or formal leadership we may expect today. They were not preachers or apostles but simply Christians who wanted others to know Christ. How refreshing!

Up to this point, followers of Jesus had been identified mainly with Jews. This move towards mission to the gentiles was of critical importance. Philip's testimony to an Ethiopian had brought the man to faith. Peter's dream in Joppa had opened his eyes and the conversion of Cornelius confirmed Peter's conviction that the loving-purposes of God, which they had discovered through Christ, were for all people. The Christians who came to Antioch, had deliberately gone among the gentiles to let them know this. The Christian community in Antioch grew.

11 v22-26 When news from Antioch reached the Church leaders in Jerusalem, they sent Barnabas to investigate. Like some of the

'unofficial evangelists', he was himself a Cypriot-Jew. He was overjoyed as he recognised the hand of God in this momentous new venture but, as the work grew, he decided to seek another to share the leadership. Although nine years had passed since Paul had been sent away to Tarsus (Acts 9 v30), Barnabas went to find him, believing that Paul would be the right man for the job. His passion for mission, his open heart and ability to minister to gentiles, as well as to Jews, would be ideal. Paul was ready to respond to God's call.

The first time the label 'Christian' emerged was in Antioch. It's been suggested that it was used in derision. Perhaps it was but I think that it stuck, out of necessity. Some Jews were followers of Jesus but many Jews were not. Some gentiles were also followers but many were not. Christianity was not to be a sect of Judaism. It was not right to think of two groups. A collective term was needed : they became known as Christ's people – Christians. Paul wrote to the Galatian Church –

> 'There is no longer Jew or Greek, …slave or free, …. male and
> female. For all of you are one in Christ Jesus.' (Gal. 3 v 28)

11 v27-30 Some prophets from Jerusalem arrived in Antioch. It seems clear that Christians held the prophetic ministry in high regard, as they had taken to heart the likely impact of an impending famine, which had been of great concern to Agabus, one of the prophets.

In v 28, Luke verifies that the famine came when Claudius was Emperor (AD 41 – 54). Josephus confirmed this in his description of relief supplies being taken to Jerusalem between AD 44 and 46. It was decided that the church must take action, as Christians were determined to give support to those who would be facing hunger and poverty. The aim was that each one would send as much as he/she could (v 29). Money was collected from among the Christians in Antioch and taken to Jerusalem, to support those hardest hit by the famine.

Practical response to social need went hand in hand with Christian evangelism, from the beginning. We continue to recognise this as a vital and integrated part of Christian ministry. The church in Antioch did not appoint administrators to deal with the money, although at Pentecost the church had recognised the importance of administrators in Christian ministry. Barnabas and Paul, the chief evangelists, seemed to regard it as part of their own ministry, to take the aid to Jerusalem.

Poverty

Niall Cooper, Director of Church Action on Poverty, in a public statement in 2017 wrote –

'All people are of intrinsic worth. All people are of equal value in the sight of God; in fact the Bible is even stronger about this: all people are made in the image and likeness of God. Yet we are constantly bombarded with messages which deny this. Increasingly, people are valued only for their wealth, skills or economic worth. Rather than affirming our interdependency, society is divided into those who are 'hard working' and those who are 'dependent' - with the former encouraged to revile the latter. People are not just blamed for their poverty but for being a 'drain' on the rest of society.

At Church Action on Poverty we believe in the power of ordinary people to make change for good. Through campaigns like 'End Hunger UK', and by working with local churches, food banks and others, we can be a powerful movement for change.'

Generosity

I have been moved by the generosity of the Turkish people to thousands of Syrian refugees, in the camps that have been established along the Turkish/Syrian border, near to Antakya, old Antioch. Some say that they are the best refugee camps ever built. Thanks to Simon Reeve and his BBC2 TV documentary (2017), we were able to see rows of small, basic, prefabricated houses, each with electricity and water. Many have televisions and satellite dishes. Over 20,000 people live together in each camp, forming small functioning towns. The camp featured in the programme had five schools, a hospital with emergency facilities, two mosques, shops and supermarkets, street lights and play areas. No doubt, the Turkish authorities directed the BBC to the best of the camps but it was impressive and, given the circumstances, the people were content.

The camps are right on the Syrian border, so the residents express sorrow as they hear continuing brutal attacks on Aleppo, a few miles away, by the so-called Islamic State. The provision the camps make available to vast numbers, who would otherwise be desolate, must be at enormous cost to Turkey. Perhaps the politicians have political interest in the project. I am aware of many things for which I could not praise the current, more authoritarian, government in Turkey, but I thank God for this generosity and compassion and for the care it is giving to many thousands in need. Such care echoes the compassion demonstrated in the early church in Antioch, responding to the needs of body and the spirit together.

Galatians 2 v. 11 – 21

Paul was absolutely confident that he was right and that Peter was wrong in withdrawing from fellowship with gentiles. Previously, Peter had been mixing freely with gentiles, sharing his faith in Christ and building up theirs. The ritual demands of Judaism had been laid aside, in the interests of Christian evangelism, until the strict attitude of Jewish Christians, who had recently arrived from Jerusalem, undermined his confidence and caused him to withdraw.

The focus of fellowship between Jewish and gentile Christians was in the 'agape' meal, which had deep significance for the early church and contributes to our understanding of Holy Communion. Eating together, however, could not be reconciled with the requirements of Jewish law. Jews would regard themselves as spiritually contaminated, unacceptable to God, and ritually unclean, if they shared a meal with gentiles. Even Barnabas stopped eating with gentile Christians. Other Jewish Christians, however, followed Peter's example.

This division was, of course, in direct conflict with the Christian Gospel in two major respects. First, in unity, as we are all one in Christ. To make such a distinction in the fellowship was contrary to the gospel truth. Secondly – Paul's impatience and passion arose from the even more fundamental truth, that we come to God by His grace alone. Paul was speaking from his own experience of Christ. He had struggled with the law and found that it did not bring him into close relationship with God but, through the death and Resurrection of Christ, the love and mercy of God had brought him salvation.

It reads as though Paul was saying – "If I could have done it all myself, by my own obedience to the law and observance of the rituals or by my own effort, in any way, there would have been no reason for Christ to die." Paul was adamant that there is no life to be found in the law but, by the grace of God in Jesus, the very life of Christ Himself can be within you.

Acts 15 v. 1 – 41

Paul wrote to Galatian Christians about gentile believers being accepted into the Church, without the need for circumcision and allegiance to the Jewish law (Galatians 2 v.11 – 21). It would seem that his letter must have been sent to Galatia before the Jerusalem Council (Acts 15), as Paul makes no reference to the decision of the Council to embrace gentile Christians, or to the letter sent to the Church in Antioch.

15 v1–5 The need for the Council arose because of the insistence, by zealous Jewish Christians from Judaea, that circumcision was necessary for salvation. Paul and Barnabas got into red hot argument with the 'men of Judaea' and the matter was referred to the apostles and elders in Jerusalem. Paul and Barnabas appeared

before the Council to testify to the conversion of gentiles in Antioch. People in Phoenicia and Samaria were thrilled to hear of it, except for some converted Pharisees, who still insisted on strict observance of the full Mosaic law.

15 v6–12 After a long discussion among the Jerusalem Church leaders, Peter spoke of his own experience, ten years earlier. He described how the Holy Spirit led him to the gentile, Cornelius, who accepted God's gift of grace and committed himself to the way of Christ. Peter explained that the Grace of God is the heart of the matter. Then Barnabas and Paul recounted true stories of God bringing gentiles to faith in Christ and service in the Church.

15 v13–35 There was silence. Perhaps those listening had been moved. James, who was regarded as the leader of the Church in Jerusalem, spoke in support of Barnabas, Paul and Peter, declaring that the new gentile Christians should not be burdened with the requirements of the Jewish law. He suggested that a letter be sent to Antioch, seeking tolerance and respect in the church, between Jewish and gentile Christians.

The assembly chose Judas and Silas to go to Antioch with Paul and Barnabas to deliver the letter. The message welcomed gentiles who had come to faith by God's grace alone and it encouraged fellowship in the Church in Antioch, by offering advice to prevent Jewish practices from hindering their unity. The text of the letter was set out with care in v.23 – 29. Prayerful consultation led the council to a common mind, enabling the early church to recognise that God's Spirit was leading the church in God's work. 15 v 28 reads 'It seems good to the Holy Spirit and to us'. The message was carried in person as well as in the written word. I regard this as another vital reminder to us, with all our 21st century possibilities of multi-media and social media communication. No letter, report, glossy material, email, video, DVD, text, Facebook or Twitter can compare with the message that is carried in a personal relationship and received in a face to face encounter, in which one person can say to another, "This seems to be what God's own Spirit is saying to us. Is it also something about which we agree?"

15 v 30–41 The representatives from the Council in Jerusalem were received with joy. Their message brought relief and consolation. Judas and Silas continued speaking to the Christians in Antioch, in a spirit of encouragement. After a while, they returned to Jerusalem with their blessing.

Paul and Barnabas remained in Antioch, in ministry among the Christians there, until they were ready to continue their mission, by visiting the churches they had established. That decision, however, revived the dispute that arose in Perga, over John Mark. Barnabas was keen that Mark should go with them but Paul was not. It looks as though Paul regarded Mark as unreliable or disloyal, because he had 'given up' and left them in Pamphylia. Paul refused to take Mark. The outcome was that Paul and Silas went off to Syria and Cilicia, while Barnabas and Mark set out for Cyprus, to strengthen the growing church there.

Judging from several of Paul's letters, it seems that he later had a change of heart about Mark and recognised the strength he had brought to the church's mission. (Colossians 4 v.10, Philemon 23 v.2 and Timothy 4 v.11). Nevertheless, this was the parting of the way for Barnabas and Paul, as they did not work together again, although they both made incalculable contributions to the life and growth of the early church ... as did John Mark.

Reflection

- Some Christians, perhaps like Simeon Stylites, have unusual rituals and disciplines that don't make a lot of sense to us. In your view, does this detract from their Christian witness or convey that Christians, and Christianity, is really rather odd?

- Christians are sometimes divided by denominations, theology, church tradition, social background, politics or race. To what extent does this contradict St. Paul's conviction that we are 'one in Christ'?

- Is feeding the hungry and campaigning with the poor a political matter or a gospel imperative?

- In Antioch, a number of Jewish Christians believed that some of the essential rules of Judaism were necessary for salvation. Other Christians believed that God's grace is enough. What do you think?

Antioch in Pisidia

Lystra
and
Derbe

Lystra mound

The mound at Derbe

Excavations underway

Iconium

Fountain for purification before entering the mosque

The famous and stunning, turquoise/green tower rises above the mosque

The many kitchens, built to provide food for the poor, now house a museum of Dervish life and devotion

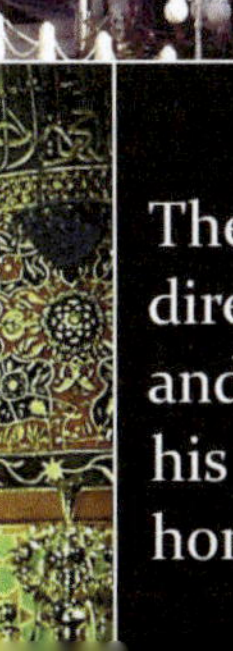

The tomb of Mevlana is directly beneath the tower and surrounded by verses of his poetry and many words honouring God

The main
street of
Konya today

The museum includes life size models.
Playing the reed flutes for whirling are
just two examples among many

Chapter 12

Pisidian Antioch to Iconium –

Lystra & Derbe … and back again!

I n the preceding chapters, our travels started on the Isle of Patmos, before visiting the Seven Churches of the Revelation. We ventured eastwards as far as Hierapolis and Colossae and then returned to the west coast of Turkey to move, stage by stage, towards the south, where the Aegean meets the Mediterranean. We paused at a number of New Testament places on the Mediterranean, as our journey took us along the southern coast, before skirting the Iskenderun Gulf and heading a little further south to reach Antioch on the River Orontes. Now, we are moving back to central Western Anatolia, to the region of Pisidia and another town called Antioch. Then we'll move eastwards, through the centre of Turkey, before back tracking to end up in Constantinople and Nicaea.

Antioch of Pisidia

A ntioch of Pisidia was built about 3,600 ft. above sea level, towards central Turkey, beyond the Taurus mountains. It would have been a tough journey to get there, in the first century. The advantage of this location, however, was that the town benefitted greatly from two major roads that crossed there. Travellers from north to south and from east to west put this place on the map, bringing visitors, business and people of wealth, power and influence to the town. Evidence of its ancient roots emerged between 1913 and 1924, when W. Ramsey and D. M. Robinson unearthed signs of a Neolithic encampment. The city was founded between 301 and 280 BC. In 25 BC, it became a Roman military base. The Emperor, Augustus, regarded it as a second Roman capital in Anatolia and arranged for three thousand soldiers, from Rome, to move into the town. The inhabitants had grown accustomed to a variety of languages, even though the Anatolians had their own local tongue. Hebrew would have been taught in the synagogues. By New Testament times, Greek was widely spoken and Latin was in use for legal and official matters. Antioch is another good example of the way in which the place and the people contributed greatly to the spread of the gospel. Evangelism was being fuelled, not only by the zeal of the apostles, but also by the cosmopolitan nature of the people of Antioch and its strategic position for travellers from north, south, east and west.

An Arab invasion virtually destroyed the city in AD 713 and, although there was an attempt to rebuild, it did not recover its elegance or success. Some people stayed until late in the 12th century but the building of a new town, Yalvac, less than a mile to the south, brought Antioch to an end.

The Archaeological Site

The Augustus Temple was built on the highest land, by the Emperor, in honour of Cybele, a mother goddess. By AD 400, what remained of the temple was in use as an open-air church. On the west side of the town, was another large church, dedicated to St. Paul. Some mosaic floors remain but the walls have long gone. At least three quarters of the city has not been excavated. However, there are some remains of a large theatre and a stadium, a fine aqueduct, a decorative fountain and a Roman bath, as well as some scattered stone carvings, quite a number of which include a bull's head.

Paul's one and only Sermon!

Acts 13 v 14 -52

13 v14-43 No ....I am not suggesting that St. Paul preached the same sermon everywhere, although every message did enshrine the one and only Gospel of God's Grace. But this is the one and only full length report of St. Paul's preaching. Having arrived in Antioch, he and his companions went to the synagogue on the Sabbath, where the leaders of the synagogue invited them to bring a message of encouragement. Paul spoke, summarising the Old Testament story of the Hebrew people and quoting John the Baptist and a number of Old Testament scriptural references. He declared that Jesus had come as the fulfilment of God's saving purposes but that the rulers in Jerusalem had failed to recognise this. They had rejected Jesus and crucified him. Many witnesses, however, testified to 'the final fulfilment of God's plan', in that God raised Jesus from death and He had been with them for some weeks afterwards. Paul explained that it was imperative for them to recognise that forgiveness and freedom comes through Christ, which the Law of Moses could never have brought. He appealed to them to believe.

After the meeting, many devout Jews, as well as gentiles, spoke personally with Paul and Barnabas, asking them to return the next Sabbath and address the people again.

Paul the Preacher

It is true that we have only this record of St. Paul's preaching and yet it is clear that, in almost all of his New Testament letters, he is proclaiming the Good News, in every way he can. He refers to God's hand in Hebrew history, he quotes the prophets, he draws on Greek philosophy and he understands the culture and experience of his various readers. Paul uses poetry, expounds deep and complex theology but, in contrast, he also writes about love - simply, profoundly and beautifully. He tells of Christ crucified for us ... to bring us back to God, forgiven, loved and free. He opens his heart in witness to the truth and recounts his own testimony of the life-changing power of God in Christ. He praises God for the faith and courage seen in the lives of other believers. He speaks of the presence and action of Christ in their service.

Paul's preaching is intelligent and articulate. He speaks boldly and yet with humility. His knowledge is extensive and his thinking is frequently original. Nevertheless, despite his burning desire to open hearts and minds to the love of God in Jesus Christ, he seems to recognise that there is something about the task that is beyond him – something spiritual for which even the most eloquent language cannot be enough. He knows that his words cannot contain the full wonder and power of God's grace in Jesus Christ – an experience that, I think, every earnest preacher knows at some time. 'Thanks be to God,' wrote Paul, '... for His *indescribable* gift.'(2 Corinthians 9 v 15).... the unspeakable, inexpressible, unutterable, overwhelming gift of God in Christ. The sole purpose of Paul, in his preaching, was that others might receive this gift. He could give all he had but he was aware that faith in Christ was God's gift, given by His Holy Spirit - not by the preacher.

13 v44-52 Luke tells us that, on the next Sabbath, the whole population of the city came to hear Barnabas and Paul. That's possibly a bit of an exaggeration, although it seems that a very large number were there. The Jewish leaders were infuriated by the popularity of the intruders and by the response from some of the Jews, as well as gentiles. In anger, they berated them. Paul and Barnabas declared that God's message was also for gentiles, again quoting Hebrew scriptures about 'being a light to the gentiles'. The gentiles listening were delighted. It's no surprise to read that, consequently, the Jews had become even more aggressive. They manipulated some of their Jewish women to stir up trouble for the Christians. These women greatly valued the ethics and discipline of Judaism, as it had provided them with some guidance and protection from depravity. In turn, the women pressurised their men (some of whom were quite influential) into hounding and dragooning Paul and Barnabas, until

they were driven out of the district. They went on their way to Iconium.

2 Timothy 3 v 11. When writing to Timothy, Paul refers back to the hostile troubles he faced in Antioch and the love and patience that sustained him.

Galatians 4 v 12 – 15. It is not immediately obvious to us that Paul was writing to the Christians of Antioch in Pisidia or to those in Iconium, Lystra and Derbe. These towns were all part of the Roman province of Galatia. His letter was intended for all Galatian Christians. It mentions that Paul was ill when he preached the gospel in the synagogue at Antioch. We don't know to what Paul was referring when he spoke of having 'a thorn in the flesh' (2 Cor. 12 v 7) but ancient traditions suggest that he suffered from burning, crippling headaches associated with malaria. If that is so, it could explain why he decided to face the hard mountain trek to Antioch in Pisidia. The town was at the highest point, where the air is fresh. Paul would then have been away from the malaria-ridden coastal districts – giving himself a chance to recover and continue his mission.

Iconium (Konya)

Konya, an attractive modern city, has grown extensively since its New Testament days. It is about half way between a north/south line from Ankara to Cyprus. Glance at a map and you'll see that it is another town where main roads meet from all directions. Since ancient times to this day, Iconium is and has always been, a place where trade routes converge. It's also a town to which Muslim and Christian visitors make their way, from all directions.

Archaeological research indicates that Konya is a very old city. Hittites lived there in the third millennium BC, followed by Phrygians, Lydians, Persians and Greeks before the Pergamum King, Attalus III, made a gift of the town to the Romans. Over the years, it was occupied by

Byzantines, Mongols, Seljuks, Ottomans, Seleucids, Pergamenes and Crusaders. Quite a chequered history!

From 1176, Konya was the capital of the old Seljuk Turkish Empire. Today, visitors seek it out as a religious centre, primarily because of Mevlana Celaleddin Rumi and the Whirling Dervishes. Much of the splendid architecture preserved in the central area is from the Seljuk and Ottoman periods. There is very little to see from Roman times but Christians still visit because Paul and Barnabas came here from Antioch of Pisidia and, for a while, received very good response to the preaching of the Christian message (Acts 14 v 1 – 7).

The second century story, entitled 'The Acts of Paul and Thecla', suggests that Paul may have faced considerable embarrassment while he was in Iconium. It was about the daughter of a leading citizen who was infatuated with Paul. She became a Christian and was determined to be baptised by Paul, incurring her father's wrath. The story says that she broke off her engagement to another man because of her love for Paul. It seems that a row broke out and they were brought before the city officials. The judgement was that Paul should be whipped and cast out of the city, and Thecla burned. However, very heavy rain fall saved her from the flames. She followed Paul and, disguised as a man, hoped that she would be able to stay with him – but no luck. Much of the story seems unlikely but there may have been some foundation for it. No doubt, the exaggerations provided amusement for some second century readers.

Acts 14 v 1 – 7 Luke's account begins by telling us that the visit to Iconium turned out to be rather like the experience in Antioch. Paul and Barnabas spoke with conviction at the synagogue, to a large crowd of Jews and Greeks, many of whom became Christian believers. The location of the synagogue has not yet come to light and may never. Jews who did not accept the word of the apostles stirred up reactionary feelings in the Jewish community. Paul and Barnabas, therefore, decided to stay longer, to strengthen those who had come to faith and to build up the Christian community.

Unyielding disunion developed among the people, with Jews and Greeks supporting each side. Some of the more influential were among those opposing the apostles and, in collaboration with the city authorities, they planned to stone them. Word of this reached Paul and Barnabas who, together with their companions, fled from Iconium to Lystra and Derbe, for safety.

Mevlana

The name given to Celaleddin Rumi by his many followers was 'Mevlana'. It means 'our master'. His 13th century mystic-movement, which had far-reaching influence on Turkish Islam, became known as the 'Dervishes'. 'Dervish' means 'poor'. Rumi, who originally came from Afghanistan in 1227, found that the society in Konya was tolerant, scholarly and an ideal environment in which he could develop his thought as poet, humanist philosopher, Islamic mystic and teacher. Many responded positively to his teaching.

Rumi married and had two sons. After his wife died, he married again and had a third son. Later, he met a poor man, Semsuddin Tabrizi, a dervish teacher and leader of a mosque. This man's love for people left a deep impression in Rumi's life, as well as the man's searching-sincerity in prayer. As their relationship deepened, Semsuddin became like a father to Rumi. On 5th December 1248, whilst he and Rumi were in conversation, Sems disappeared, after responding to a call at the back door. He was never seen again. Rumours suggested that he had been abducted and killed by one of Rumi's sons. Rumi was left bereft. Later, at 37 years old, he fell deeply in love but the lady went away. Consequently, he harboured an increasingly profound sense of loss that influenced him greatly. Coming to the conclusion that the secret of all existence is love, he set out on a search for 'the true God'. His convictions pervade his poetry. He wrote 25,618 verses, nearly all about love.

None of the great religions met his need. Eventually, he found the secret within himself, in his conviction that love is greater than any religion. He welcomed people from all religious traditions and from none, and from all social backgrounds. He invited all to be united with God. One of his sayings in the monastery, now museum, near to his tomb, typifies his open attitude -

"Come, come again, come! Infidel, fire worshipper, pagan,
Whoever you are, however often you have sinned, Come!
Our gates are not the gates of hopelessness.
Whatever your condition, Come!"

The Whirling Dervishes

The whirling ceremony is a devout act of worship. Each time I have been present, I've been moved by the sincerity, and challenged by the earnestness, with which the participants are seeking harmony with God. Rumi found that the sound of the reed flute represented the soul's unending search for something beyond ourselves. He therefore arranged for whirling to be accompanied by the flute. Talking with Dervishes has led me to understand that within the whirling, which begins slowly and gently, they aim towards unity with the cosmos and openness to God in all directions. As the speed of whirling increases, they may be taken into a state of ecstatic, eternal love. The right hand is raised to receive blessing from God as they whirl, and the left hand held towards the earth, to symbolise the free flowing to the world, and to all other beings, of everything they receive from God. They jump as an expression of rising to God and they stamp to crush selfishness under their feet. As they bow, the Dervishes endeavour to be in complete submission to God.

At the death of Mevlana, in 1273, people from many religious backgrounds joined the funeral cortege - Christians, Jews, Muslims and pagans. They came out of deep respect, to honour his vision of love for the world and to acknowledge the moral impact of his movement.

The Dervish orders were abolished by law in 1925, as part of Ataturk's programme to secularise Turkey. The monastery and the tomb then became a museum.

The famous turquoise green tower, above Mevlana's resting place, is stunning. I am always tempted to photograph it again and again, from every possible angle. The fountain, around which the Dervishes whirled, is in the courtyard. The main building enshrines many Dervish tombs, decorated and draped with richly embroidered cloth, each with its distinctive turban on top. Mevlana's tomb is covered with verses of his poetry and the walls of the museum decorated with many words honouring God, inscribed in beautiful calligraphy and rich colours. The kitchens, meeting rooms and monastic accommodation are filled with a fascinating exhibition of the life of the Dervishes, including life-size models illustrating their attire, their whirling, devotional life, study and practical work.

Mevlana 13th Century

"I tried to find Him on the Christian cross, but He was not there;
I went to the Temple of the Hindus and to the old pagodas,
But I could not find a trace of Him anywhere.
I searched on the mountains and in the valleys
but neither in the heights nor the depths was I able to find Him.
I went to the Caaba in Mecca, but He was not there either.
I questioned the scholars and philosophers
but He was beyond their understanding.
I then looked into my heart and it was there,
where He dwelled, that I saw Him
He was nowhere else to be found."

Reflection

I mentioned that I have been moved and challenged by the Dervish ceremony and conversation with them. Consequently, some matters emerge that you may like to explore.

- When I read Mevlana's invitation for 'all to come', on the monastery wall near his tomb, I ask myself, 'Do we, as Christians convey the same openness and inclusive spirit? Should we? If so, how?'

- Is a theology which concludes that 'the secret of all existence is love' too simplistic or unduly open to wild interpretation ?

- The Dervishes I've met were not monks. They came from home or work to the ceremony. Like us, they live in the world, not in a secluded monastery. Do you think it is possible to undertake a personal and earnest search for God, whilst embroiled in worldly life and work?

- Dervishes find deep communion with God and harmony with creation as they whirl. Christians speak of personal relationship with God. Can Christians also find that depth of bonding, rapport, unity, communion with God? How? Where do they find it?

Lystra & Derbe

Lystra was about twenty miles south east of Iconium. There's nothing to see there now - just a mound. That's a bit of a disappointment but, as far as it has been ascertained, this is the unexcavated site of the city. Searches nearby, in the village of Klistra, found a cross on a wall of what was probably a church, a winery and a few ruins which were probably houses. The city, however, is well and truly buried beneath the earth. A statue in honour of Zeus and Hermes was unearthed in the 19th century but little else has been seen. The small museum in the village of Hatunsaray, just south of Lystra, has a few Lystra items on display.

The Roman road, which was followed by Paul and Barnabas, runs from Ephesus to Sardis, on to Antioch in Pisidia and to Iconium, before reaching Lystra and Derbe. From there, it continues on its way through the Taurus mountains towards Tarsus. Parts of that highway were risky for travellers as, frequently, bandits would have been waiting in hiding. These dangers may have been a reason for Caesar Augustus to station soldiers in Lystra around 6 BC., although he was also dealing with trouble from tribes in the south.

As there seems to have been no synagogue or Jewish community, it is likely that the majority of the population were gentile. The people were not educated and knew nothing of the Jewish scriptures. The idea of there being one God may have been entirely new and strange. The language of local people was Lycaonian. Very few would have spoken Greek. As Paul was able to address the crowd, it is probable that he had been familiar with Lycaonian.

'Stand up Straight' :

Acts 14 v 8 – 18

There was a lame man in the crowd at Lystra, listening intently to Paul as he preached. Paul was aware of the man's intense attention and, although the man had not walked since birth, Paul looked straight at him and said, "Stand upright on your feet." The man stood up. The crowd went wild, when they saw him walking around, declaring that the gods had come down. They called Paul 'Hermes' and Barnabas 'Zeus'.

The high priest from a temple, just by the town, prepared a ceremony to welcome Paul and Barnabas and to worship them as 'gods'. The apostles went spare, tearing their clothes and rushing at the crowd. It would be blasphemy for them to be worshipped. Frantically, they tried to convince the people of their humanity and that they were messengers. Their message was an invitation to turn to the one true living God. I imagine that it was with a gasp of relief that Paul and Barnabas just managed to prevent sacrifices being made to them.

Left for Dead :

Acts 14 v 19 - 28

Some of the protesting Jews from Iconium and Antioch had pursued Paul and Barnabas. They seized this moment as an opportunity to wind up the crowd and get them to join in stoning Paul. They did their best to finish him off. Paul was dragged out of the city, battered and bruised. Many thought he was dead but, while some of the disciples formed a protective ring around him, with help, he was able to get up and walk back to safety in the city, without being seen. The next day, Paul and Barnabas moved on to Derbe. As they preached in Derbe, many came to Christian faith and joined the followers of Christ. Paul and Barnabas then returned to Lystra. What incredible courage and commitment!

On his second missionary trip, Paul went again to Lystra. It was here that he met Timothy (Acts 16 v 1 – 3). They became good friends and Timothy joined Paul for the rest of that mission. Later, Timothy accompanied Paul on his third mission journey, to Ephesus and Corinth (Acts 18 v 5), and was still alongside him in prison (Hebrews 13 v 23).

To return to their first mission : Paul and Barnabas helped to strengthen faith among the new disciples in Lystra. Then, moving back to Iconium and Antioch in Pisidia, they appointed and dedicated elders to give leadership to each church, before returning to the region of Pamphylia. There they preached in Perge, before going south to the port at Attalia, ready to sail across the Mediterranean, back to Antioch, in Syria.

On their arrival, the community of the church was called together to hear an account of how the apostles had been working in God's mission, and particularly about the significant response from gentiles. This was the church community that, before they set out, had prayed for them and entrusted them to the grace of God for the mission. Paul, Barnabas and their companions stayed in Antioch for a while, within the Christian fellowship there.

Derbe

You have probably spotted that we've said nothing about the city of Derbe. That may be because there's very little that we can say. I would not recommend that you make a journey there as, like Lystra, Derbe is still an unexcavated lump in the ground near to Karaman. Archaeologists are even cautious about expressing certainty about this being the site of Derbe, until more evidence is available to confirm its identity. There are a few minor ruins nearby but the New Testament town is yet to be unearthed. An altar stone was found that included the name 'Derbe' but one item is insufficient evidence.

About a century before Paul and Barnabas were in Derbe, a Tyrant ruled from this town. Antipater Derbetes was more generally known as 'Antipater the Pirate'. When Cicero was Governor of the neighbouring province of Cilicia, he was wined and dined by Antipater in Derbe. As this was the last Roman town on the road going east, there would have been a custom's house at the border. As some excavations are underway, more information may be coming to light even now, as you read. However, this work is inevitably slow. It may still be a little early to book your ticket to the view the latest display of New Testament evidence confirming the authenticity of Derbe.

Reflection

If you can, imagine the joy, excitement and thanksgiving among the Christians who gathered to hear the report of what God had been doing among gentiles … not among their own kind, not in their own town, not to bring any benefit to their local church community and yet there was joy amongst those who had commended Paul and Barnabas to the Grace of God for the task, now completed.

- How long is it since that kind of report was delivered to your local church and greeted with joy? Can you think of an event in mission that has brought similar joy to the church?

- Are there any distinctive factors in the mission of the apostles that make it different from ours? Of course, we live in very different times and in strikingly different contexts but is there anything here in Luke's report that could help us?

- Think of some projects you know or have heard about where the emphasis is on witness and evangelism or service and caring, or community action for justice and describe the ways in which they are an important part of Christian mission.

- Earlier in this chapter, we focused for a moment on Paul the Preacher. Do you think preaching is important today? Why? Look again at those paragraphs about Paul and ask what can we draw on today, to bring the Christian message alive? Then ask, what role does the Holy Spirit have in preaching?

Cappadocia

Haunting,
multi-coloured,
fairy-tale
panorama

Geological
Wonderland!

Homes ...... hewn from the soft tufa rock

Churches
around Goreme Valley

El Nazar Church hewn out within the rock and completed with frescoes

Tokali Kilise – Church with a buckle Elaborate pillars and arches carved within a huge rock.

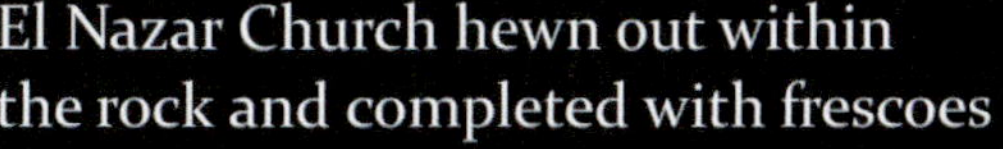

Pasha Bahche – 'Monks Valley' associated with Simeon Stylites

Karanlik Kilise

The Dark Church'

The Transfiguration
of Christ

A section of the monastery
has collapsed, although
the chapel is still dark,
thus preserving the
condition of superb
frescoes

Frescoe of the Crucifixion of Christ

Christ the Pantocrator – the Lord over all

Kaymakli
Underground City

Elaborately decorated entrance
Sultanhani Caravanserai

Kaymakli Church with a central altar

Nemrut Dagi

Model of how the statues of the gods were originally set up - Antalya

Antiochus I -
on top of the
mountain
among the gods
Zeus

Chapter 13

Cappadocia and Nemrut Dagi

Driving south east from the airport at Ankara, towards the Cappadocia basin, just when the sun was getting lower in the sky, I seemed to be entering a fantasy landscape - a geological wonderland! It was magnificent. As far as I could see - a unique, haunting, multi-coloured, fairy-tale panorama, shaded pale green, yellow, grey, mauve-pink and reddish brown: all evidence of mineral richness.

Lava from three local volcanoes covered the hills and valleys many centuries ago, leaving soft tufa rock and harder layers of basalt. Extensive erosion has produced a staggering variety of formations, in some places looking like rippling sand, in others like giant cones. Many of the cones are wearing 'cocked hats', while others are balancing great rocks on their heads. There's a huge rock toadstool and two tall boulders looking like giant sentinels striding across the landscape. Another formation, seen frequently around the area, is described locally as a 'fairy chimney'. They all blend together to form this amusing, beautiful and fascinating part of God's creation.

The variety of shapes result from the differences in the hardness of the rock. The darker basalt erodes more slowly than the softer, porous, coloured, volcanic tufa. Rain causes vertical erosion, and rivers, which have at times been at very high levels, cause horizontal erosion. Then the severe winter wind has rounded things off. Research indicates that, following a huge volcanic eruption about thirty million years ago, a massive inland sea in central Turkey evaporated, leaving the interior area of Cappadocia open to the air. The geological, historic and religious significance of this part of central Turkey seems to have been overlooked, until it was rediscovered by a French priest in the 1920's – 30's.

Troglodyte Living

The central area of Cappadocia is located in a triangle with Avanos to the north, Urgup in the east and Nevsehir in the west. It is likely that the natural caves throughout the area were inhabited centuries before Christ. Assyrian traders were there in the middle bronze age, 19th Century BC. From 1750 to 1200 BC, this was Hittite territory. In the Persian period between about 500 – 300 BC, a road was constructed through Cappadocia, from Sardis to Susa. Cappadocia was a Roman province by 17 AD and became part of the province of Galatia in 72 AD.

Acts 2 v 9 tells us that people from Cappadocia were in Jerusalem on the Day of Pentecost. They heard Peter's testimony and some are likely to have responded to his appeal. There's evidence that early Christians hid from persecution, in the caves of Cappadocia, and of Jews fleeing there after the fall of Jerusalem in AD 70.

It's disturbing to see, on our TV screens, news of hundreds of Christians and others, in the east, being driven from their homes by bombs and hostile action. Many manage to make temporary homes in refugee camps or create makeshift shelters in secluded places. Charles Dickens used the term 'houseless' rather than 'homeless' to describe people who have nowhere of their own. I'm sure he was right, as I have been amazed at the capacity of the human spirit, when I've seen parents make homes for their families in hovels.

One town where we lived, in the UK, was being used by the authorities to provide housing for 'homeless' families. Frequently, those families found themselves in 'bed and breakfast' accommodation, crammed into one grotty room. A call for breakfast came from a van each morning and they'd have to take plates into the street. Humiliating social care! We made contact with them and spread the word to gather a group, so that they could give each other support and together make representation to the authorities about their degrading conditions. At that stage, BBC Television took an interest too, as it turned out that there were more than a hundred families living in this way – 'houseless' families, who opened my eyes to the determination and loving-care of home-making, even in dire circumstances. I suppose that is the spirit that turned the strange rocky shapes of Cappadocia into homes and communities.

Over the years, more sophisticated dwellings, hewn out of the soft rock, succeeded the use of natural caves. The rock houses had several rooms, with vertical walls and flat ceilings. Stairways and passages connected two or three floors, and there were cut-out windows, balconies, ventilation shafts and chimney holes. Even today, some still look like multi-storey blocks or like high-rise apartments. A few are still inhabited, although deterioration has reduced that to a small number. It's quite an adventure to explore the rock communities and pop into some of the empty houses, climbing the stairs and squeezing through the corridors.... where it is safe to investigate. It's equally fascinating to explore caves that provided homes for some of the earliest Christian monasteries, although monks moved out when the Turks moved in. Some Christians remained until 1923, when there was an exchange of population between Turkey and Greece.

Goreme Valley

From the third and fourth centuries, many churches were carved out in Cappadocia. Over 3,500 have been identified : all hewn from the rock. 350 of them have been found in one valley alone – Goreme. A number of the monks came here from Caesarea (now Kayseri, about forty miles east of Goreme) where Basil the Great had founded the Basilian monastic order. Basil left his mark on monasticism, setting up clinics to feed and nurse those who were poor or sick, reforming the liturgy, establishing rules of poverty, chastity and obedience and attracting many who sought an ascetic life. This monastic culture was, therefore, brought into Goreme valley.

Christians retreated to Goreme valley during the Arab invasions in the 7th and 8th century. For safety, at that time, some monastic communities dug underground shelters, which grew into extensive underground cities. Crusaders settled here in the 11th and 12th century, increasing the number of churches and decorating many with beautiful frescoes, primarily of New Testament scenes. Sadly, large numbers of them were damaged during the Islamic period, when faces were obliterated. Nevertheless, what remains is outstanding.

Cave Churches

Visitors love this valley. It's often busy and rather noisy. Some guides talk loudly and incessantly. You can hear their every word from the chapel opposite and the one next door. There have been a few occasions, however, when I've been able to sit alone quietly and imagine Christians, from long ago, worshipping around me. Perhaps about twenty or so could have been comfortable in most of the chapels. I'd think of them growing in fellowship and seeking to work out Christian living in their society. I'd ponder on them preparing for mission or for the possibility of facing suffering and persecution. I had space to absorb the frescos and admire the care that had been lovingly carved into pillars and arches, to create a place conducive to worship. Those moments brought me a sense of being part of a much wider and deeper fellowship, stretching through the centuries, as though being in touch with something almost eternal.

The columns and arches were not necessary for structural purposes but were sculptured from the rock to make a cave into a church, with domes, naves and transepts in some, pews and altars in others. Some of the frescoes are from an early period and less sophisticated : others date from the time of the Iconoclasts (726 – 843). Those painted in the 'Archaic Period' (950 – 1050) can usually be identified because they are arranged in a series, telling a story from picture to picture, rather like a comic strip. The finest paintings remaining were the work of the Crusaders.

In the rock cut churches, very few faces have been painted in profile. Decorations have often been extended by draped clothing or the wings of angels. Unfamiliar symbols have been used, especially in paintings from the iconoclastic period, when reproducing the human form was not acceptable. These are a few of the symbols in the chapels ...

Fish	A well-known symbol of the followers of Jesus.
Palm leaves	Representing heaven or eternal life.
Vine	Communion with Christ or the blood of Christ.
Dove or Pigeon	Peace, love, innocence or fertility.
Cockerel	White cockerel for good fortune, black cockerel for the devil.
Peacock	The Resurrection.
Lion	Victory and salvation.
Rabbit	Sexuality, the devil or magic.
Birds	Symbols of Paradise.
Pomegranates	Eternal life.
Snakes	Satan or temptation.

Some of the Churches in Goreme Valley

Goreme Valley is a UNESCO World Heritage Site and this area, with a concentration of churches, is protected as a museum and supported by the Turkish Government. Many of the rock churches are, therefore, available to see and walkways, available to assist. Here is a brief description of some.

Kizlar Convent : Just inside the entrance to the museum area, the high ruin on the left was the convent. It's not in a safe condition to enter, now, but evidently it was a huge complex, five levels high. Rooms on the two lower floors provided space for three hundred nuns – living, sleeping, working, laundry, storage, cooking and eating. The chapel was on the third floor and the two smaller areas at the top were used as lookouts, to keep them safe.

Elmali Kilise – The Apple Church : Four pillars and a dome, similar to Byzantine architecture, have been sculptured to form this 11th century church. The frescos include 'The Last Supper', 'The Betrayal of Christ' and 'The Crucifixion'. It has been suggested that Jesus is holding an apple in one of the paintings, although I think the round object is intended to represent the world. It is, perhaps, more likely that the name 'Church of the Apple' was adopted because of an apple tree nearby.

Carikli Kilise - The Church with the Sandals : Iron stairs, replacing the eroded stone steps, lead to the entrance. The frescos are 13th century, although the church may be earlier. The design includes four domes and a wealth of decoration. The Archangel Gabriel is in the south apse. There's a Nativity scene and, separately, Mary and Child in the north apse. There are frescos of the Baptism of Jesus, the Transfiguration, Palm Sunday, the Crucifixion, the Ascension and the Apostles. In the dome, there are three Archangels as well as Matthew, Mark, Luke, John and Christ the Pantocrator (Lord of all).

Karanlik Kilise : I was amazed by the quality of frescos in this church. You have to pay an additional fee to enter the inner church to see them but it's well worth while. It was the chapel of a monastery which included a number of other rooms and chapels. Part of the dark interior can now be seen from outside, as a section of the façade has collapsed. It is called 'The Dark Church', as inside there's very little light from the one small window. Consequently, the paintings have been preserved in brilliant condition. Although they are dimly lit, the frescoes are clearly visible. The church is one of the most beautiful. It has been constructed as though supported by four columns, with a small dome each side and a larger one in the middle. There seems to be some dispute about the date of the building and the frescos. One source records that the building dates from the 13th century, while another says that the frescos are from the 11th century, but I think the artists would have had a little problem. Take your pick.

Some of the paintings represent Palm Sunday, The Last Supper, The Betrayal of Christ, The Crucifixion, The Resurrection, St. Mark, St. John and a wonderful portrayal of The Transfiguration of Christ … and the best portrayal I have ever seen of Christ the Pantocrator (Lord over all), in the dome.

Yilanli Kilise - The Church of the Serpent included a refectory complex of three rooms: one room for dining, with a long stone table, a kitchen and a storeroom. The narrow worship area is divided into two sections, with a barrel vaulted roof. There is a tomb inside. The 11th century frescoes are mainly in red ochre. St. George battling with the dragon and St. Theodore confronting a snake, that's clutching the 'damned' in its coils, make this church a favourite for some. St. George is venerated within Islam as well as in Christian tradition. Some frescoes are framed rather like icons. There are soldier saints fighting the forces of evil. Constantine and his mother Helena are shown holding a cross that was claimed to have been found in a pit near to Calvary. St. Onesimus and St. Thomas are included, as well as a hermit saint, Onofrio, who is portrayed naked (but neatly kept respectable by a palm branch). There was uncertainty about his/her gender. St. Basil the Great, bishop of nearby Caesarea, is portrayed and so is Christ.

St. Barbara Kilise : There's a legend that tells of a young woman, Barbara, who was shut away and later killed by her father, because she had become a Christian. St. Barbara became the patron saint of architects and stone masons. So it seems appropriate that a church was dedicated to her. You'd find her on the west wall. The church was constructed in 11th century with two columns and three apses. The decoration is mainly simple and symbolic, including red geometric designs, a number of crosses with animals and birds, Christ enthroned, St George and St. Theodore (two soldier saints on horse-back) fighting a dragon and a snake, as well as Christ the Pantocrator in the apse, giving His blessing.

Tokali Kilise – The Church with a Buckle : I would suggest to anyone visiting Goreme Valley that this is a church not to be missed. The frescoes are unbelievable. Their colours are vivid and all set into a vibrant deep blue background. The blue colour certainly distinguishes this church from others. It is the biggest in the Goreme valley and dates from the 10th century, although it has been carved into an older church and enlarged at various stages. It has three apses, a small chapel and a crypt. It is surrounded by pillars, as though supporting arches. The whole Gospel story of Christ is told in the art work, probably more than you could identify in one visit. The entrance to the church is outside the museum gate, opposite the parking area.

Cappadocia around Goreme

Zelve

I took my wife for an unusual stroll around Zelve, on a bright and sunny April morning, when we had a few days in Cappadocia. It was unusual because we were making our way through dark tunnels, climbing through holes and using iron stairways that had been added for safety. It was like mooching around a ghost town or an abandoned housing estate. The houses had been carved inside twisted rock cones of various sizes, all in rows and all deep pink rock on one side and very pale green on the other. The lava came from Mt. Agaeus, which can be seen in the distance. The neat layout of the rock cones could almost lead me to imagine that there had been an ancient volcanic town planning department, designing them in rows overlooking the canyons that branch out from the entrance area. The dwellings were still occupied until the early 1950's but centuries of erosion and some uncertain rumblings from the volcano encouraged people to move out to the new town.

In the first canyon, on the left, there's a small church. Despite its crumbling wall, paintings of a cross, a fish and a deer have survived. In the canyon on the right there's a mosque, which began its life as a church. 'The Church of the Grapes' is in the third canyon. It is the oldest example of architecture and Christian art-work in the area. There's also a grinding wheel for grain in one cavern, and hundreds of homes and storehouses.

Pasha Bahche

To be in Pasha Bahche (Pasabag Valley) is like finding yourself in 'fairy land'. 'Monks Valley', as it is known, is the place to see the finest examples of the so called 'fairy chimneys'. Erosion of the rock has created fascinating chimney pot shapes, giving rise to the ancient legend suggesting that this place was once inhabited by fairies. Much more reliable evidence shows us that, for many years, monks lived in the valley. They made their dwellings and meeting places at high levels, inside the 'chimney pots'.

At the top of a stairway, a large rock supports three high chimneys which were hollowed out to form a chapel and some other rooms. This pinnacle is associated with the Monk Simeon Stylites, who lived near to Antioch in Syria and whom we described earlier. He inspired the monks of Pasabag Valley to follow his example of a simple lifestyle and passionate faith. The rock formations in this valley enabled the monks to make their homes at the top of huge rock columns, to some extent reflecting Simeon's domestic arrangements. They followed his pattern of teaching, preaching and serving the people. There is a series of paintings in the chapel depicting scenes from Simeon's life. In other rock dwellings, a number of items from the time of the monastic community have also been found.

Cavausin

A huge rock castle stands at the centre of the old village. Ancient Cavausin grew up around it. Other small towns in the area developed in the same way, to provide protection for Cappadocia. Erosion and a subsequent landslide destroyed part of the castle edifice, leaving many rooms and corridors without walls. The village itself is now a little distance from the town, because of seismic concerns in the area and the possibility of further rock falls. Part of the Church of St. John the Baptist remains. Its three naves and columns are carved into the rock.

Uchisar

Driving through this area you can't miss the gigantic rocky skyscraper, with all its open windows, rising above the small town of Uchisar. This fortress is about 200 ft. high and, together with similar formations at Ortahisar and Cavausin, provided an effective line of defence for Cappadocia. The Hittites made good use of these facilities, followed by the Persians and the Macedonians. They were used again, later, by the Byzantines and by Muslims when they made moves to settle in Cappadocia.

A deep tunnel had been hewn from the rock, in those early times, stretching hundreds of yards through the mountain and under houses, to guarantee a water supply, should there have been a siege. Parts of it remain. Walls have collapsed year by year and many homes have been abandoned, although a few are still occupied. Some rock houses have rather grand, carved facades, and many of the natural formations are both intriguing and beautiful.

Kaymakli

Underground City

It was staggering to discover that hundreds of people lived underground in parts of Cappadocia.

In Tunisia, I'd seen sunken housing in pits and, in Rome, catacombs where Christians had sheltered but I had not come across communities that had lived on many levels below the surface. In this part of Turkey, where the tufa rock makes it possible, and comparatively safe, thirty six underground cities have come to light. They provided shelter from hostile attacks, blizzards and prolonged periods of frozen weather. We cannot be certain when the earliest tunnels were constructed, although the first known record was made by Xenephon, a Greek soldier and historian, in the 5th century BC. He added that livestock, poultry and goats were also living underground.

Kaymakli underground city is in the centre of the town, about fifteen miles south of Goreme. Visitors can go into the elaborate system of passages and stairways connecting living rooms, dining areas, sleeping facilities, wash rooms, wine stores, burial chambers and an underground chapel – all hewn from the rock, in the same way as the homes and churches of Cappadocia. Deep shafts were carved out to reach the water table. Air vents were cut, frequently to 300 ft., and designed to enable good circulation. The air inside the labyrinth of tunnels is remarkably fresh. Large rocks, like millstones, weighing 150 – 200 st, were set into rough grooves and, for security, they could be rolled to block passage ways and seal off entry.

To provide space, it is thought for about 3,000 people, Kaymakli city was dug to eight levels deep and covers an arca of about one and a half square miles. Access to only about 10% of the first five levels is open to visitors. Yet, from the inside, even 10% seems quite extensive. In some places, the passages become a bit narrow and, in others, you have to bend low - but the lighting is good. Having led a couple of people who expressed problems with claustrophobia, I think that anyone, who is fit enough and would like to visit, can do so with a little care and support.

In Derinkuyu underground city, five or six miles further south, a Christian mission school occupied the first two levels. Long tables had been cut into the rock and facilities for baptism are evident.

It is thought that the maze of tunnels in Kaymakli is, or was, connected underground to the Derinkuyu tunnels but the connection has not been found. It is estimated that other similar underground cities are also linked. However, clear evidence has not emerged.

Spirited Cappadocians

1 Peter 1 v 1 - 2 & Acts 2 v 1 - 13

Peter the Apostle sent this letter, probably from Rome, though it is thought that Silas or Silvanus acted as his scribe. He was writing to Christian Jews who had been scattered throughout Anatolia, mainly because they needed to escape persecution and suffering. The letter's focus is upon the attitude of Christians to the suffering of innocent people. Peter also seeks to give guidance to servants and those they serve, as well as to husbands and wives.

When he addresses his readers as 'God's chosen people', is he speaking to them as the 'Hebrew people' or does he have new Christian thinking in mind, as Christians are called to be God's new chosen people? The common factor is then not racial or ethnic identity but 'the blood of Christ' and the Holy Spirit. Jewish Christians throughout Asia Minor were becoming integrated with gentile Christians in a number of local communities.

Acts 2 v 1 – 13: Pentecost

It is misleading when these verses are described as 'the Coming of the Holy Spirit'. The scripture is clear in speaking of the Holy Spirit's action at creation and through the prophets. The Gospels regard the Holy Spirit as responsible for the conception of Jesus, His Baptism and for leading Him into the wilderness to be tested. The Spirit was present and active before Pentecost. Before you read these verses ask yourself, 'What is Holy Spirit?' Think of your understanding of the Spirit without using biblical texts or creedal language.

2 v 1 The Day of Pentecost was fifty days after the Passover. It was a big Jewish festival, like the Feast of Tabernacles. Festivals required that all male Jews, who lived within 20 miles of the Temple in Jerusalem, were legally bound to attend. At such times, there would not have been much room to move in Jerusalem. The Pentecost festival was also called the 'Feast of Weeks', as the fiftieth day followed a 'week of weeks' (i.e. the day following – 7 x 7 days).

Pentecost had two purposes. It was like a Harvest Festival, when worshippers brought the first fruits of the harvest. It was also a celebration of the law being given to Moses on Mt. Sinai. It was declared to be a Holy Day, in Leviticus and Numbers, on which no servile work should be undertaken. The law required those within 20 miles to be there for the feast but other Jews, who were deprived of temple worship (because they had been dispersed many miles from their holy city) made long pilgrimages to be at the festivals. Those from Cappadocia would have travelled about 800 miles.

Acts chapter two tells a wonderful and powerful story. It is not complete by v 13, as sometimes presented, because Peter then stood up and preached to the crowd, bringing meaning to what had happened. The great Pentecost question to the Apostles leapt out from among the people, "Brothers, what shall we do?" (v37) Offering the promise of God's Spirit, Peter appealed to the crowd, "Repent and be baptised, every one of you, in the name of Jesus Christ." (v37-40) About three thousand people responded.

Many Christians would like to know exactly what happened on this day but nobody knows exactly. In art, music, poetry, drama, preaching and writing many have brought creative imagination to the text but, although it is right to explore the scripture and understand as much as we can, we do so, knowing that explanation is beyond us.

2 v 2 The wind, a gale, strong and forceful, filled the house. The biblical word for Spirit is the same as the word 'wind' or 'breath' ('ruach' or

'nephesh' in the Old Testament and 'pneuma' in the New.) Jesus used that link in John 3 v 8, when he said to Nicodemus,

> 'The wind blows where it likes, you can hear the sound of it but you have no idea where it comes from or where it goes. Nor can you tell how a man is born by the wind of the Spirit.' John 3 v 8 (J.B.Phillips)

What is unquestionable about Pentecost is that the Holy Spirit, God's living presence, came powerfully upon them, among them, within them. We cannot explain 'how' but the 'wind' helps to describe the experience.

2 v 2-3 'Tongues of fire resting on them.' Fire was an ancient symbol of the presence of God. The 'burning bush' serves as a vivid reminder. John the Baptist talked of Jesus as 'One who would baptise with the Holy Spirit and with fire'. The use of the word 'appeared' may be suggesting that they saw what looked like tongues of fire. Luke may not have been speaking literally but, nevertheless, the experience was profound.

2 v 4-13 Where were the disciples at this point? Verse two tells us that they were seated in a house. Should we assume that, by verse four, they had moved into the Temple, as Luke describes a great crowd gathered around them? (Not possible in the house.)

The disciples addressed the people in different languages and visitors 'from all over the world' understood them. This is too often referred to as 'speaking in tongues' but the text is clear that it was not 'glossolalia', as heard later in the Church in Corinth (1 Cor. 12 v 3f and 14 v2f.) 'Speaking in tongues' produced sounds that could not be understood without interpretation. Here the people were 'amazed' (v12) and 'excited that each heard in his own language' (v 6). The areas from which people had travelled are listed (v9 – 11). Their languages would have been predominantly Aramaic-Hebrew or Greek, though in vastly differing dialects.

Mission

The people did not know what to make of this miracle, because 'the whole world' as they knew it, were able to hear, understand and respond to the Christian Gospel. Was this a dramatic, unforgettable launch of God's mission to the world? That certainly seems to be what is unfolding throughout the Acts of the Apostles .... God's mission to the world.

The presence of an early Christian community in Cappadocia could suggest that some of those who went to Jerusalem, for the Pentecost festival, took the Gospel message back home and shared it with others. There is no record of any mission visit from an apostle. It is suggested that Paul may have travelled through Caesarea (Kayseri), in Cappadocia, on his journey to Rome, but that was much later and there's no reference to it anywhere.

Acts 2 v 10 tells us that visitors from Rome also came to Jerusalem at Pentecost. Is it possible that they, too, took the Christian message back home? Over twenty years later, Paul wrote his wonderful and weighty letter to Christians in Rome. He had not previously been there, nor had Peter or any of the apostles. Did the Christian community in Rome grow from the witness of some who had found faith in Christ at Pentecost? If so, this could mean that, in the same way, witness had been shared by many other visitors, from various locations, when they returned after Pentecost. The outcome could therefore have been that small Christian churches had sprung to life all over. That Pentecost was possibly the launch of Christian mission is an exciting thought, especially if those who spread the word were 'ordinary' people who had a desire to tell others about Christ.

The Message and the Response

2 v 14-42 When Peter preached to a great crowd of Jews, he spelt out the Christian message as being the fulfilment of the highest hopes of the Hebrew faith. He built upon the prophecy of Joel (Joel 2 v28 – 32) and the words of David (Psalm 16v 8 – 11 and 110 v 1)

concluding with his personal witness to the Risen Christ. Then Peter appealed for repentance and baptism and for the people to receive God's forgiveness and His Spirit.

Three thousand were convinced by Peter's witness that day and we're told that they were baptised. I am quite sure that they were not all baptised on that same day! It had already been quite a full day. It would have been overwhelming and impossible for so many to receive meaningful baptism in the remaining time.

This brings to mind the astonishing response to an appeal, at a celebration rally in Zimbabwe. It was customary in the local churches for a few people to come forward spontaneously, without invitation, to kneel in dedication, at the end of a Sunday service, particularly if it was a special occasion. As there were something like fifteen thousand people of all ages, from all over the country, in the stands around the sports arena on that special occasion, I made it clear that the invitation was to those who were making their first open, personal response of commitment to Christ. Some experienced Christians were ready to talk with them and pray with them. As we sang, a number of people made a move from the stands into the arena, then some more, followed by many more and finally very many more. It seemed that everyone was coming, instead of specifically those who had not done so before.

A steward, who was helpfully guiding the people, as they came to kneel on the grass, became overwhelmed because there was such a crowd. I think he panicked. He called out to me, 'Send them back! Send them back!' Of course, they could not be sent back, although it was impossible for each one to have personal prayer. That would have taken days. However, it *was* overwhelming. The inspiring sight of hundreds of women, men and young people, from different tribes and every part of the country, flooding the arena and kneeling, still and silent, raised my spirit. We shared a prayer of dedication for all, asking God's Spirit to stay with us, to give His guidance and deepen our dedication and Christian service.

I am sure that Peter and other Apostles would have been thrilled to see the response from the crowd at Pentecost. It would not have been possible for each one of three thousand to receive a personal baptism on Pentecost day. Baptisms must have lasted for several days. Consequently, very many from the great crowd who were in Jerusalem throughout Pentecost did not rush home the next day but may have remained for several days – enjoying the fellowship, learning more about the faith and preparing for a new kind of future.

That's not all of Pentecost!

2 v 42 'They devoted themselves to the apostles' teaching and fellowship, to the breaking of bread and the prayers.' It seems that new believers needed to learn more, to grow in faith, to share in fellowship and to become the church, before they could be ready to go home and witness to others. This may also have been necessary in preparation for baptism. Pentecost was not all over in one day! And there's more ...

2 v 43-47 These verses describe the continuing Pentecost process of Christian discipleship. v. 46 speaks of a 'day by day' development of worship, breaking bread, sharing meals and praising God ... with more people joining in. The sharing was tangible as well as spiritual (v 44f). They made their material belongings available to everyone and sold their personal effects to make sure that no one was left in need. Their new experience of the Holy Spirit was leading Christians towards a holy life style. It is seen here in the generosity of believers, in their conviction of every person's value and in their practical care for those in need. It's a challenging thought but it says that '*all* believers' were involved in this radical action.

Perhaps the Pentecost people stayed for some days or weeks in Jerusalem, before taking as much as possible of their experience back to their home. Perhaps the very brief reference to Cappadocia in the New Testament had much greater significance than is, at first, apparent to us. I am convinced that we devalue Pentecost and undermine its fullness, if we think of it only as a strange and wonderful experience in an upper room. Its completeness seems to include :

- The powerful, shattering, 'in-spiring', i.e. 'in-breathing' of God's power and living Spirit. (See also John 20 v 22)
- The preaching of the Christian Gospel to a crowd, probably in the temple courtyard.
- An appeal for repentance, faith in Christ, baptism and for openness to the Holy Spirit.
- The response of many people in baptism, in learning Christian discipleship, in becoming the Church and in radical Christian action.
- An explosion of God's mission by Christian people, as they spread back into their world, with a living faith in Christ and new way of life to declare.

Reflection

Acts Chapter two has raised a number of challenging questions to which you may have given thought, as you've been reading. Even though I am not able to reach conclusions for all of them, I still find them of great value to explore.

- Christians know that the Holy Spirit has power, promotes action, creates change, inspires people. We know what the Holy Spirit does but what **is** Holy Spirit? What do we mean by Holy Spirit? Think of your understanding of the Spirit, without using biblical texts or creedal language.

- We cannot know exactly what happened to the disciples when they were together on the Day of Pentecost. Nevertheless, think about how you understand that narrative and compare your thoughts with those of other people.

- Do you think that complete Pentecost includes the things listed above?

- Was Pentecost the launch of God's mission to the world, first carried home in word and action by 'ordinary' Christians? Do most everyday Christians share their faith in word and action today?

- The graphic description in Acts 2 v 1 – 4 gives us vivid images of the outward signs of the Holy Spirit coming in power. What are the outward signs of God's Spirit taking action among Christians and in the world today?

Sultanhani Caravanserai

A caravanserai functioned like a hostel, offering protection and board for merchants, their goods and their animals, when travelling the main routes throughout Anatolia. Caravanserais were set up under Seljuk rule (1071 – 1243 AD) and continued to be in use for years. They were built about 20–25 miles apart, the average distance a loaded camel would be able walk in a day.

The Sultanhani Caravanserai, about 25 miles before Aksaray on the road from Konya, is the biggest and probably best preserved in its original form. There are still 120 others in existence but some have been adapted as restaurants or hotels. Four different sources have indicated four different construction dates of Sultalhani - 1226,1229,1232 and 1236, but that gives us an idea of the period. It was built under the direction of Seljuk Sultan Alaattin Keykubad. It is a huge, imposing fortress-like structure. I was not surprised to learn that, in emergency, the Seljuk state had reserved the right to use the facilities for military purposes.

There was one entrance only, usually rather grand, to a Caravanserai. The sculptured masonry surrounding the large gateway, here, was richly ornamented. The entrance was big enough for a heavily loaded camel. Once inside, the camels and other animals could be taken through the spacious courtyard, into a vast, cathedral-like shelter at the far end. Goods could be safely stored. On the left were kitchens, shops, Turkish baths and sleeping accommodation. A small mosque, mounted on pillars, was a central feature of the courtyard. A coffee house, library, doctors and veterinary attendants, food and provisions for the animals were available - all provided at caravansaries by the state authorities.

Travelling merchants were allowed to stay for three nights only, at no cost to themselves. These facilities were not for the high-flyers alone but also for the workers, who loaded camels or tended the animals, and for small business merchants. Even a state insurance system was established to cover losses that may be brought about by theft or disaster.

The Seljuks understood the importance of trade, for the wealth of the nation. That included local, national and international trade. They shaped their economic policies around the need for successful trade and were aware that supporting the welfare of the merchants and their employees was economically beneficial. It maintained a more secure and peaceful society. The economy flourished under Seljuk rule.

The caravanserais could be mistaken for castles, palaces or ten star hotels! I have been impressed by their quality and more greatly impressed by the Seljuk's concern and provision for the welfare of the workers.

Reflection

- Why is it that a 13th century Muslim state can be aware of the economic value of giving support to the nation's workers and yet, in the 21st century western world, with a long tradition of Christian culture, some of these things are still rather a struggle? The Seljuks regarded the welfare of working people as a major factor in policy making and ensured that generous provision was made to sustain their wellbeing.

- Today, some UK employers begrudge paying the minimum wage. Too many full time workers have to depend on 'benefits' and food-banks. Many employed people are on 'Zero hours contracts' which, at times, can mean there is no work and, therefore, no income. Many others are categorised as 'self-employed' and, therefore, do not receive payment when they are sick; they are not paid for annual leave; no pension contributions are made by their employer. They may be deprived of rights given to other workers and yet they are, in every respect, under the same authority as those who are regarded as fully employed.

Why is it necessary for unions and professional associations to campaign, protest or strike, to secure open negotiation about various matters relating to the working conditions and the income of employees?

- It would seem that these things would not have been acceptable in Seljuk Muslim practice towards workers. Is there anything in Christian faith that would persuade us to challenge these factors in UK employment practice today?

Nemrut Dagi

The mountain, Nemrut Dagi, is in a range of mountains north east of Adyiaman, in south-central Turkey. With little more information than that, I set out to find it, because I wanted to see the colossal heads which had been set up at the top of the mountain. To say that it was a scary adventure is an over-restrained understatement. The undulating approach road through the mountains was a pleasant drive, although it seemed to go on for ever and the fuel gauge, on the basic little car I'd hired, was seriously beginning to worry me. Worry matured into panic : the roadway narrowed, the smooth surface was transformed into a bumpy, ruggedly-excavated track and I was already miles from a filling station. The car was into a steep climb, struggling up the mountain, with solid rock on one side and a sheer drop on the other. I was dreading the thought of an approaching vehicle, as there was no room to pass, except for hewn-out spaces now and then ... but I wouldn't have been able to reverse down to find one ... and live!

As the gradient increased, the strain on the engine increased – so did my anxiety. Thankfully, I didn't know, then, that the summit is over 7,000 ft.

Eventually, I did arrive at an area where a few vehicles had been parked. Breathing a sigh of relief, I was able to leave the car and climb the final 50 ft. to the top. A superimposed summit had been constructed on the highest surface. It is like a gigantic cone made of thousands and thousands of small boulders and stone chippings, 164 ft. high by nearly 500 ft. diameter. It is a tomb, the burial place of Antiochus 1st. His reign over the Kingdom of Commagene, on the eastern edge of the Taurus mountains, came to an end about thirty years before Christ.

A terrace had been built on the east and on the west side of the tumulus (the burial mound of boulders.) Giant statues of the gods, each around 30ft. high, are sitting on the terraces, guarded by a lion and an eagle. The heads had fallen but they have been set upright on the ground. The gods, seated in two rows, back to back, looked out upon the world, east and west. There's Apollo, Tyche, Zeus and Heracles, and seated among them is ... Antiochus. I've learned that the statues somehow also represent Mithra, Helios, Hermes and others, in order to include gods of the Persian and Macedonian ancestors of Antiochus. It looks as though every detail of his instructions had been carried out to the letter. An altar platform had been erected, as well a huge stone sculptured frieze, with some mythological and astronomical significance. The frieze also includes a relief of Antiochus shaking hands with each of the deities in turn.

To design and erect this was a remarkable, creative project and, considering the weathering they must have suffered, the statues remain in extremely good condition. Nemrut is now a UNESCO World Heritage site and there are plans to ensure its preservation.

The sun was getting low in the sky, heralding a 'Turner sunset'. I really wanted to stay until it was sinking beneath the horizon but I feared the downward track. The whole scene was eerie and mystical but I was spell-bound by the place. The tombs of the Egyptian pharaohs and the temples of Abu Simbel are almost beyond belief but the scale of this operation, the audacious ambition of Antiochus, and the soaring, transcendent, remote, haunting reality of Nemrut Dagi took my breath away.

Reflection

- Nemrut is clearly not a New Testament site. I have included it, however, because it's a great place to know about, even more so because it speaks graphically to me of our human nature and causes me to reflect on the contrasting nature of God, as discovered in Jesus Christ. Antiochus was obviously a man of great wealth and power. At the summit of this mountain, you can see how he used an enormous amount of that wealth to amplify his own grandeur and glory, even after his death. This man set himself up at the top of the world ... among the gods. A few years later God demonstrated in Christ that He reaches to the bottom of the world. He set himself among humankind with all our weakness and failure. He did it because of His limitless love.

'He did not cling to his prerogatives as God, but stripped himself of all privilege by consenting to be a servant and being born as mortal man. He humbled himself by living in utter obedience, even to the extent of dying on a cross.- the death of a common criminal.' (Philippians 2 v 6 – 8)

- Discuss these thoughts noting the important differences between Jesus and Antiochus.

Constantinople

The Church of St Irene
(Divine Peace)

St John the Baptist
The oldest church in
Istanbul. Byzantine
monastery AD 462

The Church of St Saviour
in Chora (below)

Mosaic of Christ over the
entrance to the Nave and
a frescoe of Church Fathers

St Sophia
Hagia Sophia (Divine Wisdom)
Pillars and arches surround the ground floor supporting great gallerys
Mosaic of Christ
A number of mosaics picture the Emperor with Christ

The Blue Mosque
(Sultan Ahmet Camii)

The Gate of Peace
Entrance to Topkapi Palace

Buyuk Mecidiye Camii
Mosque beside the Bosphorus
at Ortokoy

The Byzantine Hippodrome

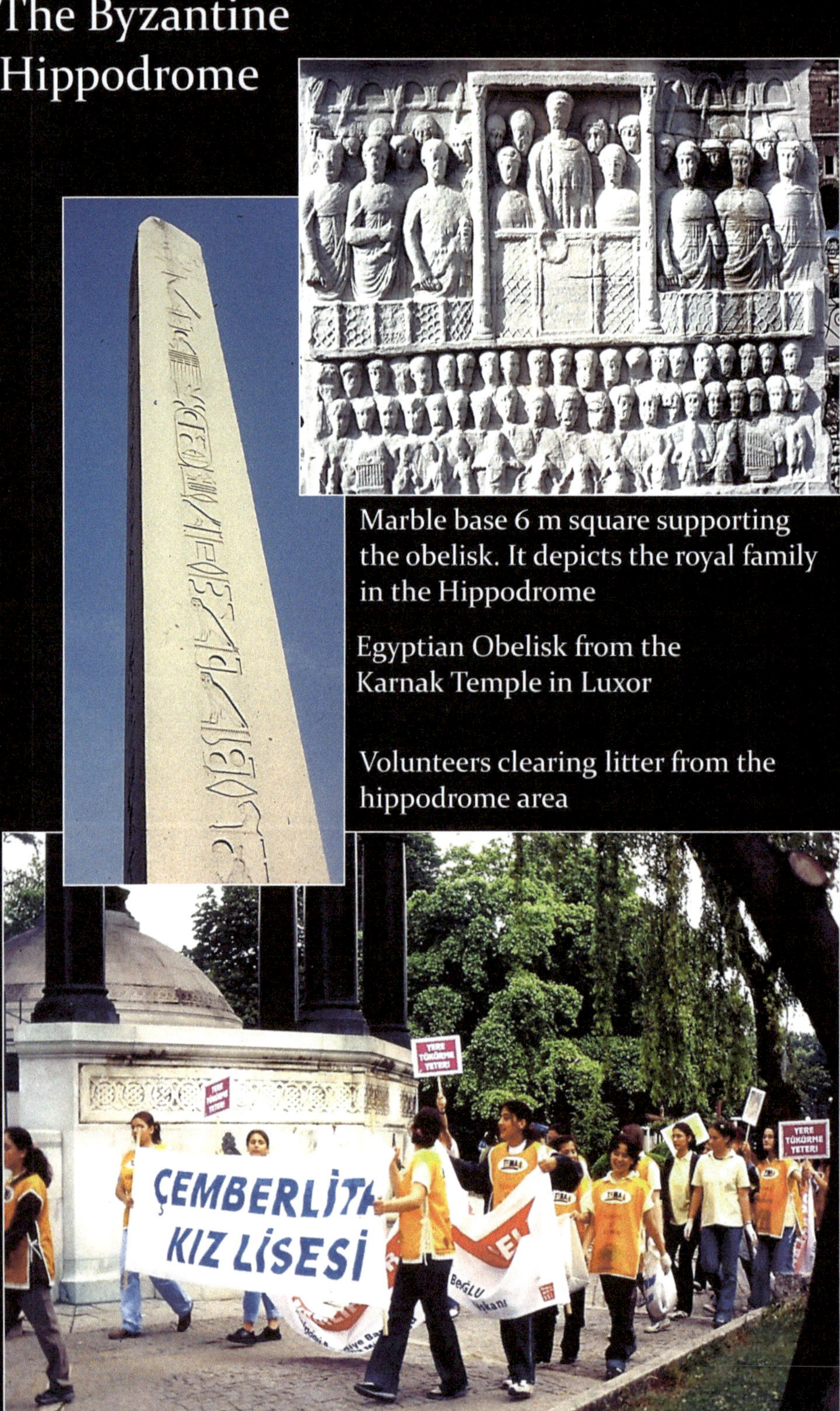

Marble base 6 m square supporting the obelisk. It depicts the royal family in the Hippodrome

Egyptian Obelisk from the Karnak Temple in Luxor

Volunteers clearing litter from the hippodrome area

The Bosphorus

Enjoy a cruise on the Bosphorus to see Ciragan, old Ottoman Royal Palace and Dolmabahce Palace - summer residences of the sultans

Galata Tower (1348)
overlooks the Golden Horn

Ottoman Gravestones : Size of Turbans
indicate the status of the dead, a Hat
- the Sufi order, a Fez - a public servant

Valens Aqueduct
(4th Century)

Colourful flower stalls can be
found around the market

Lion from the
Ishtar Gate.
Archaeological
Museum Istanbul

Byzantine Frieze of
sheep at the entrance to
previous Haghia Sophia
building, dedicated
in 415 AD

Chapter 14

Constantinople

Istanbul is the place to go in Turkey. Put it on your 'must do before I die' list. It stands out as one of the world's most magical cities, packed with history and intrigue. The breath-taking panoramic view from the Bosphorus strait is indelibly imprinted on my memory – bridges, towers, domes, palaces, mosques and minarets. There's a wonderful blend of ancient and modern, east and west, historic and contemporary. It's a lively, colourful town of welcoming people, busy markets, historic monasteries, museums and churches and enough to absorb your mind for months.

What's in a Name?

Semistra was the first settlement in the area, on the Golden Horn, at some time during the first millennium BC. Lygus town grew up on Seraglio Point in the 9th century BC., in the area which was known as 'the old city'. 'The old city', however, is now regarded as old Byzantium which, according to Strabo, was established in that location by Byzas, in 667BC. The city adopted his name. It's a splendid spot surrounded by water on three sides: the Bosphorus, the Golden Horn and the Marmara Sea.

Constantine chose this place as his new capital, when he became emperor of the whole Roman Empire in AD 324. Rebuilding began in the city and by AD 330, he renamed it Constantinople. An informal name also came into popular use -'New Rome'. Constantinople became the capital of the Roman Empire in the east. The city was claimed by the Muslim Ottoman Empire under the Turkish Sultan Mehmet II in 1453. Five new names were then tested for the capital over a period of time and the sixth one renamed the city - Istanbul. When Ataturk established The Turkish Republic in 1923, the capital was transferred to Ankara and so Istanbul didn't suffer another change of name. It continues to be the largest city in Turkey, with a population of over ten million and still greatly influences life throughout the nation.

The Empires

The continents of Europe and Asia meet in Istanbul. When you cross the bridges over the Bosphorus, you move through the gateway from west to east while you're still in the same city. Culture, fashion, business, education and political influence cross the bridges too, both ways. In recent years, religious and political tensions have been shifting back and forth at quite a pace. Istanbul is guardian of treasures and inheritor of culture, wisdom and intellectual legacy from three great Empires: the Roman, Byzantine and Ottoman Empires. No one could estimate the accumulative contribution this has brought to western life.

The old city was built on seven hills. Its walls were constructed under the leadership of Byzas, in order to safeguard the town's security and provide protection from the world. Through the years, the city's boundaries spread far and wide. In the last couple of decades, it has become abundantly clear that the ideas, abilities and enterprise of increasingly educated younger people have been releasing positive energy and influence, far beyond its former boundaries. I only hope and pray that more recent political changes in the nation will not rebuild walls that hinder the extensive, healthy sharing of the potential and promise that is evident throughout Turkey.

Christian City

At the last count, there were 157 Christian churches in Istanbul today. (There are also 17 synagogues, 10 monasteries and over 2,000 mosques, including a gigantic new mosque in the city). Until Islam was imposed by Sultan Mehmet, in 1453, and churches compelled to become mosques, Istanbul was regarded as a great Christian city.

Constantine embraced Christianity in AD 313. He was born in Serbia, educated in the court of Diocletian and fought in his army. In 305 AD, he joined his father in Britain. His father was an accomplished, high ranking, military man, who called his son to assist his campaign against the Picts, north of Hadrian's Wall. Constantine developed great military skill. His father's health deteriorated throughout that year. Before his death, in July 306, he declared, in York, that Constantine was now 'Augustus'. This elevated status led to him being Emperor, giving Constantine authority in France and Spain. He rallied his troops in York and led successful campaigns across Europe, to establish himself in Rome. That could explain the fine statue of Constantine the Great beside York Minster.

The Emperor Constantine had early contact with Christians, before a vision of a cross in the sky prompted him to claim the faith for himself. It seems to have coincided with his move from Rome to Byzantium, to locate himself at a more strategic centre of the Empire. He made Byzantium/Constantinople the second capital of the Roman Empire. He also established Christianity as a state religion. Constantine set up the first Ecumenical Council, in AD 325, at his palace in Nicea. As the Council came to an end, he brought the first big delegation of bishops to visit Constantinople. The second capital of the Empire was creeping towards being the second capital of the Christian Church.

In AD 381, Theodosius 1 invited the second great Ecumenical Council, with its host of bishops, to meet at the Church of St. Irene, in Constantinople. Ten years later, in AD 391, he went further than Constantine, by forbidding pagan observance.

St. Irene (Divine Peace)

Constantine enlarged a church ready to receive his delegation of bishops in AD 325. It was then consecrated as the first Cathedral Church and dedicated to St. Irene (Divine Peace). It stands just inside the main gate of Topkapi Palace. This building served as the Cathedral until the Church of St. Sophia (Divine Wisdom) was built in AD 360. After Hagia Sophia was destroyed by fire in AD 404, St. Irene was reinstated as the Cathedral, for ten years. In AD 564, St. Irene was also damaged by fire and partially rebuilt under Justinian. Later, in AD 740, it was rocked by an earthquake but it still stands.

Unlike most churches all across the land, this church is one of very few that was not converted into a mosque, by law, when the Ottomans came to power in 1453. It was used for a while as an arsenal and then as a military museum, for some years. Despite rough treatment during those years, you'd be amazed by its extremely good condition. Now it is a concert hall for the Istanbul International Festival of Classical Music. Generally, it is not open to the public, which is a disappointment as visitors are not able to see the columns and arches, lining each side of the nave, or the huge cross painted on the curve of the domed ceiling of the apse, above where the altar would have been.

Hagia Sophia (Divine Wisdom)

My first impression was that it would be very difficult to worship regularly in this place. It is vast, like an empty echoing aircraft hangar. There were some hundreds of people but they looked lost in the enormous space. I felt that it would be impossible to create a sense of close fellowship, during worship in that church. Such first impressions can too easily mask its magnificence and cause anyone to overlook the awesome architecture, its overwhelming sense of history and the realisation that thousands of Christians worshipped there for a thousand years. Add to that the fact that Muslims prayed in that building for nearly 500 years and, surely, we'd realise that this must be holy ground.

The first building was dedicated in AD 360. Its style was rectangular, like a basilica. It was constructed with a wooden roof that probably hastened the building's collapse, when fire swept throughout, in AD 404. A second church was built by Theodosius but that also burned down, in AD 532. Immediately, Justinian commissioned the present building. It was completed in five years and at the dedication in AD 537 the Emperor announced –

> "Glory be to God who hath declared me worthy
> to accomplish such work.
> O, Solomon, I have surpassed thee!"

It is true that he had sponsored the biggest building in the world. Even today, it remains the world's fourth biggest church ever to have been built, but to who's glory?

Architecturally, St. Sophia is a complex building but of most elegant proportions. The vast, majestic but shallow dome was seen as such a marvel, that people were reluctant to trust it and go inside, fearing that it might collapse. Later, great flying buttresses were added to strengthen the structure and provide additional support for the dome, during earthquakes.

Internal Splendour

One hundred and seven colossal columns inside are thought to have come from pagan temples around the country. Eight green columns were probably from the Temple of Artemis (Diana) in Ephesus. Rare and beautiful marble facings added to the internal splendour, as did some of the mosaics. In the gallery, there's a famous mosaic of Christ with Mary and one of John the Baptist. Another mosaic includes the Empress Zoe (1028 – 1054) with her husband, the Emperor. When Zoe arranged for her husband to be killed, the Emperor's face was changed to accommodate her second husband. Following his calamitous death, the face was changed again to that of Constantine IX, her third husband. He managed to outlive her. Above the main entrance, which was the Imperial Gate, there is a mosaic of Christ the Pantocrator on a jewelled throne, dressed as an emperor! A number of other Christian frescoes in the building are having a few layers of plaster removed and are being carefully uncovered.

Two huge marble jars were brought from Pergamum in the 16th century. Great wooden plaques were mounted at gallery level, in the 19th century, bearing the names of Allah, the prophet Mohammed and other religious leaders. There's a stone from the Temple in Jerusalem and a stone from Hezekiah's tunnel, also in Jerusalem, all part of the building's treasury.

To see the fine restoration, the marble panels, mosaics and frescoes is impressive but that cannot compensate for the inevitable impression of an internally faded building. Nevertheless, imagine if you can, the once vivid colours and glittering brilliance of the angels around the dome, with Christ the Pantocrator, in the centre, high over all. Imagine the contrast of rich hues and the glinting gold of more mosaics, still concealed, on other walls. Add to this, the gleam of shining marble panels, in a variety of shades, set into stone alongside the Corinthian columns. Include in your thoughts, bright sunlight streaming through the high windows and the sound of a great choir reverberating throughout the building. The acoustics are spectacular, with eleven seconds of reverberation. Visualise the priests and deacons, psalmists and servers, all in full regalia, entering the building in ceremonial procession, leading the Emperor to worship. That's how it was. It may not be your chosen style of regular worship but that was the magnificence and source of inspiration to be found in Hagia Sophia.

A Place of Prayer

Leaving St. Sophia, you could easily overlook the immense doors, clad with bronze, which have been there since the time of Justinian. Outside the entrance, displayed on the ground, is a length of frieze from the second building. The skill of the stone mason can be seen in his line of sheep, representing the apostles and a recurring biblical theme of sheep and shepherds. Much of the interior decoration and the statues were stripped by the Crusaders in 1204. A wooden minaret was added and then replaced with bricks when this church became a mosque. The other three were built later in the 16th century.

Hagia Sophia has a beautiful, spacious setting, surrounded by grass, colourful shrubs and flower beds. The two large fountains create dancing rainbows, as the sun catches the spray that's cooling the air. It is a glimpse of elegance and grace against its backcloth of blue made by the sky merging into the sea.

There are times of the day when this scene is not quite as serene. From around 5 am., intoned 'calls to prayer' are amplified from the minarets of the Blue Mosque, next door, competing with those from Suleymaniye Mosque nearby, as well as with other calls to prayer that can be heard from a distance. On some mornings, the chanting is beautifully harmonised : on others, you may wish that Imams could be selected for the quality of their singing voice. Hagia Sophia is, of course, a museum and no longer a place of worship for Christians or Muslims.

In Istanbul, I have been moved by the sight of large mosques, overflowing with working men at the time of Friday prayers, filling the forecourts and spilling onto the pavements. They have been bent low and fully engaged in devotion. Sadly, I have to acknowledge that, in very many of our churches, the 'prayer meeting' is about the smallest gathering.

If ever you are ever able to visit St. Sophia, you may find it hard to feel that you're in a place of Christian worship, especially if you're caught up in the crowded, bustling atmosphere of tourists. Before you leave, however, try to spend a few moments imagining this vast church full of worshipping Christians. Listen to their praise echoing in the dome and add your own prayer to theirs.

The Church of St. Saviour in Chora

The frescoes in this church are exceptional. The most outstanding and significant of them date from early in the 14th century. An outside glance could suggest that this is a rather plain building and yet, inside, almost every wall and ceiling is covered with mosaics and paintings of the highest quality, in fascinating detail.

The church was built as part of a Byzantine monastery, some say from the 4th century. Other archaeologists emphasise that there's no tangible evidence of the Chora monastery before the 7th to 8th century. The last major restoration and redecoration of the building was in the 14th century. Many of the mosaics feature the life of Christ or the Virgin Mary. There is one of St. Peter and another of St. Paul. The side chapel (or mortuary chapel) is filled with quite theatrical representations of The Last Judgement, Heaven and Hell and the hope of Resurrection. I smile at the imagination of the artist, portraying a whimsical touch in the work. For example, a serving maid who is preparing a bath for a baby is shown testing the temperature of the water with her elbow. In another, girls seem to be competing with the Virgin Mary, as they prepare threads for a purple veil for the temple. Their faces are thought to betray signs of jealousy and scorn. In the judgement, the devil is escorting souls to hell. One of them is taking a regretful backward glance, while another is politely standing aside to offer his friend the chance to go first. Jesus stands in the place of judgement but his face is calm, patient and suffering with the souls.

The monastery church became a mosque in the Ottoman period. It was comparatively late, in 1948, when the building was designated a museum. Nevertheless, each time I have been there, I have found that I could not have escaped the sense of being in a place of Christian worship.

The Oldest Church

The Byzantine Monastery of St. John the Baptist was founded in AD 462. I am not suggesting that it would be a good place to visit, as there's very little of it left. The apse of the monastery church flanked by two lofty walls still remains. If anything else has survived, it is buried or it has become completely overgrown. It's interesting that the monastery was established by a Roman aristocrat, Studius, whose name was given to the large complex, which became known as 'Studion'. Monastic life here had been governed by strict discipline, including the unchallengeable exclusion of women from its buildings, at all times.

The monastery became the University of Constantinople and its major faculty continued to be theology. Twice it sustained considerable damage. First, from the Latin invasions in 1204 and then the Ottoman conquest in 1453. The monks were forced to leave in 1462 and the church became a mosque, under the direction of the Sultan. Fires, earthquake and looting of the empty buildings brought the monastery and the church to its final end, leaving just the sturdy but damaged walls and apse of the church, as testimony to what had been a great institution.

Byzantine Hippodrome

The Hippodrome was in front of where the Blue Mosque now stands. It was built in AD 203, on an area which local historians think had probably been used, since before New Testament times, as a gathering place for the people of the town. Later, it was reconstructed by Constantine, when transforming the city into his capital. This stadium was enormous: 1,575 ft. long and 384 ft. wide. 100,000 spectators could watch circuses, chariot races and gladiator battles. It provided a superb venue for great civic gatherings and it even became the place where two violent riots wreaked havoc.

The hippodrome was raided and ransacked by the Crusaders in 1204. They left it virtually demolished. Today, a large paved square covers some of the area. A few monuments from the centre of the track have been rescued and are back in place, including part of an Egyptian obelisk from the Karnak Temple in Luxor. The obelisk was broken in transit. Its base is decorated with an impressive relief of Theodosius and his courtiers. A serpentine column, which has lost its head, has also been re-erected in this area, and a column of stones that was used by soldiers, over the centuries, to practise scaling the heights.

Now, it seems that the square has reverted to its earliest use, as an informal place for people to gather, to relax and meet friends. Visitors take photographs of the stunning sights all around, as they enjoy being in Istanbul. Once, when I was there with a group, listening to our guide running over some bits of history, we were enveloped by a few dozen young people who came into the square on a 'Keep Turkey Tidy' campaign. They were picking up litter and, in good humour and high spirits, they were recruiting us to participate. We were compelled to shelve the history and join in, hunting around for litter.

At another time, I bumped into people from various regions, eager to be photographed in their traditional, colourful costumes. On summer evenings, the hippodrome becomes a stage for street-performers who amuse the crowd or for buskers making music, while others take it easy and watch the sun go down.

The central places of interest in Istanbul have little or no direct New Testament link. It is, however, such an important city and phenomenal place to visit, that I'll say a few words about places that I think are the primary sites to see.

The Blue Mosque

The beautiful Blue Mosque dominates the skyline, with its six towering minarets and 260 windows that illuminate its gloriously glazed interior. Officially, it is the Sultan Ahmet Mosque. It was constructed by the Sultan in1609 – 16. Its more popular name has stuck because of the 21,000 ceramic tiles, glazed with predominantly blue flowers, that cover the lower half of the internal walls and galleries. They were produced in Iznik (ancient Nicaea) which is famed for its ceramics. The inner courtyard is surrounded by 26 columns supporting 30 domes. This is where worshippers would wash in the splendid fountain before entering the mosque for prayer.

For centuries, this was the Imperial Mosque. A procession from Topkapi Palace would lead the Sultan and the people to the mosque each week, for Friday prayers.

The Underground Palace

The Yerebaten Sarayi Cistern, in the central area, is described as a 'palace' because in Turkish, its name, Saray, means Palace and because it's built like one. There are 336 columns with Corinthian capitals and arches. It is 460 ft. long, 230 ft. wide and very deep. Many of the columns and the stone foundations supporting them came from crumbling temples. Medusa heads provide the base for two columns in a far corner. It is thought that the builder was possibly a Christian, who hid the heads of these pagan gods in a secluded spot. The cistern was constructed under Justinian 1, in 542, to provide water for the city, at times of drought. Walkways and good lighting enable visitors to explore. .

Topkapi Palace

This palace, now museum, displays the finest and most decadent example of Ottoman wealth and splendour. The surrounding walls were completed in 1478, although there have been some alterations and additions since. About 4,000 people lived within its boundaries. Ahmet III had an elaborate Ottoman fountain, with an overhanging roof, built in the first courtyard. The courtyards also housed a hospital providing 120 beds, the bakery, the arsenal, the mint, some dormitories and storage rooms.

The 'Gate of Peace' is at the entrance to the third courtyard. It was built with octagonal towers as the entrance to the administration centre, where council meetings were held regularly.

The Harem, at the far end of its courtyard, housed hundreds of women. Murat III is believed to have had 1,200 harem women, by whom he fathered 103 children! It's not surprising, then, that there was difficulty in deciding the true succession. It was usually solved by the eldest son, who would arrange the slaughter of his potential rivals. As it was later thought that perhaps this practice was rather too barbaric, they locked up the younger sons in Topkapi prison. The Harem was disbanded in 1909.

The Kitchens Everyone who lived in the palace was catered for by the kitchens. Each kitchen prepared a different quality of food for each station in the hierarchy. This explains why the ten large kitchens were necessary, each with its own oven, chimney and dome.

The Treasury A fine exhibition of jewels and other treasures are displayed here. Among them are some of the biggest emeralds and diamonds in the world. Other treasures have also been carefully preserved – the famous Topkapi dagger and the sword and seal of Mohammed, along with a tooth and his beard. A hand and arm of John the Baptist and some bones, regarded as being from his skull, are also on display.

The Fourth Courtyard Beyond the ornate kiosks and terraces are some wonderful views of the Golden Horn, in one direction, and the Marmara Sea in the other.

The Bosphorus

This historic waterway winds its course from the Black Sea to the Marmara Sea. A trip on one of the cruise boats for a couple of hours, from Istanbul, is both soothingly restful and photogenically exhilarating. At the northern end, where the Bosphorus meets the Black Sea, are the 'clashing rocks', where Jason and the Argonauts faced navigation difficulties when searching for the Golden Fleece.

Elegant bridges span the Bosphorus. Some breathtakingly grand palaces line the shore, such as the famous Dolmabahce Palace, with a white marble frontage, or the Kirmizi Yali, a well preserved red mansion. There are extravagant summer houses of the Sultans and fortifications on both the European and the Asian sides of the river. A fascinating array of vessels sail the Bosphorus, carrying visitors from all over the world, who usually wave happily to other visitors sailing by.

The Egyptian Bazaar

The bazaars are intriguing places. They are like a complex of tunnels above ground. The Egyptian Bazaar was built in 1664. Restoration in 1940 was drastically necessary, after earthquake rumblings and crumblings, together with other damage and the wear and tear of nearly three centuries. Initially, the spices and herbs sold there were from Egypt, or came through Egypt, but today many other foods are available. From the Pandeli Restaurant, on the first floor, there are superb views of the Gallata Bridge.

The Grand Bazaar

From the Byzantine period, the area where the Grand Bazaar stands had been a place for trading, like an open market. The Turks built the oldest part of this grand covered market, in 1455 – 61, to stimulate economic development in the city. Success has led to considerable extensions so that now there are over 4,000 shops from which to choose. Jewellery, leather-goods, clothing, carpets, lamps, traditional crafts, electrical goods, souvenirs and the best Turkish apple tea are all available ... and more. There are also quiet tea houses where visitors can escape to enjoy a rest, away from the bustle and bargaining.

Reflection

- The Emperor Constantine established Christianity as a religion of the state, in AD 325, enabling the Christian faith to become more open, respected and acceptable. This helped the faith to spread quite rapidly through the Roman Empire. Was this a good move? Why?

- Some years later, in AD 391, Theodosius strengthened the place of Christian mission throughout the Turkish nation and the Empire, by bringing pagan worship to an end by law.
  Do you think this was the will of God?
  Is it right for a nation to have an established faith and state church today? Why?

- What impression is being given to the world, on state occasions, when the church is prominent, caped, trimmed with gold braiding and its representatives are alongside the powerful? Is this an appropriate indication of the Church giving rightful care and support to those who have been appointed to civic authority under God, entirely in the spirit of Romans 13 v 1 – 7?
  Alternatively, does this indicate that the Church is part of the establishment and on the side of the rich and powerful, rather than standing with those in need, as Jesus did?

- Do you hear warnings for us today in the words of dedication announced by the Emperor Justinian, at the opening of the final building of Hagia Sophia in AD537 "Glory be to God who hath declared me worthy to accomplish such work. O, Solomon, I have surpassed thee!"

  If you do hear warnings, to what could they apply in the churches today?

Nicaea

The Istanbul Kapisi - seen from within the city. This gate marks the northern boundary of Nicaea and is part of the city wall, built by the Greeks in 300BC

The Green Mosque (Yesil Camii) The minaret clad in coloured tiles

The Archaeological Museum Formerly a hostel for wandering dervishes, set up in 1388

An example of fine Iznik ceramics. Vivid combinations of colours and highest quality, since about 1470

Lake Ascania, Nicaea (Iznik)
The site of Constantine's palace (remnants of what may be foundations at the shore) – venue of the first Ecumenical Council AD 325

The apse of St Sophia – venue of 7th council AD 787

St Sophia, Nicaea

Chapter 15

Nicaea

and the great Ecumenical Councils

n the first chapter, I mentioned Tezer, a Turkish young man who was sitting beside me on a flight to Istanbul. He had been in the UK, at the Birmingham International Exhibition Centre, as part of a staff team from a Turkish Company. He and his colleagues, who were sitting behind, had obviously had a great time. They were laughing and joking about the ups and downs of their week's work, until the two behind dozed off to sleep. In conversation with Tezer, I mentioned that I'd be staying in Istanbul. "If you are going to Istanbul you must visit Iznik," he said, enthusiastically. "We have recently been there for our honeymoon." What a coincidence! I had been around Istanbul a number of times and on this visit, Iznik was the very place I had come to see. Tezer was delighted. He reached for his laptop and, within seconds, I was looking at pictures of the very places I was planning to visit … though I would not have thought of ancient walls and decaying church buildings as ideal honeymoon scenery.

The enthusiasm of this young man, and his photographs, gave me an excellent introduction. Now I would recognise exactly what I was looking for. He wanted to know why I was interested and I explained. With a twinkle in his eye, he pointed to one of his photographs. It was the ruins of the Church of St. Sophia, at the central cross roads in Iznik. In this town, then called Nicaea, two of the great ecumenical councils had been convened. He was pointing into the apse of the church, where the bishops had gathered for the second of them. "This," he said, smiling, "this is the place where they decided to make Jesus into God. … Now he isn't, now he is. Now he isn't, now he is!"

He was pulling my leg, of course, but that led us into quite a complex conversation. It was fascinating. I was intrigued by the knowledge and interest of a young Muslim in the early formation of Christian doctrine. Within days, I was on a bus at sunrise, making my way around the eastern side of the Marmara Sea, to see the places he had shown to me. The small town of Iznik is about 160k journey, south of Istanbul.

The First Ecumenical Council

Nicaea, the ancient name for Iznik, is not a New Testament site. It is not mentioned in the Scripture but on May 20th AD 325, Constantine the Great welcomed members of the first Great Ecumenical Council to his imperial palace on the shores of Lake Ascania, in Nicaea (Iznik). Constantine hosted the meeting and gave the opening address, urging the church to live in peace and unity. It seems that he regarded Christianity as a means of uniting the Empire. This Council was the first clear indication of a close relationship developing between church and the state. The Emperor had financed and hosted the Council, organising transport for the 220 bishops (out of 318) who attended. He had arranged a splendid banquet on July 25th to conclude the Council, following its two month session ... and we may think that our church meetings are frequently too long!

The Nicene Creed

Nicaea gave its name to the basic, historic creed of the Christian Church, the Nicene Creed. That Creed emerged from this Council meeting. None of the many other religions in the Roman Empire had previously had a statement of faith. There was purpose, however, in seeking to find a form of words that would be acceptable to the whole church, especially as there were different understandings of the nature of Jesus. That purpose was to unite the church. Unity was of special interest to Constantine, as he was anxious to hold the Empire together. It would be fair to note, however, that he was not the only one who had political interest in the close relationship developing between him and the church. The bishops were most keen to encourage a closer bond with the Emperor, to make use of his imperial power for the church.

The process of consultation to reach a statement of faith, that would be acceptable throughout the church, was turbulent. Conflicts arose, primarily, about the nature of Jesus. The proceedings were far from united. Arius, a priest from Libya, claimed that Jesus, the Son, must have been inferior to God who is Father. He regarded the Son as a demigod, with a human body but not human nature, created for the salvation of the world. He was supported by Bishop Eusebius of Nicodemia but sharply opposed by Alexander, Bishop of Alexandria and by Athanasius. The frenzy of argument developed into ecumenical fisticuffs, when our kind and cuddly Santa Claus, Bishop Nicholas of Myra, could not contain himself and gave Arius a punch on the nose.

Holy Trinity

The Council came to agreement on wording that said Jesus, the Son, was 'of one substance with the Father'. There were different understandings of 'substance' but the church has held to the agreement that Father and Son are of the same essence and that Jesus is not a separate or inferior god. The arguments didn't stop, however. This matter was to come up at later Councils and, it seems, found its way into daily discourse. Gregory of Nyssa records –

> It you ask a man for change he will give you a piece of philosophy about the Begotten and the Unbegotten; If you enquire the price of a loaf, he replies: 'The Father is greater and the Son inferior'; or if you ask whether the bath is ready, the answer you receive is that the Son was made out nothing'.

To this day, Christians wrestle with the nature of the Holy Trinity. Changes in language, in popular psychology about 'persons' and 'individual identity', together with increasing unfamiliarity with the

Christian faith, easily lead to misunderstanding or to ridicule from those intent on undermining Christian Theology.

I feel concern when I hear a blessing from 'God the Father, God the Son and God the Holy Spirit.' It seems to convey the notion of three Gods. I would prefer to say 'God, who is Father, Son and Holy Spirit,' thus retaining our faith in One God, who has three ways of being God, and so avoiding any suggestion of polytheism (i.e. many gods). Thinking about the Trinity, I have picked up, from somewhere, the thought that a man can have three ways of being himself – father to his children, son to his parents and brother to his siblings. I don't suggest that this is a perfect parallel, nothing can be, but it embodies three ways of relating, three different ways of loving and serving, three ways of being the one person. This helps me a little in understanding the nature of God. The thought of God as 'Trinity' also conveys and interpersonal relatedness within the Godhead. This was especially evident during the incarnation, as Jesus related to God as His Father and the Spirit as His guide and inspiration. Such relatedness bears witness to the interaction, variety, life and movement enshrined in God's own nature. Nevertheless, biblical witness to one God, who is eternally Father, Son and Holy Spirit, was clearly enshrined in the early Christian Creeds and has continued to be a central matter in Christian faith.

The great significance of this first Council, at Nicaea, is that the first statement of Christian orthodoxy was agreed. It was also at this Council that the Emperor first appeared to act as head of the church, as well as head of state.

If there had not been a late rearrangement, we could be discussing the Ancyran Creed. Constantine had made arrangements for the Council to meet at Ancyra (Ankara) and changed the plan at a late stage, before calling the Council to Nicaea.

The Church of St. Sophia

Constantine's Imperial Palace, the venue of the first great Ecumenical Council in AD 325, once stood on the eastern shore of Lake Ascania (Iznik). A few submerged stones from the foundation of the palace can be seen at the edge of the lake today but it's not possible to get any idea even of the outline shape of the building. It was no bother to me at all that Tezer made an error in one small detail, in that the major agreements about the nature of Christ were made by the first Council when meeting at the Palace. It was the Seventh, not the first Council, that met at the Church of St Sophia in Nicaea in 787.

The shell of St. Sophia still stands at the centre of the town where the main north - south road crosses the main road from west to east. The remaining walls of the building are easily visible from outside but the site is not usually open to visitors. The remains of a fine mosaic floor and, protected by a glass screen, a fresco of Christ with John the Baptist and Mary have been preserved. The church was built in the time of Justinian. It became a mosque in 1331, long before the edict requiring churches to make that change. The building was damaged by an earthquake in 1065, and suffered two fires in the 15th and 16th centuries. Some rebuilding and restoration took place but it was increasingly neglected, before being destroyed in 1922, in the conflict between Greece and Turkey. What remains of the building is now a museum. The only congregation for many years has been a loyal family of storks that nest in the broken minaret each spring.

Nicaea the Town

The modern town of Iznik is still surrounded by the city wall which, with a little patching here and there, has been standing since 300BC. There were four great, decorated stone gateways, three of which remain, although some Byzantine towers have been added. The Istanbul Gate in the north and Yenisehir Gate in the south are joined by a road running straight through the town . Lefke Gate is on the eastern side but the western gate is no longer standing. Walking from one end to the other takes only about 20 to 30 minutes. In fact, I found that it's easy to walk around the town and see everything of interest, in a full day. You can usually pick up a snack near the centre of town to get you through the day, as long as you are not as scatty as I was, in forgetting that it was Ramadan, and finding there was no food available anywhere, in the middle of the day.

During the period in which Pliny was Governor of Bithynia (AD111 – 113) he lived in Nicaea. He was in correspondence with Emperor Trajan because he was disturbed by Christians in his province. When he asked what he should do about them, Trajan counselled him to be merciful but to maintain his authority as Governor. Pliny took a harder line, however, and executed Christians who would not express scorn for Christ or who refused to bow down to the Roman gods and statues of the Emperor. Nevertheless, the numbers of Christians continued to increase and they would not let go of, what Pliny described as, their 'base and excessive superstition'. Again Trajan advised him to avoid hassling the people and stirring up opposition.

The Seljuks took over the town in 1081. It was then recaptured by the Crusaders in 1097, followed by a period in which it was capital of the Byzantine Empire. For fifty years, it was regarded as capital of the Empire of Nicaea. The Ottomans added the town to their Empire in 1331.

The Lake

I suggested that the old town may not have been the ideal spot for Tezer and Gulpin to spend their honeymoon but beside the lake, adjacent to the town, would have been a different story. Lake Ascania is surrounded by olive trees, fruit gardens and grapes vines. Iznik is in a popular and successful grape growing area - yet another beautiful and relaxing corner of Turkey. The fresh water is calm and the fish are plentiful. It looked so inviting that I even fancied a visit to the excellent lakeside fish restaurant ... but it was Ramadan, a time of fasting until evening.

There are a few other interesting places in this small town that caught my eye -

Yesil Camii (The Green Mosque)

The Green Mosque, a 14th Century building near to the eastern gate, is not as grand as the Green Mosque and the Green Tomb in Bursa but the minaret is a sight worth seeing. It is decorated with green and red Iznik tiles.

Archaeological Museum

This building, near to the Yesil Camii, is regarded as the finest in Nicaea. It was opened in 1388 as a hospice for Dervishes. There are five domes over the arched entrance into the central domed room that leads to two side rooms, each also with a dome. The exhibits include some surprising earthen-ware burial caskets from the Hittite period. Each casket is like a very big egg, or perhaps a womb, containing the remains of a body in a foetal position. I had never seen anything like it before or even heard about this tradition of burial. You can also see Roman articles and Seljuk/ Ottoman ceramic tiles.

Iznik Ceramics

Since the Ottoman period, from 1470 to 1561, Iznik has been famous for its ceramic tiles, pottery vessels and plates. Good examples of Iznik ceramics can be seen all over Turkey. Perhaps the finest are in the Blue Mosque (Sultan Hamet Mosque) that was completed in 1616. 21,043 ceramic tiles were used in decorating the inside walls and pillars. The most impressive designs are in brilliant cobalt blue and white, combining elements from Arabesque and Chinese traditions.

The tiles produced between 1560 and 1620 are valued as the very best in quality, clarity, design and colour. The rich red colour used at that time is considered to be unique and, therefore, has never been produced anywhere else.

Seven Ecumenical Councils

First Council (325) – Nicaea

B asic details about the first council and the venue have been given above but one fascinating recorded snippet of information was that the host, Constantine, who was frequently present in the council meeting, appeared each time in a wig of a different colour. But please don't think that this might have given rise to the traditional liturgical colours that were later adopted by the church.

There were other matters on the agenda apart from the nature of Christ, though that was the predominant concern. One practical issue was the date of Easter. Some parts of the church were using the Jewish calendar to determine when the celebration should be and others were not. The decision was that Easter Day should always be on a Sunday and never coincide with a Jewish festival.

Constantine summoned the Council when he was earnestly seeking to hold the Roman Empire together, as tensions were threatening its unity. He hoped that strengthening the unity of the church could help to cement the solidarity of the Empire. Although that was not recorded from the Council, I suppose it was in the background throughout and may have influenced some areas of consultation. The Council did not fully succeed in achieving his goals. The decisions did hold things together until Constantine's death but afterwards some of the conflicts and divisions began to surface again.

Second Council (381) – Constantinople

The Council, summoned by Theodosius I (378 – 95), met in the Church of St. Irene. The building is on the left, just beyond the main entrance, inside the walls of Topkapi Palace. We noted, earlier, that it had been enlarged and dedicated as the first cathedral, when Constantine chose Byzantium as his new capital.

The Council worked on the Doctrine of the Trinity, focussing particularly on the nature of the Holy Spirit, to improve some statements in the Creed. Theologians like Gregory of Nazianzus, Athanasius of Alexandria and Basil of Caesarea, who died just before the Council meeting, had done the preparatory work but everyone wanted their personal views to be taken into account. It was following this Council that Gregory of Nyssa noted that even the baker and the maid had an opinion on these major theological matters. The debate sometimes degenerated into a lot of bickering, rather like 'Prime Minister's Question Time' in the House of Commons, on some days. The Patriarch of Constantinople complained that 'the proceedings were like the noise of wasps or magpies'. Nevertheless, the Council did confirm the Creed, adding the explanation that 'the Holy Spirit was of the same substance as the Father and the Son'.

One other bit of business at the Council was the agreement that, as Constantinople was now regarded as the 'New Rome', it's Bishop should become second In the hierarchy, after the Bishop of Rome. I think that the agreement was far from unanimous as the Bishop of Alexandria, previously the number two, would have had his nose put out of joint.

Reflection

We have already given some space to reflection on the Holy Spirit but another thought comes to mind about the nature of the Spirit. Over thirty years ago, the challenge of a young man in Australia caused me to change the way in which I refer to the Holy Spirit.

I had been speaking each evening at a national Christian youth gathering and he had been listening carefully. "Why do you speak of the Holy Spirit as 'He'?", I was asked. I hadn't realised that I did. I suppose the reasons were tradition and habit, although that was no justification. Despite the fact that very many feminine images are used to describe God's nature throughout scripture, tradition has greatly favoured the use of masculine language when speaking about God.

The language of scripture, that describes God as Father and Jesus as Son, certainly encourages that concept of God's nature but there's no reason at all why gender should be ascribed to the Holy Spirit. Qualities of love, joy, peace, patience, kindness, generosity, loyalty, tolerance and self-control are by no means predominantly masculine. (Galatians 5 v 22).

- His question taught me to avoid any suggestion of gender when speaking of the Holy Spirit. Some Christians refer to Mother God. What do you think?

Third Council (431) –
The Church of the Virgin Mary, Ephesus

The Council was still deeply preoccupied with the nature of Christ. Theologians from the Alexandrian school emphasised the Divine nature of Christ, whilst the Theologians from Antioch saw Him as the ideal human being and therefore emphasised His humanity. This led to acrimonious confrontation between Alexandria and Antioch. How could Christ be 'wholly man and wholly God'? Did he have a split personality? Did he not have two distinct natures, one human and one divine? Was he really two and not one? Surely he must have been more divine or more human and therefore less of the other? These arguments were raging for months. Leaders from different parts of the church took sides. All this was in the air, when Emperor Theodosius II called the Council to meet at Ephesus to settle the matter.

A fragile reunion enabled the participants to get through the Council and to reach equally fragile agreements but the 'cease fire' didn't last long and Theodosius had to call them back to Ephesus AD 449 to sort things out. Pope Leo described that gathering as like a 'den of robbers'. It went down in history as the 'Council of Robbers'!

Despite all these fireworks, with a few modifications, the Creed remained intact but division became inevitable. In the west, Constantinople and Rome worked together, in Africa, cooperation developed between Egyptian (Coptic) and Ethiopian churches, while in the East, churches in areas linked with Persia grew into closer union.

Fourth Council (451) – Chalcedon

Chalcedon (Kadikoy), on the Asian side of the Bosphorus, has been absorbed into greater Istanbul, over the years. There are no visible remains from the 5th Century, although the ancient town must be buried beneath later developments. So there is nothing to see of St. Euphemia, where the Council gathered. This was the largest of the Councils with 600 bishops attending.

The Person of Christ was still top of the agenda in this council. A declaration was agreed that Christ was 'Truly God and Truly man', in one 'person'. The Latin Catholic Churches and Eastern Orthodox came together on this understanding but it divided them from the Syrian Orthodox and Armenian Orthodox, which withdrew from the Council and did not return. They believed that Christ had one composite, indivisible nature.

A major bone of contention arose from the recognition of Rome and Constantinople as equally supreme in authority and importance. In practice, that gave more power to the Bishop of Constantinople, the capital of the remains of the Roman Empire, even though the Bishop of Rome was of higher status in the universal church.

Fifth Council (553) – St. Sophia, Constantinople

The great Cathedral had been rebuilt by Justinian, after devastating destruction by fire. The Council was still seeking a formula to represent the Nature of Christ that would unite the Church, but failed. Disputes continued to abound. Justinian was concerned to strengthen church unity throughout the empire and to unite Church and State under his rule. He thought that consistent beliefs held by the whole Church would be instrumental in achieving this. In 529, he closed the Platonic Academy in Athens to repress competition from pagan Greek philosophy.

The Emperor did not attend this Council but he wrote to some members encouraging them to placate the churches in Egypt, Syria and Palestine, in order to bring them into the body of the Church. However, such efforts could not succeed, as those churches objected to the agreed creedal statement about the nature of Christ. This was the first Council to describe itself as 'ecumenical', even though some Christian traditions were not represented. Future Council meetings would also be regarded as 'Ecumenical'.

Sixth Council (680 –681) – Constantinople

The Council was summoned to the 'Domed Hall' of the Great Palace, by Emperor Constantine 4th (668 – 685) in an attempt to bring fragmenting groups into unity. Again, the focus of discussion was the nature of Christ. Further attempts were made to find a formula to describe the person of Christ that would satisfy both sides of the argument. One attempt was along the lines of 'Christ has two natures, human and divine, but only one will'. As this could not be reconciled with the Gospel accounts, after long debate, it was not accepted.

The Emperor was concerned with building up the Church against the possible threats from Islam. Since 622, Mohammed had been leading the rapid expansion of Islam, a concern which had not arisen at the time of the previous Council. In 668, Mohammed's army had attacked Constantinople. Intellectual, cultural and military conflicts developed between Christianity and Islam. They are still having a powerful, negative impact on harmony in the middle-east, and indeed on the world, to this day.

Seventh Council (787) – St. Sophia, Nicaea

This second council, in Nicaea, was convened to settle a deep dispute about icons. The Latin, Catholic, western churches regarded the use of icons as a form of idolatry and the Eastern Orthodox saw them as a great spiritual aid to devotion. The Council agreed that, 'Icons deserve reverence but not adoration, which is due to God alone'. In recording the wording of this agreement there was, somehow, an error which implied that Christians could worship icons, in the same way that they worship God. This led to a deep dispute and extensive argument. In consequence, the Church divided into East and West: Constantinople and Rome. The iconoclastic movement gained momentum and many icons and beautiful art works were destroyed.

This was the last of the great Ecumenical Councils but following the death of Theophilos (829 – 42), Theodora, his wife, convened a Council meeting at St. Sophia, in Constantinople, at the beginning of Lent in 843. The focus was on the proper wording of the resolution agreed at the Council of 787 about returning icons to the church, to be reverenced but not worshipped. It concluded with a grand procession of icons which was described as 'the Triumph of Orthodoxy'. By this time, the division between Constantinople and Rome was well established - the Roman Catholic Church, in the west, and the Eastern Orthodox Church, in the east.

The Nicene Creed

As settled upon at the Council of Nicaea, AD 325
(Modified and added to later.)

We believe in one God, the Father, the Almighty, maker of all things, visible and invisible.

And in one Lord, Jesus Christ, the Son of God, begotten of the Father, only begotten, that is, of the substance of the Father, God from God, Light from Light, true God from true God, begotten not made, of one substance with the Father, through whom all things were made, things in heaven and things on earth;

Who for us men and our salvation, came down and was made flesh, and became man, suffered and rose on the third day, ascended into heaven, is coming to judge, living and dead.

And in the Holy Spirit.

And those who say "There was, when He was not" and "Before He was begotten, he was not," and that, "he came into being from nothingness," or those who allege that the son of God is: "of another substance or essence" or "created", or "changeable" or "alterable" these the Catholic and Apostolic Church anathematises.

Amen.

Congratulations!

Congratulations, if you have read through all of the chapters to this point. This last bit of history and theology may not have been the most thrilling but I hope that you have found interest, challenge, inspiration and, perhaps, moments of joy and deepening faith, within this publication, while 'visiting' places where the church grew up and thinking your way through important chapters of the New Testament.

The notes in this final chapter have excluded a multitude of detail, in order to summarise the early struggles of the church, when seeking to find a unifying statement of Christian Faith. For the church, the life-shaping events of those years and the debates about the nature of God are of supreme importance, in our understanding of developing theology and practice. Like the New Testament experience of the apostles, the wrangling and prayerful reflections throughout the church's first few centuries highlight some important questions for us, many of which we may have returned to time and again.

Reflection

- Constantine regarded the Christian Church as a means of strengthening unity in the Roman Empire. Do you think that this was an abuse of the Christian Faith, high-jacking it for political purposes? Alternatively, was it a faithful and courageous attempt, to open the Empire to God's unifying Grace in Jesus Christ, to heal, reconcile and bring genuine harmony to divided peoples?

- Constantine's role as head of the Roman Empire had the appearance of being combined with a role that seemed to be the head of the Church. Do you think that the head of State (Emperor, Monarch, President) should also be head of the Church? Why or Why not?

- What relationship do you think there should be between Church and State?

The Nature of Jesus

In the end, I am left with the view that the nature of the relationship between Jesus and God, our understanding of 'Trinity' and the way in which Humanity and Divinity both apply to Jesus, exhausts our understanding and defies explanation. Nevertheless, these things are fundamental to Christian Faith and many of us, as Christians, find that we have to try to get our heads around them. We do so with the awareness that we are on 'holy ground'. It's obvious, from the years of debate at the Councils, that these matters are not easy to grasp but how could we expect the mystery of God's eternal being to be made easy to grasp. There are times when we cannot make head nor tail of ourselves or even those we love dearly.

In our endeavour to understand, we have to remember the affirmation of Jesus that, 'The Lord our God, the Lord is one' (Mark 12 v 29). New Testament followers of Jesus did not change their minds about that, nor have we. They did not set out to invent a new doctrine or think up a new definition of God, such as 'Trinity', but the closer they came to Jesus, the more they discovered that they were in the presence of the living God. They described Him with the very words they used when speaking of God and of His Spirit in their lives. Experience had brought it upon them. It probably would not have made a lot of sense to them, if they had tried to work it out in an entirely rational explanation. Followers of Jesus Christ experienced God's reality in Him. They found God's forgiveness, His renewing power, life in all its fullness and salvation and hope in Christ. Their experience led to their conviction. Experience and testimony, not rational explanation, was their evidence.

Reflection

- How could Christ be 'wholly man and wholly God'?
- Did He have a split personality?
- Did He have two distinct natures, one human and one divine?
- Was He more divine or more human?
- Did He have two natures but one will?
- How do you understand the person of Jesus and who he was/is?
- Is our full understanding a requirement of faith and commitment?

The Holy Trinity

The roots of the Church's understanding of Trinity are, of course, embedded in the Old Testament as well as the New. Hebrew Faith is grounded in the acknowledgment that there is one Lord, and emphasises that God is one (Deuteronomy 6 v 4). Throughout Old Testament scripture, there's also clear recognition of God's action as the Holy Spirit, especially in creation and in speaking powerfully through the prophets. There is no suggestion in the Old Testament, however, that it was necessary to think of God as 'a duo' of Father and Holy Spirit. God is one. The New Testament opens with the Holy Spirit having a significant role in the birth of Jesus, His Baptism and in leading Him into the wilderness. The clear perception in scripture is that this was God at work. The difficulties for the early church, as we have said, was in understanding the nature of Jesus - in whom they recognised God incarnate. Nevertheless, there was no suggestion that God is 'a trio'. Our understanding and our conviction is that 'we believe in one God'.

Reflection

- How do we understand the Holy Trinity? Can we ever?

- Questions about the use of icons in worship came under discussion, during the Councils. We know of some wonderful, artistic creations that represent Jesus, inspiring paintings of Jesus and outstanding sculptures. We may have been moved by live passion drama or films of the Gospels. Do we consider that these visual images could be graven images?

- What is our view about icons? They continue to have an important place in eastern Christian tradition, as devotional aids in worshipping God.

- On what basis can we make our judgement?

Division

Critics accuse Christianity of leading to violence, corruption, superstition, bigotry and division, among other things. Too many divisive factors in the history of the church could be seen to strengthen that view. Accounts of some bitter arguments during the Great Ecumenical Councils could easily confirm that it has always been so.

We have not grown out of creating division. You may know of groups of Christians who have left their congregations and set up separately, because they hold different understandings of doctrine/scripture or disagree on moral or social issues.

I am not concerned, at this point, about who is right or wrong but about relationships. 'By this everyone will know that you are my disciples, if you have love for one another,' said Jesus (John 13 v 35), and yet Christians fall out over doctrinal convictions and Christian lifestyle. Constantly, we seem to be on the verge of yet another schism in the church, as Christians threaten to divide overs deeply held differences about Christian Faith or practice, instead of holding together in love.

Reflection

- Is it necessary for all Christians to hold the same interpretation of their faith, of the Creed or of certain doctrines?

- Is Christian faith about our trust in God and commitment to Christ or is it about beliefs and doctrines?

- Some suggest that the time has come for a new Creed. What do you think?

- When there's a deep division over a doctrinal matter, is it right to divide the two sides to safeguard the 'truth' or right to hold together, to preserve and promote Christian love and unity?

- How would the Church maintain unity of faith and purpose, if every Christian was free to interpret the Christian faith in his or her own way?

- If you were writing a creed for yourself, what essentials of your faith would you ensure are included? What would you prefer to leave out? Why?

Congratulations!

New Testament Turkey
BULGARIA
BLACK SEA
GREECE
CONSTANTINOPLE
MARMARA SEA
Nicaea
MYSIA
Troy
ALEXANDER TROAS
ASIA
PHRYGIA
AEGEAN SEA
PERGAMUM
THYATIRA
SARDIS
PISIDIAN ANTIOCH
SMYRNA
PHILADELPHIA
PISIDIA
Hierapolis
EPHESUS
LAODICEA
Priene
COLOSSAE
Lys
Miletus
Didyma
PAMPHYLIA
PATMOS
Perge
Dalyan
LYCIA
Attalia
Aspe
Telemessos
Xanthos
Myra
Patara
MEDITERRANEAN SEA

BITHYNIA
PONTUS
ARMENIA
GALATIA
CAPPADOCIA
Goreme
Kaymakli
Nemrut Dagi
ICONIUM
LYCAONIA
Derbe
CILICIA
TARSUS
ANTIOCH
SYRIA
CYPRUS

Bibliography

Alan, Hakan. **Churches in Turkey**. Istanbul : AS & 64 2007

Barclay, William.
    The Revelation of St. John. (2nd Edit)
    Edinburgh : St. Andrew Press 1960
    The Gospel of St. Mark. (2nd Edit)
    Edinburgh : St. Andrew Press 1974
    The Acts of the Apostles. (2nd Edit)
    Edinburgh : St. Andrew Press 1976

Barrett, C.K. **Luke the Historian in Recent Study**
    London : Epworth Press 1961

Blake, Everit & Edmonds, Anna. **Biblical Sites in Turkey** (9th Edit)
    Istanbul : SEV Matbaacilik ve Yayincilik AS 1997

Bockhorni, Reinhard. **Turkey**. London : Apa Publications 1997

Bonhoeffer, Dietrich. **The Cost of Discipleship** (6th Edit)
    London : SCM Press 1959, AS 1997

Browning, Robert. **Pauline Places**. Hodder & Stoughton : London 1989

Bruce, F.F. **The Book of Acts**.
    Edinburgh : Marshall Morgan & Scott 1965

Bryce, Trevor. **The Trojans and their Neighbours**.
    Oxford : Routledge 2006

Bonechi, Casa. **All of Cappadocia**. Firenze Italy : Bonechi 1997

Buyukkolanci, Mustufa. **The Life and Monument of St John**.
    Selcuk-Izmir : Efes 2000 Foundation 2001

Can, Turhan. **Turkey, Cradle of Civilization.**
    Istanbul : Orient Publishing House 1994

Cimok, Fatih.
   A Guide to the Seven Churches. Istanbul : A Turizm Yayinlari 1998
   St. Paul of Anatolia. Istanbul : A Turizm Yayinlari 1999
   Biblical Anatolia . Istanbul : A Turizm Yayinlari 1997

Crawshaw, Gerry. **Essential Turkey**. (2nd Edition)
   Basingstoke : A A Publishing 1994

Cross, F L (Ed). **The Oxford Dictionary of the Christian Church**.
   New York : Oxford University Press 1958

Darke, Diana. **Travellers Turkey**. (2nd Edit)
   Basingstoke : A A Publishing 1994

Demir, Omer. **Cappadocia Cradle of History**. (8th Edit)
   Nevsehir : Demir Color 1996

Dioscorides, Pedanius. **De Materia Medica**. (Lyon 1554)
   Wikipedia 2017

Edmonds, Anna. **Turkey's Religious Sites**. (2nd Edit)
   Istanbul : Damko Publications 1998

Ercenk, Giray. **History, Culture, Nature in Antalya & the Western
   Mediterranean**. Antalya : Promotion Tourism Development inc. 2012

Ergener, R. **Everything you always wanted to know about Turkey**.
   Istanbul : Dreamtours 2001

Freely, John. **The Western Shores of Turkey**.
   London : John Murray 1988

Hahn, Ferdinand. **Mission in the New Testament**.
   London : SCM Press 1965

Hanson, A T.
   The Pioneer Ministry. London : SCM Press 1961
   Tradition in the Early Church. London : SCM Press 1962

House, Christopher (Ed). **Constantine : AD 2000 years of Christianity**.
   London : Telegraph Group 1999

Inman, Nick (Ed). **Istanbul**. London : Dorling Kindersley 2002

Govier, Gordon. **Archaeology in Turkey**.
Illinois : Christianity Today 2011

Kennedy, H A A. **The Theology of the Epistles**.
London : Gerald Duckworth Co 1919

Latourette, Kenneth Scott . **A History of Christianity**.
London : Eyre & Spottiswoode 1964

McNeille, A H. **An Introduction to the Study of the New Testament**.
(2nd Edit) London : Oxford University Press 1952

Melianos, Nikos. **Patmos – The Island of Revelation**.
Athens : Heli Photo 2005

Neil, William. **The Truth about the Early Church.**
London : Hodder & Stoughton 1970

Neille, Stephen. **Paul to the Colossians**.
London : Lutterworth Press 1963

Olonga, Henry. **Blood, Sweat and Treason**.
Surrey : Vision Sports Publishing 2010

Onder, Mehmet. **Mevlana and Konya**. Istanbul : Keskin Color AS 1997

Ozeren, Ocal. **Ephesus**. Istanbul : Keskin Color AS 1998

Phillips, J.B. **The New Testament in Modern English**.
London : Geoffrey Bles 1960

Price, J Randall & House, H Wayne. **Zondervan Handbook of Biblical Archaeology**. Michigan : World of Bible Ministries 2017

Rehber. **Hagia Sophia & Chora Museum**. (8th Edit)
Istanbul : Rehber 1999

Robinson, Cyril E. **A History of Rome**. London : Methuen 1935

Stephens. **The Englishman's Greek New Testament**. 1550 (3rd Edit)
London : Samuel Bagster, 1896

Stephenson, J (Ed). **A New Eusebius** (2nd Edit) London : SPCK 1999

Stobart, J C. **The Grandeur that was Rome**. (4th Edit)
London : Book Club Associates 1987

Stott, John. **What Christ thinks of the Church**.
Illinois : Word Publishing 1990

Swan, Suzanne. **Turkey**. London : Dorling Kindersley 2006

Temple, William. **Readings in St. John's Gospel**. UK : Macmillan 1963

Tillich, Paul. **Shaking the Foundations**. London : Pelican 1962

Toubis, Michalis. **Patmos – the Holy Island of the Apocalypse**.
Athens : Michael Toubis Publications 2006

Waite, Terry. **Taken on Trust**. London : Hodder and Stoughton 1993

Wesley, John.
The Standard Sermons of John Wesley. (7th Edit)
London : The Epworth Press 1968
The Journal of John Wesley. (Ed. Nehemiah Curnock)
London : The Epworth Press 1938

Winwood, David.
Burning Heart.
London : Methodist Division of Education and Youth 1988
I Want to Begin a Christian Life.
London : Methodist Division of Education and Youth 1983

Whitham, A R. **History of the Christian Church**.
London : Rivingtons 1963

Yenen, Serif. **Turkish Odyssey**. (3rd Edit)
Istanbul : Meander Publishing 2001